THE AGE OF EVANGELICALISM

THE AGE OF EVANGELICALISM

America's Born-Again Years

Steven P. Miller

OXFORD
UNIVERSITY PRESS

OXFORD
UNIVERSITY PRESS

Oxford University Press is a department of the
University of Oxford. It furthers the University's objective
of excellence in research, scholarship, and education
by publishing worldwide.

Oxford   New York
Auckland   Cape Town   Dar es Salaam   Hong Kong   Karachi
Kuala Lumpur   Madrid   Melbourne   Mexico City   Nairobi
New Delhi   Shanghai   Taipei   Toronto

With offices in
Argentina   Austria   Brazil   Chile   Czech Republic   France   Greece
Guatemala   Hungary   Italy   Japan   Poland   Portugal   Singapore
South Korea   Switzerland   Thailand   Turkey   Ukraine   Vietnam

Oxford is a registered trade mark of Oxford University Press
in the UK and certain other countries.

Published in the United States of America by
Oxford University Press
198 Madison Avenue, New York, NY 10016

Library of Congress Cataloging-in-Publication Data
Miller, Steven P. (Steven Patrick), 1977–
The age of evangelicalism : America's born-again years / Steven P. Miller.
pages   cm
Includes bibliographical references and index.
ISBN 978-0-19-977795-2 (hardcover : alk. paper)—ISBN 978-0-19-977802-7 (ebook)   1. United States—Church
history—20th century.   2. United States—Church history—21st century.   3. Evangelicalism—United States—
History—20th century.   4. Evangelicalism—United States—History—21st century.   I. Title.
BR526.M555   2014
277.3'082—dc23   2013037929

9 8 7 6 5 4 3 2 1

Printed in the United States of America
on acid-free paper

CONTENTS

ACKNOWLEDGMENTS

As the author of a quite different volume once put it in his acknowledgments, precious few "fancy ingredients" went into the making of this book. I researched, I wrote, and I occasionally worked the resulting material into courses. Students got a kick out of Marabel Morgan and were remarkably polite upon encountering Hal Lindsey. One student, LeAnn Noland, generously shared her insights into the West Memphis Three case. The encouragement of colleagues and friends was in abundance, of course. Special thanks to Randall Balmer, Darren Dochuk, Paul Harvey, Patrick Jackson, Warren Rosenblum, Phillip Luke Sinitiere, Matthew Avery Sutton, John Wigger, and several anonymous reviewers. Thanks as well to the participants in the 2011 David Bruce Centre for American Studies Colloquium at Keele University and the 2012–2013 Danforth Center on Religion and Politics Colloquium at Washington University in St. Louis. Many others deserve a shout-out, and I hope you know who you are. Librarians at Webster University (especially Matthew Weir) and Washington University in St. Louis permitted me to pump their interlibrary loan systems at full throttle, while Liz Bilbo of the Reflections Thomas Kinkade Art Gallery, Bruce Compton of the Pew Charitable Trusts, Anna Groff of *The Mennonite*, and Duane Shank of Sojourners diligently responded to inquiries. The folks at the Southern Baptist Historical Library and Archives supported an always enjoyable visit to Nashville. Layne Amerikaner of People for the American Way, Tia Angelos of Getty, Arthur Blessitt of the Arthur Blessitt Evangelistic Association, Tricia Gesner and Cathy Gonzalez of the Associated Press, Merridith Miller of Condé Nast, and especially Charlotte Steinhardt of Oxford University Press provided valuable assistance with permissions. Many thanks to Gwen Colvin and Charlotte Steinhardt for overseeing the production process, Rebecca Gaff for proofing the proofs, and David Herholz for snapping publicity shots. My editor at Oxford, Theo Calderara, was enthusiastic from day one, and the final manuscript reflects his refining touch. Finally, I extend a note of gratitude to the post-1976 generation of scholars, journalists, and pundits whose investigations into modern American evangelicalism gave me so much to digest.

This book was a pleasure to write, and the vastly underrated city of St. Louis was a pleasant place in which to compose it. Life rarely stays on track, to be sure. Still, in the empty middle of academia, there is some solace in knowing that what was never solid cannot melt into air. Much more comfort can be found far away from the shared office. This book is dedicated to Clarissa Gaff and to our daughter Greta. The latter arrived during the final year of writing and kindly napped as I edited. There's nothing adjunct about our family.

Steven P. Miller

October 2013   St. Louis

THE AGE OF EVANGELICALISM

AN AGE, NOT A SUBCULTURE

In the first years of the twenty-first century, America was awash in a sea of evangelical talk. Influential political scientist Alan Wolfe wrote of "a sense in which we are all evangelicals now," as the religious practices of many Americans took on tones associated with born-again faith: populism, volunteerism, and (more than ever) a focus on individual needs. His eye was on the megachurch, not the White House. Yet those spheres merged in the minds of many commentators. Indeed, politics threatened to overshadow the varieties of regenerated faith that Wolfe explored. The presidency of George W. Bush offered a daily referendum on the implications of evangelical ubiquity. Perhaps the United States really was a born-again nation.[1]

America's chattering classes, empowered by cable news and the nascent blogosphere, seemed fixated on that very possibility. More than a few in their ranks saw synergy between a Jesus-touting president and a best-seller list stocked with end-times thrillers and born-again self-help books. Such hyper-public evangelicalism gave the old-time gospel a peculiar sense of novelty. What had thrust pastors Tim LaHaye, coauthor of the *Left Behind* novel series, and Rick Warren, author of *The Purpose Driven Life*, into the limelight? The mainstream media, standing targets for accusations of secular bias, came under renewed fire for failing to "get religion," as the founders of one blog punned.[2] Yet evangelicalism scarcely lacked for coverage; indeed, it sometimes stood in for American religion as a whole. The rub lay in the differing responses to the prospect of an evangelical America. Many reporters on the campaign trail made an open-minded visit to the local megachurch. Others saw more sinister forces at work. By 2006, the publishing industry had created an entire genre casting the evangelical surge as a wholesale threat to American values (and, for some, to biblical principles, too). Nonevangelicals seemed to have a stark choice: acquiescence or opposition?

As it turned out, waiting patiently also worked. The scene could hardly have been more different as the decade closed. The patriarchs of the evangelical right, many of whom bellowed triumphantly after Bush's 2004 reelection, played a negligible role in the 2008 presidential campaign. Their waning, increasingly insular voices contrasted with the newly assertive tone of progressive evangelicals eager to hitch their hopes to the eventual Democratic nominee, Barack Obama. His first inauguration thus promised to be a watershed moment. None other than Rick Warren beseeched an evangelical Jesus on behalf of a new president whose closest religious ties were with arguably the most liberal denomination in American Protestantism. Evangelicals no longer struck the zeitgeist keepers as such a unified bloc.[3]

What had changed in only a few years? How could evangelicalism shift so suddenly from the new normal to yesterday's news? On one level, the above narrative was merely the latest chapter in an ongoing media romance with American evangelicalism—a ritual of courting good copy, sparring with provocative targets, and then moving on to the next supposed silent majority. The 1980s had witnessed a similar crush of coverage about the exploits of televangelists on screen, in the White House, and in the penitentiary. This cycle of obsession and evasion points to a two-part "evangelical problem" in American society as a whole. Many Americans have not acknowledged the full impact of born-again Protestantism on their society, or they have held a one-dimensional interpretation of it. Many self-described evangelicals, in turn, have not conceded their status as something other than an oppressed or marginalized minority. These viewpoints assume that evangelicalism is a narrow lane, either to be avoided or hogged. The way through this impasse is to widen the road, treating them as part of a larger story about how and why evangelicalism mattered in recent American history.

This book explores the place and meaning of evangelical Christianity in the United States from the 1970s through the first decade of the twenty-first century. It pays particular attention to the uses that a diverse array of Americans—self-proclaimed evangelicals, of course, but also movement conservatives, secular liberals, journalistic elites, and sundry others—found for born-again faith. Beginning with the Jesus vogue of the early 1970s, evangelical Christianity was seen and heard, then seen and heard again. During these years, evangelicalism (the label commonly given to the public expression of born-again Christianity) influenced American history in profound, but only partially appreciated, ways. As befits the subject matter, this is something of a story of rebirth. Public evangelicalism gestated in the space created by the Watergate scandal of the early and mid-1970s. Out of that context emerged both a born-again president, Jimmy Carter, and his equally evangelical arch-nemesis, the Christian Right. The climax came three decades later with the presidency of George W. Bush, who synthesized the former's therapeutic Jesus talk with the latter's political agenda. Along the way came two evangelical scares, innumerable born-again spectacles, and several broad reconsiderations of the place of faith in American politics and culture.

During the Age of Evangelicalism, born-again Christianity provided alternately a language, a medium, and a foil by which millions of Americans came to terms with political and cultural changes. The influence of evangelicalism emerged not solely from the conservative end of the born-again spectrum, but rather from the interplay of its left and right factions, even while the latter almost always maintained a decided upper hand. One important product of this interplay was a renewed conviction that faith deserves a prominent place in the "public square." That belief was hotly contested, which suggests a second crucial point: Evangelical influence was pervasive enough to extend beyond avowed practitioners of born-again faith and to include its detractors and bemused bystanders as well. From the 1970s onward, evangelicalism possessed an impressive amount of sway in American culture and politics.[4]

A central premise of this study is that evangelicals are not the only protagonists in the history of modern US evangelicalism. Examples abounded of direct and indirect evangelical influence, from Jimmy Carter's born-again honesty to Norman Lear's "American way," James Davison Hunter's "culture wars" metaphor, and Jim Wallis's "God is not a Republican" mantra. There were Marabel Morgan's marriage seminars, Hal Lindsey's prophecy guides, Tammy Faye Bakker's eyelashes, and Thomas Kinkade's oil paintings. These phenomena attracted myriad voters, viewers, readers, and consumers for varying reasons. None of them make sense without understanding their inescapable connections to American evangelicalism. Likewise, they make little sense when framed primarily as products of a narrow evangelical subculture. Some were passing fads, others drove profound political changes, and still others seeped into the vocabulary of the times. But all reached well beyond the realm of Sunday School classes, revival services, and family values crusades.

The above examples highlight one of the basic stress points of recent American history. The Age of Evangelicalism was profoundly distant from the imagined Christian America of ages past. Americans at the end of the twentieth century and the start of a new one resided in a society that, by almost any measure, had grown more religiously pluralistic and, in certain circles, more self-consciously secular. Yet two of the most vocally pious presidents in American history bookended the period. To invoke Walt Whitman, American society sometimes has a way of saying "very well then" to its seeming contradictions. In the case at hand, those contradictions were very real, but they do not tell the whole story. While the prominence of evangelicalism was hardly new, it was especially salient and dynamic in the years after 1970. Growing religious diversity and secularism made born-again faith increasingly an avowed identity, as opposed to an assumed one. In the process, labels like "evangelical" and "born again" gained new significance. To the extent that secularization, or something akin to it, occurred, it served to reconfigure the influence of evangelicalism, rather than diminish it.

A simple library catalog search might support the suspicion that this story already has been told. Of books about American evangelicalism there most certainly is no end. Yet the subject remains stubbornly separated from critical parts of its very history. Three broad motifs have dominated thoughtful inquiries into American evangelicalism since the 1970s. The "up from Scopes" narrative celebrates the ascendance of evangelicalism from the ashes of the 1925 Scopes Monkey Trial. This theme, which remained a journalistic staple decades after George Gallup Jr. labeled 1976 as the "Year of the Evangelical," resembles studies of American conservatism that stop with the 1980 election of Ronald Reagan, preferring the striking aroma of initial success to the more complex (and occasionally muddled) bouquet that comes with age. More common in academic circles, the "give 'em a fair shake" model seeks to explain the evangelical subculture to an audience that, presumably, carries reflexive hostility or incredulity toward this Bible-bound "other." While such efforts are invaluable, they risk perpetuating the impulse to view evangelicals as outsiders (or to take them at their word about being outsiders) vis-à-vis an assumed American center. Finally, the "none dare call it treason" approach probes evangelicalism as an underappreciated, surging force in American culture and, by extension, as a threat to American values. It really could happen here, the argument goes. Not surprisingly, this last perspective peaked among activists and scholars during George W. Bush's presidency.

The Age of Evangelicalism does not reject the above narratives so much as it seeks to make them part of the story. I operate from the assumption that, in the end, an exposé of recent American evangelicalism is neither advisable nor possible; there is little left to expose. I offer neither an insider's scoop nor an outsider's anthropology. Nor am I preoccupied with policing the definitional boundaries of evangelicalism, filing exotic anecdotes from the front, or scoring political points. In my approach, evangelicalism is not still recovering from its nadir after the Scopes Trial. Nor is it deserving of excessive scholarly empathy. And it certainly is not a zealous fifth column about which to sound the alarm. Capturing what evangelicalism meant in recent American history involves mixing high and low, politics and culture, scholars and popularizers. It also entails being as concerned about the fruit of evangelical influence as about the root of it.

Accounts of modern American evangelicalism now stand at something of a crossroads. A number of recent histories indicate that the topic is entering a more mature phase. The authors of these important works, which have concentrated especially on political evangelicalism, generally keep their culture war cards to themselves. We can now place born-again Christianity at the heart of suburbanization, the rise of the Sunbelt, and the growth of the service economy, to cite but three examples. Attention to the evangelical left continues to grow.[5] What remains largely unstated in these histories is the logical upshot of their findings: If recent American evangelicalism has been so significant, then perhaps it is not really a subculture after all. Perhaps American evangelicalism resides at the very center of recent American history.

Grappling with that proposition requires an end to the habit of evaluating American evangelicalism on its own, self-limiting terms. During the last four decades, few American evangelical leaders were prepared to acknowledge, never mind to accept, the fullness of their relevance. When it comes to historical influence, though, modern American evangelicalism handily transcends the category of subculture. As Amy Frykholm has observed, the broad reach of even patently evangelical phenomena, such as the *Left Behind* novels, defies assumptions "that evangelicalism can be rather neatly sifted out from the rest of the population." Attempts to do so turn evangelicalism into an episodically influential force at best—a historical "jack-in-the-box," popping up now and again, to use historian Jon Butler's metaphor. A "vast and robust parallel culture" of evangelical institutions and experts continues to exist, of course. Yet its influence on the rest of America gives lie to the assumption that evangelicalism is a mere subculture. Of critical importance here is evangelicalism's dual status as both a "cognitive minority" and a "sociocultural majority."[6] In other words, its footprint has extended far beyond the number of people who might fairly be called evangelical. This book explores that tension, while also scrutinizing what evangelicalism meant to the multitudes of Americans who sought to keep as much distance from it as they possibly could.

The recent history of American evangelicalism looks different—and, in many respects, a lot more interesting—when it is not solely about evangelicals themselves. Such was the nature of evangelicalism's impact on late twentieth-century American culture and politics: It was pervasive enough that no one expression of evangelicalism could lay sole claim to it, and it involved more than just avowed born-again Christians. The meaning of evangelicalism could never be the exclusive property of evangelicals for the simple reason that born-again Christianity occupied such a prominent place in American society. No group controlled the narrative, but few could avoid a story that spanned many times and places—from the Jesus-soaked 1970s to the culture war 1990s to the Obama ascendancy, and from Washington, DC, to Colorado Springs to West Memphis. Then and there, evangelicalism was an age, not a subculture.

1 THE SEVENTIES EVANGELICAL MOMENT

Few subjects in US history have more established signposts than evangelicalism. George Whitefield's revivals of the eighteenth century, Charles Finney's of the nineteenth, and Billy Graham's of the twentieth are three of the handiest markers for the scores of commentators who have sought to understand how born-again Christianity became the characteristically American way of doing religion. The origins of many such inquiries, however, date from a more recent moment—the 1970s. By the latter half of that decade, born-again Christianity was, in the emerging parlance of those times, nothing short of a "media event." Popular newsweeklies pronounced 1976 "The Year of the Evangelicals," described the Bible Belt as "on the verge of becoming a national state of mind," and declared the growing prominence of born-again faith to be "the most significant—and overlooked—religious phenomenon of the 70s."[1] The most obvious catalyst for such attention was the successful presidential run of Democrat Jimmy Carter, who became the peanut-farming poster child for born-again Christianity. Carter's candid talk about his personal faith drew his GOP opponent, Gerald Ford, out of the prayer closet. It also caught the attention of politically conservative evangelicals, many of whom became Carter's harshest critics.

Yet the evangelical Seventies began well before the Carter presidency and the subsequent rise of the Christian Right. Those developments merely forced observers to label a trend that they had long been trailing. Before "born again" entered popular parlance and before anyone wrote of "evangelical chic," journalists and scholars hyped the Jesus Movement and analyzed a surging "third force," or "third stream," in postwar American Christianity. During much of the decade, and even well into the Carter administration, the precise political implications of the evangelical boom remained unclear and, for some observers, irrelevant. The countless popular surveys of born-again America, circa 1976, devoted as much attention to celebrity converts and evangelistic bumper stickers as to demonstrations for "family values" and against the Equal Rights Amendment.[2]

Two phenomena at the start of the decade revealed how born-again Christianity traversed American culture and politics, roaming well beyond a posited evangelical subculture. On July 4, 1970, the renowned evangelist Billy Graham delivered the flagship sermon for the highly publicized Honor America Day festivities. His cochair was comedian Bob Hope. That same year, another evangelist, Hal Lindsey, published what became the best-selling American nonfiction book of the decade, an end-times polemic called *The Late Great Planet Earth*. The cinematic icon Orson Welles later narrated a widely released documentary version of the book. The sacred blurred with the secular. Born-again faith was present in many forms—both personal and political—during the 1970s. The trend of "evangelical chic" featured a wealth of additional signifiers, ranging from the fundamentalist-hippie brew of the Jesus Movement to the therapeutic antifeminism of Marabel Morgan. As Americans responded in conflicted ways to the challenges of the times, especially the Watergate crisis that ended a presidency, the old-time Gospel took on new resonance. The evangelical Seventies were under way.

Watergate and the Crisis of Civil Religion

The evangelical Seventies began during the presidency of Richard Nixon, then managed to survive it. Honor America Day and the Watergate crisis that followed it spoke to the durability and versatility of public evangelicalism. Nixon appealed to several disgruntled sectors of the electorate, including suburban property owners, white Southern Democrats, and white ethnics. Yet his "silent majority"—alternately known as "Middle America" or the "forgotten Americans"—included more than a few of the born-again Christians to whom Jimmy Carter later proved attractive. When *Time* magazine named "Middle Americans" the 1969 "Man and Woman of the Year," it led by citing those citizens who "prayed defiantly" in the face of court restrictions on sanctioned invocations in public schools.[3]

To critics, these and other court decisions threatened precisely what Honor America Day sought to keep alive: the postwar synergy between public piety and American patriotism. The day began with a nationally televised interfaith service featuring a sermon by Billy Graham. "Let the world know," Graham declared to a crowd of more than 10,000 at the Lincoln Memorial, "that the vast majority of us still proudly sing, 'My country, 'tis of thee, sweet land of liberty.'" In his patriotic jeremiad, Graham cited a biblical mandate to "honor the nation," called for a "renewal of faith in God, equality, justice and peace for all," and invoked Winston Churchill in urging Americans to "never give in! Never! Never! Never! Never! Never! Never! Never!" Bob Hope emceed the evening's closing festivities, which drew a much larger audience of 350,000 to the Washington Monument. Graham and Hope billed the day as a nonpartisan exercise in national unity. Skeptics noted the preponderance of Nixon supporters among the event organizers, who took pains to gain endorsements from some prominent liberals, including Senator George McGovern of South Dakota.[4]

While such God-and-country rituals were hardly new features of the American political landscape, they were an especially notable component of the "consensus culture" of the early Cold War years. That culture stressed the nation's unique interfaith comity, reflecting a near-universal postwar sentiment that religion—specifically, the recently popularized notion of the "Judeo-Christian tradition"—was a positive good for American society. During the 1950s, Congress enshrined "In God We Trust" as the national motto, while politicians of all stripes took part in the newly created Presidential Prayer Breakfast. Evangelical leaders supported but by no means drove these efforts; collectively, they devoted more energy to cultivating a vast array of nondenominational, "parachurch" organizations created during the 1940s and 1950s. Yet Cold War–style religiosity contributed greatly to the "demarginalization of evangelicalism." In 1952, Graham closed his Washington, DC, crusade with a service on the Capitol steps. His presence at Honor America Day—alongside Archbishop Fulton Sheen, Rabbi Marc Tanenbaum, and African American minister E. V. Hill—suggested that at least this flagship evangelical endorsed a civic faith designed to cut across monotheistic lines and, to a lesser extent, racial and ethnic divisions as well. The postwar religion boom set the stage for the pronouncement of born-again Christianity as a vital force in American society.[5]

By 1970, though, the notion of a Judeo-Christian consensus was clearly under threat. It even had a new name: "civil religion." In a series of publications starting in 1967, sociologist Robert Bellah employed "civil religion" to describe the complex and enduring rituals, beliefs, and symbols that, from the founding of the nation onward, had reflected "an understanding of the American experience in the light of ultimate and universal reality." Bellah distinguished between civil religion and organized religion, but this difference was less apparent to the millions of American churchgoers who saw no inherent tension between cross and flag. As the concept of civil religion cycled through the periodical literature, it came to mean (as Bellah publicly lamented) "the idolatrous worship of the state" and often, more specifically, the "link between Biblical and political rightism." For critics of that link, Honor America Day was an easy target. The most visible criticism came, not surprisingly, from the New Left. Honor America Day attracted around 1,000 protesters, some of whom participated in a marijuana "smoke-in" and clashed with police. Earlier, the event committee had rejected a request to allow the poet Allen Ginsberg, a counterculture icon and practicing Buddhist, to conduct the morning service alongside Graham.[6]

If Honor America Day demonstrated the widening cultural divisions in America, it also signaled a turning point for the influence of born-again Christianity. Evangelicalism would dominate post-1960s civil religion—much to the chagrin of some evangelicals themselves. Two years after the festivities, a book appeared arguing that Graham and his constituency represented the political wave of the future. *Religion and the New Majority: Billy Graham, Middle America, and the Politics of the 70s* sparked less discussion at the time than did other analyses of the Nixon electorate (namely, Kevin Phillips's *The Emerging Republican Majority* and Ben Wattenberg and Richard Scammon's *The Real Majority*). But it was the only such work to anticipate the politicization of civil religion in the aftermath of the tumultuous 1960s. For the authors Lowell Streiker and Gerald Strober, Graham's political talent lay in his ability to affirm American decency. That gift was on display at the Lincoln Memorial. The evangelist's blend of "religious assurance with the basic moderateness of traditional American concepts of morality and action," they argued, made him "the man for this season, this trying time." For precisely those reasons, a small but growing number of progressive evangelicals worried that Graham's civil religion would sap the born-again message of any prophetic content. At the Honor America Day rally, a group of Mennonites—adherents of a historically pacifistic faith tradition—held a banner asking, "Hour of decision: God or country?" (*The Hour of Decision* was the name of Graham's weekly radio show.) To them and like-minded believers, patriotism and piety were fundamentally incompatible. Honor America Day lingered in the memories of progressive evangelical activists. The event, one critic wrote, revealed "the pernicious nature of this civil religion—the religion of Americanism."[7]

The Watergate crisis of 1973–1974 unexpectedly thrust born-again faith farther into the cultural spotlight. At first glance, it cast a shadow on Strober and Streiker's thesis. As the scandal unfolded, the same Nixon who palled around with Graham and hosted Sunday services at the White House came to look even more paranoid and corrupt than longtime critics of "Tricky Dick" had assumed. Watergate was indeed a crisis for Graham and other born-again Nixon partisans. Yet it brought the evangelical Seventies to fruition.

Watergate sparked the kind of spiritual introspection that came naturally to many evangelicals. *Christianity Today*, the flagship evangelical publication cofounded by Graham, echoed Watergate convict Jeb Magruder in viewing the scandal as a cautionary tale about secular "situational ethics." Graham's efforts along those lines—averring repeatedly that "there's a little bit of Watergate in all of us"—read too easily as a backhanded Nixon apologia. However, other prominent evangelical leaders, such as liberal Republican senator Mark Hatfield of Oregon, had a freer hand to play the role of prophet. Mentioned as a possible Nixon running mate in 1968, Hatfield became the leading GOP opponent of the administration's Vietnam policy. His relationship with the White House declined even more after a 1973 National Prayer Breakfast speech during which, with Nixon on his right and Graham on his left, the senator warned the audience not to "appeal to the god of civil religion." An "embarrassed" Graham, who had pitched Hatfield for the vice presidency in 1968, soon voiced his displeasure to the senator and complained to Nixon about such "terrible" and "inexcusable" behavior. As the Watergate crisis intensified, Hatfield gained Senate support for a resolution declaring April 30, 1974, a National Day of Humiliation, Fasting, and Prayer for Americans to "repent of our national sins." The call was modeled on a similar effort by Abraham Lincoln during the Civil War (a fact that, ironically, made Hatfield's proclamation itself an exercise in civil religion). The resolution failed in the House of Representatives, but it drew the endorsement of more than a dozen state governors, including Nixon supporter Ronald Reagan. Humorist Art Buchwald's satire of it appeared under the headline, "The Day We All Eat Humble Pie."[8]

The Watergate crisis thus facilitated new visions for evangelical public service. Disgust with Nixon inspired televangelist Pat Robertson—who, although he was the son of a former US senator, had a reputation as an apolitical charismatic Baptist—to dedicate more airtime to current events. Illinois congressman John Anderson also saw Watergate as a mandate for evangelical activism. A liberal Republican like Hatfield, Anderson linked Watergate with "the breakdown in the moral consensus of the American nation." Yet Anderson, who had come under fire from fellow believers after he suggested that Nixon consider resigning, did not despair. "The lesson of Watergate," he wrote in a book published by an evangelical press, "is not that we should withdraw from public service if we have strong moral convictions. Rather, it is that we cannot afford to be silent and passive when our political life is threatened by political opportunists."[9]

Anderson surely drew encouragement from the spate of Watergate-repentant conversions to born-again Christianity. The most famous—and surprising, even to cynics—example was Nixon hatchet man Charles Colson. His transformation during the Watergate crisis from dirty trickster to prayer breakfaster garnered no small amount of media attention and eventually spawned a best-selling memoir titled *Born Again*. Colson was by no means the only Watergate convict to strike a born-again note in the mid-1970s. Even his former bane, Watergate special prosecutor Leon Jaworski, eventually published a memoir highlighting his faith journey. Jaworski wrote the book at the behest of evangelical power broker Bill Bright, who mailed 4,000 copies to government officials.[10] While the Watergate crisis penetrated the defenses of civil religion, the evangelical brand remained far from tarnished.

Why Liberal Churches Aren't Growing

With time, evangelicals and nonevangelicals alike came to see the 1970s as a born-again moment. The growing profile of evangelical Christianity potentially challenged the vision of what sociologist Daniel Bell and others called the emerging "postindustrial society." That descriptor became a staple of the genre of "futurology" (sometimes rendered as "futurism"). As popularized by Alvin Toffler, futurists saw themselves as practicing the social science of anticipation; they highlighted trends that eventually merited labels like "globalization," "post-Fordism," and "postmodernity." What Toffler did not initially envision, however, was much of a role for religion amid "the roaring current of change" (surprisingly, not even in resisting or mediating that change). For all of their cutting-edge predictions, Toffler and most of his peers hewed to the assumption—traditional for a generation or more—that modernization meant secularization. Toffler, for understandable reasons, was not inclined to see connections between his *Future Shock* and Hal Lindsey's *The Late Great Planet Earth*, both of which appeared in 1970. Yet the two best sellers reflected an interest in "prevision" that cut across elite and popular lines.[11]

Meanwhile, a number of leading liberal Protestants (often also called "mainline" Protestants) feared that they were in for a future shock of their own. They worried that the mainline denominations (including the largest branches of Presbyterianism and Methodism) had lost their status, long taken for granted, as the guardians of American society. Prominent sociologist Peter Berger led the choir of concern. Berger viewed his sociological and theological prerogatives as separate hats; in many of his works, though, they coordinated like shirt and tie. Berger the scholar made his reputation in part as an exponent of secularization theory, putting special emphasis on pluralism as its catalyst. Yet Berger the Lutheran layman was far from pleased with the secularization he observed among his fellow liberal Protestants. In the late 1960s, he foresaw a future in which "religious believers are likely to be found only in small sects, huddled together to resist a worldwide secular culture." A new perspective surfaced in his prominent 1971 address to the Consultation on Church Union, a liberal Protestant project created a decade earlier to promote the ultimate ecumenical goal of a single church united on Reformation principles. Berger criticized mainline Protestants for not making a clear-enough distinction between themselves and what an influential work of 1960s theology celebrated as the "secular city." "I think many in our churches today can be described as *in search of a culture with which to identify*," Berger emphasized. He did envision "a possibly powerful reversal of the secularization process." Yet it was likely to come from other, more conservative corners of Christendom. "*If* there is going to be a renascence of religion," he stressed, "its bearers will *not* be the people who have been falling all over each other to be 'relevant to modern man.' . . . Put simply: Ages of faith are not marked by 'dialogue,' but by *proclamation*." Berger later helped to organize the 1975 Hartford "Appeal for Theological Affirmation," a high-profile repudiation of the perceived trend away from "transcendence" in American theology. His religious concerns ultimately caught up with his scholarship. Starting in the mid-1970s, Berger spent the rest of his career qualifying and finally retreating from secularization theory. He cited the growing prominence of evangelicalism as a major reason for his scholarly change of heart.[12]

Fellow liberal Protestant Dean Kelley documented the numbers behind Berger's worries. His influential 1972 study, *Why Conservative Churches Are Growing*, focused on those churches that continued to expand well after the postwar revival. Examples included generic evangelicals, as well as Mormons, Jehovah's Witnesses, and other historically marginal Christian groups. The book's distinctiveness lay not in noting the numerical decline of mainline Protestantism since the mid-1960s but in describing the process as a zero-sum game that theologically conservative churches were winning. Kelley, a Methodist minister who worked for the National Council of Churches, hoped to encourage "a certain wry appreciation of the qualities liberal churchmen have found so objectionable in the nonecumenical, nonmainline church bodies." He echoed other in-house critics of liberal Protestant churches, including Berger, Jeffrey Hadden, and Richard John Neuhaus, in speculating that in many respects those churches were "not very religious at all." That is, as Kelley put it, they were not "explaining the meaning of life in ultimate terms." Kelley was deeply invested in the survival of mainline Protestantism, but he confessed that his arguments had "given some aid and comfort to members of the rapidly growing churches by recognizing them as doing something right rather than dismissing them as superstitious zealots." His somewhat stiff work of sociology became one of the most widely cited studies of late twentieth-century American religion. Its thesis was conventional wisdom among chroniclers of the evangelical boom in the 1970s and beyond. As if to confirm the new common sense, the evangelical-friendly New International Version translation of the Bible quickly outsold its English-language competitors after its full release in 1978.[13]

Kelley's argument drew strength from two religious trends that were in full bloom by the time his book appeared: the charismatic movement and the related Jesus Movement. Both revealed the broadening of the evangelical spectrum at the start of the 1970s. The charismatic movement, sometimes called "neo-Pentecostalism" in recognition of the existing and still-thriving Pentecostal tradition, began in the late 1950s and early 1960s within a few mainline Protestant churches. The long-term effects of the charismatic revival, however, were felt most profoundly in born-again circles. Its embrace by evangelical celebrities, such as singer and actor Pat Boone, helped to introduce many previously wary evangelicals to Pentecostal beliefs and tendencies, including Holy Spirit baptism and, for a minority of charismatics, the consequent gift of glossolalia, or "speaking in tongues." The holy-roller stereotype endured, to be sure, especially after the 1972 release of the Oscar-winning documentary *Marjoe*, which traced the antics of a Pentecostal child preacher turned adult tent-revival con artist. By 1975, however, upwards of five million Americans practiced some form of charismatic Christianity.[14]

Included in that group were many converts to the Jesus Movement, whose participations alternately were known as "Jesus People," "Jesus freaks," and "street Christians." The Jesus Movement emerged during the late 1960s in the Bay Area and Southern California. It quickly spread across the continent. Its rise accentuated the porous boundaries between the three great traditions in postwar American evangelicalism: hard-line fundamentalism, spirit-filled Pentecostalism, and comparatively moderate "neoevangelicalism." Most initial leaders of the Jesus Movement either possessed ties to conventional evangelical mission networks or cultivated them. For example, Jack Sparks founded the Berkeley-based Christian World Liberation Front with early support from Campus Crusade for Christ, while Don Williams started the Salt Company coffeehouse as a mission of Hollywood Presbyterian Church. Chuck Smith, who gained attention by conducting mass seaside baptisms in Orange County, began his career as a pastor in the International Church of the Foursquare Gospel, a Pentecostal denomination founded by celebrity evangelist Aimee Semple McPherson in the 1920s. Other Jesus Movement ministers drew inspiration from street evangelist David Wilkerson. The Pentecostal minister recounted his work among New York City gangs and drug addicts in a 1963 book, *The Cross and Switchblade.* At the end of the decade, his story reached a wider audience through a movie starring Pat Boone, a Jesus Movement booster. Despite ongoing links to established evangelical institutions, significant portions of the Jesus Movement blended into, and in turn influenced, the counterculture, celebrity, and cult scenes of California. The Jesus Movement thus struck some observers as a novel creation, while others saw it as the old-time gospel translated into hipster speak. Either way, by 1971, it was on the radar screens of the national news-weeklies and television networks.[15]

Although the Jesus Movement proved to be a short-lived phenomenon, its legacy endured in secular and evangelical circles alike. For the latter, it was an important medium through which countercultural elements found their way into heretofore straitlaced congregations. The process was sometimes awkward. A Jesus Movement riff on the New Testament rendered the apostle Paul's parting words to the Corinthians as "Maranatha! Right on! Jesus' love be with you all." Accounts appeared from converted drug users and antiwar radicals, such as Jerry Halliday, whose testimony featured a stoned phone call to Pat Robertson's fledgling television show, *The 700 Club.* Halliday cast his story as a challenge to "church people" squares. Yet pew dwellers could take solace in the Sunday School–friendly message that lay between such cheesy youth ministry antics as a detailed list of all drugs consumed and a play script titled "Let the Son Shine In." A recurring concern about the Jesus Movement in mainstream evangelical circles involved not its innovation, but its simplistic reduction of Christianity to the "One Way!" of Jesus. Perhaps the most visible expression of the movement was a fist thrust forward, Black Power–style, only with the index finger pointed toward heaven. Jesus Movement slogans easily became commodities in the hands of marketers. "Jesus Rock," for example, helped to inspire the genre of contemporary Christian music. With time—and with an assist from evangelical elites, such as Billy Graham—the culture of the Jesus Movement surfaced in more mainstream forums. Emblematic of the transition was Explo '72, an evangelical youth festival and evangelism conference sponsored by Campus Crusade for Christ and held in Dallas. Graham, who addressed the event, billed it as the "Christian Woodstock." Others called it "Godstock." Even as evangelical traditionalists fretted about the merits of Jesus rock, President Nixon maneuvered unsuccessfully for an invitation to join what would have been a sympathetic crowd. On the final day, an audience of 180,000 listened to an array of explicitly Christian musicians, along with performances by bona fide celebrities, such as Johnny Cash and Kris Kristofferson. Campus Crusade for Christ soon ran hour-long excerpts from Explo '72 on television stations nationwide.[16]

The Jesus Movement was part of a broader craze for all things Christ in early 1970s popular culture. The trend expressed itself in such diverse (and by no means always born-again friendly) forums as the popular rock opera *Jesus Christ Superstar* and numerous covers of the gospel song "Jesus Is Just Alright," most prominently by the Byrds and the Doobie Brothers. The album version of *Jesus Christ Superstar* preceded the premiere of the musical itself, meaning that many churches and schools put on unauthorized concerts well before the show hit Broadway. The Jesus craze featured its own extensive lists of celebrity converts, including Cash, Fleetwood Mac guitarist Jeremy Spencer, and frequent *Laugh-In* guest Tiny Tim. One convert, Noel Paul Stookey (of Peter, Paul, and Mary fame), composed "The Wedding Song (There Is Love)," which became a staple in American wedding ceremonies, while another, Barry McGuire (best known for "Eve of Destruction"), switched to Christian music. By 1971, as *Jesus Christ Superstar* began its run on Broadway and the comparatively orthodox *Godspell* did well Off Broadway, the proliferation of "Jesus songs" spawned a send-up by Sha Na Na, asking, "Are you on the Top 40 of your Lordy, Lordy, Lordy?"[17]

The charismatic revival and the Jesus Movement stood at the intersection of evangelical missions and what historian Amanda Porterfield has described as "countercultural efforts to reenchant the world." Contemporaries noted the overlap between 1960s radicalism and 1970s spiritualism. The growth of the Jesus Movement resembled the drift of significant portions of the New Left toward what was becoming known as "New Age" spirituality. Former Students for a Democratic Society firebrand Rennie Davis, who protested Honor America Day in 1970, famously joined the Divine Light Mission, while ex-Yippie radical Jerry Rubin's spiritual journey ranged from self-actualization seminars to acupuncture and sex therapy. The Jesus Movement's overarching message of "a fundamental change within" sprang mostly from traditional evangelical sources and was not one of religious inclusiveness. In mostly unacknowledged ways, however, its emphasis on conversion jibed with the question posed by a yoga practitioner in the early 1970s: "But how can we have a peaceful society if there's no peace within us?" By then, the influence of popular born-again Christianity had outstripped the ability of evangelical gatekeepers to control the narrative. It was a national phenomenon waiting to be named—and counted.[18]

Evangelical Chic

The Jesus Movement anticipated the boom in public evangelicalism that came to constitute one of the most significant cultural trends of the 1970s. During the height of the 1976 presidential campaign, columnist Garry Wills wrote that "evangelical chic is impending." Besides Jimmy Carter, the pollster George Gallup Jr. was the most important driver of the new media meme.[19]

The Gallup organization put its statistical stamp of approval on the evangelical Seventies. In late August 1976, prompted by Carter's self-description of his faith, the company made its first attempt to calculate the total number of born-again Christians in the United States. It used a straightforward, if broad criterion: an affirmative response to the question "Would you say that you have been 'born again' or have had a 'born again' experience—that is, a turning point in your life when you committed yourself to Christ?" A surprising 34 percent of all respondents—around half of all Protestants in the sample—answered yes. The widely cited math added up to almost 50 million adult born-again Americans, whom Gallup and many journalists influenced by the report rhetorically converted into "evangelicals." This implicit definition of "evangelical" as "born again" included members of conservative Protestant groups, such as many among Carter's Southern Baptists, who might not have identified with the former label. Gallup, an active Episcopalian who described himself as "evangelically oriented," used his organization's findings to counter the contention "that we are entering a post-Christian era." To the contrary, many Americans were comfortable with the idea of a born-again president. In an address to his fellow Episcopalians during the height of the election season, Gallup declared 1976 the "Year of the Evangelical." *Time* magazine reported on Gallup's speech, and a *Newsweek* cover story in late October further popularized the term (and pluralized "evangelical"). "[I]sn't it time for us to bring our religious feelings out of the closet?" Gallup asked. His organization's numbers, along with the lessons he drew from them, figured prominently in mid-1970s analyses of born-again America. The 1976 poll included evidence that the number of "hard-core" evangelicals was much smaller—18 percent of the sample—although Gallup and his journalist interlocutors did not initially highlight this qualifying evidence. The Gallup organization eventually employed a more demanding statistical definition of "evangelical," bringing down the proportion of adult evangelical Americans to 20 percent in a 1978 poll commissioned by *Christianity Today* magazine. Even with those lower numbers, Gallup predicted that the 1980s would be "the decade of the evangelicals, because that is where the action is." A generation of evangelical activists eagerly cited (and, in some cases, exaggerated) Gallup's math when making the case for born-again political engagement. Academics began to take notice as well. Gallup's personal ties with evangelical elites expanded as his organization increasingly focused on religious polling.[20]

Evangelical chic also drew momentum from the continuing run of 1970s conversions, which extended well beyond the realms of Watergate felons and Jesus Movement baptisms. The phenomenon was particularly pronounced in the arena of professional sports, where the popular Dallas Cowboys featured a Christian coach (Tom Landry, a Methodist) and quarterback (Roger Staubach, an outspoken Catholic whose autobiographies were published by an evangelical press). *Time* described "the liniment-and-locker-room chapels that seem to have converted half of the players in the National Football League." The evangelical media, for its part, happily embraced all such converts, highlighting flirtations with born-again Christianity by rock guitarist Eric Clapton and other celebrities. June Carter Cash, spouse of newly born-again Johnny, received the "Wife and Mother of the Year 1974" award from Youth for Christ, and she extolled the virtues of spousal submission in an evangelical publication.[21]

Other prominent celebrity converts included former Black Panther leader Eldridge Cleaver, as well as Bob Dylan. Cleaver, who had a religious experience while living in exile in France, formally converted during a prison stay following his return to the United States in 1975. He quickly graduated from radical to evangelical chic, fortified with the blessing of Billy Graham and the financial support of conservative activist and evangelical philanthropist Arthur DeMoss. The recovering radical avoided extended prison time and enjoyed a brief moment in the evangelical sun, complete with an organization (Eldridge Cleaver Crusades), film (*The Eldridge Cleaver Story*), updated autobiography (*Soul on Fire*—a play on his classic *Soul on Ice*), and appearance at Jerry Falwell's Thomas Road Baptist Church. "I just wish I could be born again every day," Cleaver told *People* magazine. The eccentric and mercurial Cleaver was an awkward fit for an evangelical establishment that was eager to embrace him. Ever the entrepreneur, he promoted a line of codpiece-detailed pants for men at the same time that he plunged into mission work. Cleaver's subsequent religious sojourns, including turns as a Moonie and a Mormon, took him well outside the born-again nest.[22]

Bob Dylan's evangelical phase followed a 1978 encounter with Jesus. In his trademark cagey fashion, Dylan described it as "a born-again experience, if you want to call it that." Dylan, who then lived in Southern California, had a seeker's receptiveness to faith and spirituality; years before, he pointed Noel Paul Stookey toward the Bible. Still, Dylan's Jewish background made him a surprising candidate for Christian conversion. Through a girlfriend, Dylan got in touch with a nearby charismatic Vineyard church, led by Ken Gulliksen and closely connected to Chuck Smith's Calvary Chapel. The post-conversion Dylan voiced the apocalyptic concerns of that scene. Occasionally disgruntled concertgoers heard Hal Lindsey–inspired commentaries on the Book of Revelation. Other fruits of conversion included an explicitly evangelical album, the presence of Jews for Jesus pamphleteers outside of concerts, an appearance on behalf of the evangelical relief group World Vision, and a harmonica solo on an album by pioneering Christian artist Keith Green. Longtime fan Jimmy Carter took note of Dylan's Christian turn and talked of inviting him to the White House. By 1983, though, Dylan had begun to rediscover his Jewish roots.[23]

The pinnacle of evangelical chic was the sudden fame of Ruth Carter Stapleton. A charismatic Christian and teacher of "inner healing," Stapleton chafed at the label "faith healer." She played an influential role in the religious journey of her brother, Jimmy, and she later publicized his piety during the 1976 campaign. Her profile grew precipitously after the election. During the first two years of the Carter presidency, Stapleton addressed the West German parliament and hosted a $1,500-per-table Manhattan benefit for her new retreat center, Holovita. The fund-raiser mostly attracted liberal elites, including Norman Mailer, who tolerated an evening of polite bemusement to stay in the White House's good graces. A *Village Voice* writer, "quite unprepared for evangelical chic," marveled at the sight of Stapleton "addressing a ballroom full of pampered pagans."[24]

Stapleton's notoriety crescendoed when she ministered to the pornographer Larry Flynt, whose unabashedly raunchy *Hustler* magazine was a leading target of antismut groups in the 1970s and 1980s. "I think we have a lot in common," Flynt recalled Stapleton saying during their first phone conversation. "We both think sexual repression is bad for people." Starting in 1977, Flynt went through a brief but memorable born-again period that saw him flying Stapleton in his private jet (painted a prurient pink) and giving a public confession at a church where she was scheduled to speak. Journalists compared Flynt's conversion to Charles Colson's and noted that the former was out on bond pending criminal charges that might net him twenty-five years in prison.

Rather than fully repudiate his ways, however, Flynt merged Christ with career, briefly turning *Hustler* into what one chronicler called a "sex-for-Jesus grab bag of dildos and crucifixes." Flynt soon reverted to "porn-again" status. He kept in touch with Stapleton, though, and she prayed at his bedside following an assassination attempt in 1978.[25]

The Me (and Jesus) Decade

What explained evangelical chic, however fleeting, faddish, and even campy it sometimes seemed? At some level, as one thoughtful critic charged, "Born-again became a buzzword that could be applied to anyone who had made a comeback." Even then, plenty of announced conversions technically were reversions to Christian upbringings. Clearly, though, born-again faith was a fixture in the larger therapeutic turn, a widely cited trend that historian Christopher Lasch famously skewed in his 1979 book, *The Culture of Narcissism*. Lasch pointedly distinguished the newer mode of the "therapeutic" from the older category "religious." "People today," he wrote, "hunger not for personal salvation . . . but for the feeling, the momentary illusion, of personal well-being, health, and psychic security." Lasch's analysis left no room for the Dean Kelley–Peter Berger narrative of conservative church resurgence. In different ways, though, all three linked religion with doctrinal resoluteness, as opposed to cultural resourcefulness. They did not acknowledge how evangelicalism's answers might address real-life needs. Three years before Lasch's book appeared, journalist Tom Wolfe lampooned the 1970s as the "'Me' Decade." The less-remembered second half of Wolfe's *New York* article announced a "Third Great Awakening." Others proposed a synthesis: the "Thee Decade." At a time when self-help books like *I'm OK, You're OK* made up around 15 percent of all best sellers, evangelical and evangelical-friendly books proliferated within the genre. As evangelicals embraced the therapeutic turn, other Americans proved responsive to the therapeutic side of born-again Christianity.[26]

Nowhere was therapeutic evangelicalism more evident than in books addressing marital sexuality. Evangelicals did not shun the sexual revolution of the 1960s and beyond so much as they "simply made it their own." The consensus argument among the countless evangelical sex and marriage guides (usually, the two genres were conflated) was that, in the words of pastor and popular author Bruce Larson, sex should be "enjoyed but always in the context of responsibility." Most such books offered elaborate details on the first part of Larson's formula, while assuming the parties in question were married—to each other.[27]

The most influential evangelical sex guide during the final quarter of the twentieth century was the 1976 book *The Act of Marriage: The Beauty of Sexual Love*, by Tim and Beverly LaHaye. Tim, a fundamentalist Baptist pastor in San Diego, and Beverly, an outspoken social conservative, took the marriage advice they were already dispensing in traveling Family Life Seminars and converted it to manuscript form. The book sold 178,000 copies in its first year and 500,000 copies by the end of the decade, emerging as a standard text in conservative evangelical pre-marriage counseling sessions. Although the LaHayes soon became prominent figures in the Christian Right, their book was decidedly focused on the bedroom, not the ballot box. *The Act of Love*, Tim stressed, "should be read only by married couples, those immediately contemplating marriage, or those who counsel married couples." The husband-wife authorial team—an arrangement common to the genre—offered a vision of sexuality that, if quite traditional when compared to the "key parties" of 1970s lore, was hardly a paean to Victorian mores. To be sure, the LaHayes assumed that wives would stay at home, viewed solo masturbation as selfish, and found oral sex unnecessary (although not un-Christian per se). Yet they specifically attacked the "old Victorian nonsense that a 'nice lady doesn't act as if she enjoys sex.'" To the contrary, the authors maintained an abiding concern with female orgasm. In the modern era, they argued, most wives either expected to—or should expect to—receive vaginal or clitoral stimulation from their husbands, who needed the know-how necessary to satisfy such new, but fair, standards. Because the LaHayes filtered their celebration of modern sexual awareness through the lens of traditional marriage, though, their book had several features that set it far apart from the booming secular sex-guide industry. Their focus on female orgasm, while common to that industry as a whole, translated into a special emphasis on the wedding night and honeymoon—namely, the preparations necessary to ensure that the presumably virginal and fragile bride did not have a traumatic first experience. If the LaHayes sought to demystify female sexuality, their elaborate instructions left little room for experiential learning. Recommended preemptive measures included surgical breaking of the hymen and Dr. Arnold Kegel's "vaginal exercise program." Still, the LaHayes and their peers insisted that Christian couples quite simply had better sex. They cited an extensive 1974–1975 survey of *Redbook* readers, which found that "the greater the intensity of a woman's religious convictions, the likelier she is to be highly satisfied with the sexual pleasure of marriage."[28]

While the LaHayes drew scant attention from nonevangelical readers, Marabel Morgan's 1973 self-help guide for wives, *The Total Woman*, was impossible to ignore. The best-selling nonfiction book of 1974, it sold more than three million copies by 1977, by which time revenue from Morgan's nationwide network of seminars had reached $1.5 million. Morgan described herself as a born-again Christian and published the hardcover version of her book with an evangelical press. "There was no bolt of lightning, only peace," she said of her born-again experience. "I was tickled to death." The final "assignment" in *The Total Woman* is to read a "modern translation" of John Chapter 3 (which contains the verse from which the term "born again" derives) and to accept Christ's "free gift of life."[29]

As with the LaHayes' book, *The Total Woman* remained memorable for its telling quirks. Morgan's book and seminar have lingered in the popular imagination for their fixation on the close of the husband's workday, which was also the pivotal moment in the wife's transition toward a fulfilling evening. Morgan and her fans suggested numerous creative strategies for greeting their hardworking husbands. Possibilities for a six o'clock surprise included "pink baby-doll pyjamas" and "the no-bra look." "What about it, girls?" Morgan asked her readers. "Are you in a marriage rut? Would your husband pick you up for his mistress?" One critic quipped, "A man married to a Total Woman wouldn't know whether he'd be coming home after work to Lolita or Bathsheba." Morgan's ideas echoed those of Helen Andelin, a devout Mormon whose 1963 book and long-running companion class, *Fascinating Womanhood*, offered advice on how to become a "Domestic Goddess." *The Total Woman* was much more candid about sexual intimacy, however, even as it diluted kinkiness with Christian humor. One Southern Baptist woman, Morgan wrote, "welcomed her husband home in black mesh stockings, high heels, and an apron. That's all. He took one look and shouted, 'Praise the Lord!'" Such strategies worked in *The Total Woman*, but not in the popular Fannie Flagg novel *Fried Green Tomatoes at the Whistle Stop Café*, which appeared a decade removed from the peak of Morgan's fame. Both the novel and its film adaptation feature frustrated protagonist Evelyn Crouch greeting her dolt of a husband at the door wearing nothing but cellophane. He shoos her inside.[30]

Morgan's quirks concealed the source of her popularity and relevance. *The Total Woman* posed an existential question that, in its own way, cut to the core of the therapeutic turn: "Have you ever sat across from your husband in a crowded restaurant and wondered, 'What on earth can I say to this man I live with, with whom I am intimate?'" Morgan's solutions were often glib to the point of evasiveness, sating the male ego rather than transforming it. They did, though, serve to update the modern housewife for the sexual revolution, offering what one sympathetic reviewer termed "hints for the unliberated Christian woman." In Flagg's novel, the "Complete Woman" is contrasted with a feminist group session in which women use mirrors to "study their vaginas," something Evelyn is "too scared" to do. Morgan offered a way for her fans to come to terms with sex in the 1970s. She did not attack promiscuity or soaring divorce rates, but rather she spoke to the emerging conventional wisdom: "Good sex is a must for a good marriage." "It isn't that sex holds [a marriage] together," she told *Christianity Today*. "But sex is very, very important." If many readers agreed with her biblically based argument for submitting to husbands (or, as she rephrased it with a nod to the evangelical-friendly Amplified Bible, "adapting" to them), they likely took some solace in her assurance that "for me, the principle very rarely applies." Moreover, Morgan clarified in therapeutic terms, "adapting is my voluntary decision."[31]

Critics tended not to perceive this more pragmatic side of *The Total Woman* and its sequel, *Total Joy*. They made easy sport of what historian and prominent liberal Protestant Martin Marty called "fundies and their fetishes." Marty conjured up an end-times scenario of "the enraptured raptured from their trampolines, he as a dime-a-dance ticket taker and she in raincoat and gorilla mask." Yet Morgan's reach extended well beyond the sociological parameters that Marty had in mind. She claimed that her message was not initially directed to Christians but "to a friend of mine who doesn't even believe there's a God. My whole purpose was to get her attention so that I could help her to find life." By 1976, Morgan had received full profiles in the *New York Times*, *Redbook*, *People*, and other major periodicals. One Total Woman devotee admitted that she enjoyed looking at *Playgirl* magazine, while another listed her tactics for self-improvement as "pottery, transcendental meditation, Total Woman." Not all conservative evangelicals embraced Morgan. Many Christian bookstores initially sold *The Total Woman* behind the counter, if at all. A contributor to *Moody Monthly*, which chose not to run advertisements for the book, attacked the biblical basis of the "advice that 'anything goes' on the marriage bed (or 'under the dining room table')" and lamented its "wide acceptance" among evangelicals. Morgan's success among nonevangelicals, too, highlighted the critical role of popular evangelicalism in mediating the sexual revolution by giving it a traditionalist spin.[32]

The political upshot of Morgan's popularity was less clear. To many observers, *The Total Woman* symbolized the "counterrevolution" against Gloria Steinem's *Ms.* magazine. Its reputation for antifeminism came with good reason. Morgan called herself "a wife and mother first and foremost" and argued that married women should, if possible, stay at home while their children were young. The first acknowledgment in *The Total Woman* is to gospel singer and former beauty queen Anita Bryant, a fellow south Floridian. Bryant, an outspoken Christian and Total Woman seminar alum, gained notoriety in 1977 for leading a successful effort to overturn a gay rights ordinance in Miami-Dade County. At some level, Morgan's books functioned as therapeutic complements to the activism of Bryant or, even more prominently, Equal Rights Amendment opponent Phyllis Schlafly. A Princeton University group tried to arrange a debate between Morgan and feminist icon Betty Friedan, whose *The Feminine Mystique* preceded *The Total Woman* by precisely ten years. Morgan's concern with the marital health and psychological well-being of homemakers, though, scarcely placed her on the fringes of 1970s discourse about family life. In his inaugural address, Jimmy Carter described the American family as "the basis of our society." Morgan's star rose amid a national near-consensus that the family was in a state of crisis.[33]

The success of child psychologist James Dobson pointed to the overlap between this nationwide discussion and conservative evangelical understandings of the family. Dobson served on the faculty of the University of Southern California School of Medicine during the 1970s. He built a therapeutic empire, eventually housed in the organization Focus on the Family, on the back of his 1970 best seller, *Dare to Discipline*. As with the LaHayes' rejection of Victorianism, Dobson's call for increased discipline in American homes and schools reflected secular influences even as it rejected their more radical 1960s-era manifestations. Dobson took great pains to differentiate between "discipline" and "punishment." His "parent-centered" approach called for love applied within a system of clear and consistent parental hierarchy. "Little children," Dobson stressed, "are exceedingly vulnerable to the teaching (good or bad) of their guardians, and mistakes made in the early years prove costly, indeed." While *Dare to Discipline* went through countless reprintings over two decades, it was very much a product of Nixonian law-and-order discourse. Parents should "sell themselves" to their children as "worthy of respect," Dobson wrote. "If they are not worthy of respect, then neither is their religion or their morals, or their government, or their country, or any of their values." The book's popularity endured because it offered practical ideas for balancing discipline with rewards. Still, Dobson clearly rejected the "permissiveness" associated with postwar parenting guru Benjamin Spock. Spock's work had already come under fire amid the youth revolt of the late 1960s, when a *Newsweek* headline asked, "Is Dr. Spock to Blame?" *Dare to Discipline* quickly found a place in the Nixon White House library. By the mid-1970s, Dobson was a regular guest on television talk shows.[34]

The LaHayes, Morgan, Dobson, and other evangelical self-help gurus had a wide reach. They put their own spin on the familiar feminist slogan "the personal is political," blessing conjugal pleasure and (for the more dour Dobson) parental discipline within the economically, socially, and spiritually stable confines of husband-headed households and self-conscious heterosexuality. *Dare to Discipline* and *The Total Woman* were two of many books during the 1970s that emerged from evangelical publishers and then received mass-market paperback distribution from secular presses. Those houses took note of an expanding audience that often flew beneath the radar screen of conventional best-seller lists (partly because of the segmented Christian bookstore market and partly because of a preponderance of backlist sales). The Pocket Books edition of *The Total Woman* had a reported first print run of two million.[35]

The success of Dobson and Morgan, however, paled in comparison to that of Hal Lindsey's prophecy primer, *The Late Great Planet Earth*. It was the stealth best seller of the decade. The book sold 1.5 million copies in its first two years and more than 10 million copies by 1979. Most early sales came from evangelicals, in keeping with Lindsey's past association with Campus Crusade for Christ. When the trade publisher Bantam released a mass-market edition, though, it resurfaced alongside occult and New Age books in secular stores, an ironic nod to the fact that Lindsey cast biblical prophecy as a superior rival to "present day astrologers, prophets, and seers."[36]

Lindsey offered a highly detailed application of premillennial dispensationalism, an eschatology—or theological view of the end-times—that had gained popularity in evangelical circles since the late 1800s. Premillennialists believe that the literal return of Jesus will precede the millennium, the 1,000-year reign of Christ anticipated in the Book of Revelation. Among a small but influential group of Protestants, a particular type of premillennialism, called dispensationalism, took root. By no means did all premillennialists embrace the dispensationalist scheme of history—but that grand narrative came to have an outsize presence in evangelical popular culture. Dispensationalists divide human history into several time periods (or dispensations) during which God related, relates, or will relate to humans in different ways. The theory provides one way of explaining apparent discrepancies between the Old and New Testaments. Most dispensationalists believe in the end-times concept of the "rapture." By this, they mean that believing Christians will physically depart from the world before the actual second coming of

Christ. Lindsey called it "the ultimate trip." The years between the rapture and the second coming will be a period of tribulation for those who are, as a later fiction series put it, "left behind." Lindsey had studied dispensationalism at its leading center, the fundamentalist Dallas Theological Seminary. While lacking the scholarly credentials of his seminary mentor John F. Walvoord—who published his own best-selling analysis of prophecy in 1974—Lindsey offered an accessible but orthodox version of the eschatology updated for the headlines. For Lindsey, the end-times clock started ticking with the 1948 founding of Israel, the "paramount prophetic sign." Further confirmation came with Israel's victory in the 1967 Six-Day War, which put it in control of Jerusalem's Old City and galvanized the latent Zionism of many American evangelicals who hitherto were wary of the secular Israeli state. The road to Armageddon—the climactic battle preceding Christ's return—will feature Russia (what the prophet Ezekiel meant by "Gog"), China (leader of a 200 million–strong "Oriental army"), and a revived Roman Empire (i.e., the European Common Market and its allies). The last entity will produce a "future fuehrer," known in biblical prophecy as the Antichrist. Lindsey's argument was, according to one analysis, "confused and contradictory, saved from total incoherence by the doctrine of the rapture."[37]

All the same, *The Late Great Planet Earth* resonated with the zeitgeist. It reflected both the assertiveness of the Jesus Movement and the mainstreaming of countercultural lingo already evident on popular television shows like *Laugh-In*. Lindsey called his UCLA-area headquarters the J. C. Light and Power Company. His book functioned, in the words of one scholar, "like an imagined rap session," employing subheadings such as "Dead Men Do Tell Tales!" (in reference to ancient historians who corroborate biblical accounts) and "Scarlet O'Harlot" (in reference to the Book of Revelation's Whore of Babylon). Some readers would have recognized the title's similarity to another product of the Golden State, Curt Gentry's 1968 novel, *The Last Days of the Late, Great State of California*, which looks back after a giant earthquake has destroyed the state. Such strained hipness did not detract from *The Late Great Planet Earth*'s popularity, in part because it helped to smooth over the book's zealotry. Lindsey tapped into a larger mood. "Storm warnings, portents, hints of catastrophe haunt our times," Christopher Lasch wrote in *The Culture of Narcissism*. "The question of whether the world will end in fire or in ice, with a bang or a whimper, no longer interests artists alone." Lindsey's sales figures also reflected the popularity of "devil films," such as *The Exorcist* and *The Omen*, which drew entertainment value from the spectral side of Christian theology. Within more explicitly Christian circles, the 1972 end-times film

A Thief in the Night, in which believers are raptured to heaven but the protagonist is left behind to suffer, began its long march toward a purported 300 million viewers.[38]

The documentary version of *The Late Great Planet Earth* explicitly translated Lindsey's prophecies into the present tense. The movie, which was a Hollywood hit in early 1979, suggested how 1970s evangelicalism could synergize with almost any subject. Famous director and actor Orson Welles hosted the hour-and-a-half shuttle run between Jesus Movement apocalypticism and antigrowth liberalism. Welles had a long-standing interest in forecasting; he also narrated the documentary version of Alvin Toffler's *Future Shock*. Welles's narration uncritically linked pessimism with eschatology, while Lindsey's sermonettes filled in some of the theological blanks. "The big question becomes," Welles stated at one point, "when will the seven-year countdown [to Armageddon] begin?" A large portion of the movie consists of interviews with futurists and scientists, most of whom likely could not have distinguished dispensationalism from Deuteronomy. Still, their hyperbolic gloominess about population control and environmental catastrophe was oddly in tune with Lindsey's declaration that the status of the United States was likely to decline. (Lindsey hedged slightly because of the dilemma—for a fundamentalist, at least—that the Bible does not mention the western hemisphere.) In a decade that saw oil shortages, the Yom Kippur War, and the Munich massacre, many readers and viewers had reason to heed Lindsey's admonition to "keep your eyes on the Middle East." His end-times scenario included mass Jewish conversions to Christianity, and he made a point of evangelizing to Jews, who formed a disproportionate presence in the Jesus Movement. At the same time, Lindsey emphatically saw the nation of Israel as a manifestation of God's will—a fact that helped to explain the appearance in the documentary of future Israeli president Chaim Herzog.[39]

In straddling several genres—testimony, propaganda, camp, and science fiction among them—the documentary version of *The Late Great Planet Earth* demonstrated the place of evangelical perspectives in popular futurism. *New York Times* critic Janet Maslin dismissed the film's "grim but sketchy hypothesis." But many Americans bought into more sophisticated versions of the pessimism theme in 1979. The best-selling book of that year was historian Barbara Tuchman's *A Distant Mirror*, a narrative of the Plague-filled fourteenth century. Bob Dylan's pastor had turned him on to Lindsey, and Dylan's gloomy 1979 song "Slow Train Coming" warned of "foreign oil controlling American soil" and "sheiks walking around like kings." As the 1970s came to a close, another prominent futurist, Jeremy Rifkin, saw born-again Christianity as a sign of the times. "America is moving from a growth period to a decay period," Rifkin argued. He interpreted the "evangelical-Charismatic movement" as "the single most visible and significant response" to the resultant economic, social, and cultural changes. Perhaps postindustrial America was giving religion a new relevance. Toffler, for his part, by then acknowledged the existence of the " 'born-again' movement" but cast its believers as "scrambling for salvation in a society they picture as decadent and doomed." Toffler remained, in effect, a believer in secularization theory, while Rifkin saw a "second Protestant reformation" on the horizon. Both, however, worried about "the religio-politics that may well lie ahead," with its "authoritarian streak" and potential for "fascism."[40]

During the evangelical Seventies, born-again Christianity came to occupy a prominent place in discussions about the direction of America. Commentators on evangelicalism, puffed up by book contracts from Harper and Row and other trade publishers, could confidently declare that it was "really the mainline brand of American Christianity." Not all evangelical leaders celebrated this development. Many had spent the postwar years creating "a nonsectarian evangelical consensus" centered on such forums as *Christianity Today*. Now, one contemporary observer argued, "the age of monolithic unity (perhaps always exaggerated)" was "as dead as the idea that evangelicals are an obscure group of religious fanatics to whom no serious observer of American life need pay any attention." Indeed, the two deaths went hand in hand. Whatever evangelical consensus had existed was cracking up just as born-again Christianity was coming out. Then, as since, evangelical writers policed the boundaries of orthodoxy and warned about the cost of becoming "respectable and even fashionable." *Christianity Today* editor Harold Lindsell published a cranky but influential 1976 screed, *The Battle for the Bible*, which excluded from "evangelical" anyone who did not hold firm to biblical "inerrancy." Others regretted the antics of increasingly popular television ministers, such as Jerry Falwell. An evangelical satirical magazine, the *Wittenburg Door*, poked fun of "The Totaled Woman" (as well as its own initially inadvertent misspelling of Luther's home city).[41]

Such divisions did not dilute the influence of evangelicalism, though; they simply dispersed it. A prominent evangelical magazine ranked Lindsell's book as the third most important religious story of the bicentennial year. First place was the reemergence of evangelicals as—"for the first time in 50 years—the dominant religious force in the country." Second place went to the growing "efforts to motivate Christians into the political arena." The latter two narratives were well on their way to seeming synonymous to many Americans.[42]

The direction of evangelical political influence remained uncertain as the avowedly born-again Jimmy Carter assumed office. Three years earlier, amid the Watergate crisis, future Christian Right figurehead Pat Robertson's zeal for evangelism still contrasted with his father's fame as a senator. "After my conversion to Christ," Robertson stated, "my political outlook changed completely. As it now stands, I'm not political in thinking but spiritual—except that I hope Bible-believing people will be placed in positions of political responsibility." Soon, though, Robertson and others began seeing politics as a mission unto itself. Carter's presidency provided the ironic impetus for this new direction.[43]

During the height of the Watergate crisis, Republican congressman John Anderson addressed an audience of evangelical power brokers. His message to the annual meeting of the National Association of Evangelicals was at once familiar and novel. It reflected the optimism, along with the anxiety, latent in 1970s evangelical politics. Anderson began with a narrative staple of American evangelical self-analysis: the steady struggle against great obstacles—in this case, the financial prowess and cultural cachet of liberal Protestant elites. Then his tone shifted. "Well," Anderson declared, "things have changed. Now *they* are the 'kooks'—and *we* are the 'beautiful people.' *Our* prayer breakfasts are so popular that only those with engraved invitations are allowed to attend. *Our* evangelists have the ready ear of those in positions of highest authority. *Our* churches are growing, and theirs are withering." This was no time to gloat, though, for the "new evangelical majority in American religion bears a heavy responsibility for the nation's future." With power came burdens.[1]

The same year saw the publication of an essay collection bearing the excitable title *Politics and Religion Can Mix!* In it, an eclectic group of prominent politicians affirmed the title's thesis, remaining comfortably within the confines of an American civil religion that others viewed as being under duress. Liberal Republican ex-senator Margaret Chase Smith of Maine and conservative Democratic governor George Wallace of Alabama agreed that God was a wonderful resource in times of crisis. Nelson Rockefeller, better associated with a second marriage than with a second birth, recalled his Christian upbringing. Jimmy Carter, the ambitious governor of Georgia, affirmed the central place of Jesus Christ in his life. But it was another rising Southern Democrat who best articulated the central theme of the book. Florida governor Reubin Askew, known both for his moderate politics and his work with the evangelical organization Campus Crusade for Christ, employed a familiar adage that found new life in the next presidential campaign. "I have often stated," he wrote, "that, while I believe in the separation of church and state, I do not believe in the separation of church and statesman."[2]

The above examples point to the divided mind of born-again politics during the 1970s. Some evangelicals delighted in their newfound prominence, others fretted that Christians were losing influence in a secular society, and still others worried that evangelicals remained wedded to conservatism. Increasingly, however, American evangelicals of all political persuasions saw an opportunity to do something about the state of their nation. In the wake of Watergate, a consensus formed that born-again faith could contribute something good—perhaps even essential—to the body politic. A dignified and heartfelt evangelical language of public service and responsibility began to enter American politics. A different form of evangelical politics soon followed, one shaped less by the ethical challenges that came with Watergate and more by the moral changes connected with the 1960s. No one embodied the first form of evangelical politics more than Jimmy Carter. Barely on the national radar screen when John Anderson gave his speech, Carter assumed the presidency two years later. A centrist by inclination, he nonetheless drew from a left-leaning tradition of born-again public witness. This evangelical left competed with its much larger right-wing counterpart to shape the meaning of born-again politics in the last quarter of the twentieth century and beyond. Neither the evangelical left nor right mapped neatly onto the ideological spectrum. Yet neither camp proved able to transcend America's limited vocabulary of liberal versus conservative. Instead, they influenced the meaning of those labels.

The ideological sorting out of evangelical politics did not culminate with the Year of the Evangelical, but rather flowed from it. In the process, politics became the dominant lens through which a generation of Americans encountered and evaluated born-again Christianity. Evangelicalism remained a cultural force independent of campaign cycles and Sunday morning news shows. Still, more than any other factor, the prominence of evangelicalism in post-Watergate politics made born-again Christianity significant to nonevangelical Americans. Over time, many Americans came to associate evangelicalism with Ronald Reagan, not Jimmy Carter. Looking back from the twenty-first century, the significantly greater success of the evangelical right seems foreordained. Yet from the vantage point of 1974, Anderson and Askew had little reason to anticipate that outcome. In one of the richest ironies in recent American political history, the catalyst for their disappointment was the election of a president who shared the initials of his Lord and Savior.

The Evangelical Left

At the beginning of the 1970s, the category "evangelical" was not an espe-
cially useful indicator of where a given official fell on the political continuum.
In Congress, John Anderson occupied the center, with Democratic senator
George McGovern of South Dakota on his left and Republican senator Barry
Goldwater of Arizona on his right. The first was an active evangelical, the
second a former evangelical, and the third an unenthusiastic Episcopalian.
When Anderson edited his own volume about Christians in politics,
McGovern contributed a chapter on "The Politics of Hunger." Goldwater
titled his essay "The Politics of Morality." McGovern urged Christians to
support progressive federal legislation, while Goldwater criticized liberal cler-
gymen for equating godliness with government. As McGovern emerged as a
viable presidential candidate in 1972, the rhetorical momentum was on his
side. McGovern and many of his supporters did not hesitate to enlist Jesus in
the case for withdrawing from Vietnam to focus on problems at home. The
son of a Wesleyan Methodist minister, McGovern had briefly occupied a
Methodist pastorate of his own as a seminary student. McGovern's campaign
manager, Gary Hart, came from a morally austere Church of the Nazarene
background. By the 1970s, neither McGovern nor Hart could be classified as
evangelicals. But they understood the language of born-again faith no less
than did Richard Nixon, himself of evangelical Quaker stock.[3]

Still, when a group called "Evangelicals for McGovern" surfaced after the
Democratic convention, heads turned among reporters accustomed to covering the Billy Graham–Nixon alliance. The small but vocal organization
reflected the decentralized nature of the McGovern campaign. A fund-raising
letter argued that McGovern's Wesleyan upbringing had "helped produce a
candid, decent man, who can restore credibility to the presidency and reorder
our national priorities." Evangelicals for McGovern explicitly sought to "end
the outdated stereotype" that "conservative-theology-equals-conservative-
politics." The McGovern campaign took notice. After some wrangling, the
candidate secured an invitation to speak in Illinois at Wheaton College, the
alma mater of Graham himself and the flagship institution of evangelical
higher education. Both McGovern's theology and politics were decidedly
more liberal than the Wheaton brand. Speaking to a crowd dotted with pro-
Nixon posters, though, McGovern voiced Christian sentiments that few in
the audience were likely to dispute. "We all stand for the constitutional principle of the separation of church and state," he asserted. "But we should all
stand against the distortion of that principle into the practice of the separation

of faith from politics, the separation of morality from government." McGovern described his pious upbringing and praised past evangelical crusaders for social justice. "Because spiritual currents are moving across this land," McGovern declared, "I am hopeful for our future." He closed by citing Puritan minister John Winthrop's "city upon a hill" sermon and the Old Testament prophet Micah's call "to do justly, and to love mercy, and to walk humbly with thy God." McGovern's mini-sermon at Wheaton highlighted his increasingly prophetic tone toward the end of the campaign. The Democratic nominee "has turned more furiously evangelical than any major party candidate since William Jennings Bryan," noted *Newsweek* in an article titled "McGovern's Politics of Righteousness."[4]

In the end, McGovern fared even worse among evangelicals than with the electorate as a whole. Nixon gained an estimated 84 percent of evangelical Protestant votes while crushing McGovern by a margin of more than 20 points. In his concession speech, McGovern turned to the Book of Isaiah: "They that wait upon the Lord shall renew their strength." This would not be the last time that a majority of evangelical voters would side with the less pious but more conservative candidate. In November 1972, though, many progressive evangelicals thought time was on their side.[5]

They had reason for hope. By the early 1970s, more and more evangelical thinkers were emphasizing what they called "social concern," in contrast to the traditional priority of soul-saving. A leading theologian touted "the rediscovery of the social implications of the gospel on the part of many evangelical leaders today." The overwhelming assumption—inside and outside evangelical circles—was that this trend heralded a political turn to the left.[6]

The "young evangelicals," as members of the evangelical left were sometimes known, rejected the conservatism of their twentieth-century biological parents and embraced the activism of their nineteenth-century spiritual forbearers. While the "neoevangelicals" actually had pioneered the renewal of evangelical social concern starting in the 1940s, they possessed an overwhelmingly right-leaning political outlook that did not waver under the strain of Watergate. Theologian Carl F. H. Henry—whose 1947 tract *The Uneasy Conscience of Modern Fundamentalism* ironically served as a source of inspiration to the evangelical left—wrote an "Open Letter to President Ford" in 1976. Henry railed against "taxes that snatch away one day's earnings in every five" and "the flagrant schemes of welfare opportunists." The younger generation fought back by "discovering a heritage" of evangelical social activism that was much more radical than what Henry had in mind. The Anabaptists of the early Reformation—dissenters from Catholic and Protestant state churches alike—provided one source of inspiration. The most usable past was the world of antebellum American reform. As one young evangelical argued, "19th century evangelism stimulated in the people a concern for social issues which resulted in the abolition of slavery, prison reform, humane treatment for the mentally ill, and improved working conditions for industrial laborers. There was at that time no dichotomy between spiritual renewal and social compassion." What had happened to the abolitionist legacy of Charles Finney, the Tappan brothers, and the early administrators of Oberlin and Wheaton Colleges? Following the arguments of evangelical scholars Timothy Smith, a historian, and David Moberg, a sociologist, progressive evangelicals spoke of a World War I–era "Great Reversal." They referred to the process by which fundamentalists, reacting against the perceived excesses of the Social Gospel and theological liberalism, turned away from social issues and toward a narrower focus on proselytization, individual salvation, and doctrinal essentials. The subsequent association of conservative politics and evangelical Christianity burdened the latter with an "unequal yoke," in the words of historian and activist Richard Pierard. Some evangelicals made the above arguments in support of a less partisan (i.e., less Republican) approach to politics. Others embraced a New Left–infused, "Post-American" brand of prophetic radicalism (per the name of a leading magazine of the evangelical left).[7]

While Evangelicals for McGovern attracted media curiosity, the real coming-out moment for the evangelical left occurred a year later when around fifty evangelical activists and leaders convened during the Thanksgiving holiday at an inner-city Chicago YMCA hotel. The resulting Chicago Declaration of Evangelical Social Concern eventually attracted a broad array of endorsers, including a former editor of *Christianity Today* and the president of the National Association of Evangelicals. It was, in the words of organizer Ron Sider—who had been the driving force behind Evangelicals for McGovern—a "propitious moment" for "the new evangelical majority." Religious and political trends were working in its favor. "Externally, liberal theology and its ecclesiastical bureaucracy are in serious trouble," Sider asserted. "In addition, the disruptive events of Vietnam and Watergate are freeing evangelicals from an automatic acceptance of traditional socio-political presuppositions." The Chicago gathering caught the notice of prominent media outlets. Marjorie Hyer, a *Washington Post* reporter writing in the liberal *Christian Century*, gushed, "If 40 million evangelicals in this country should start taking seriously all those problems that every religious convention resolutionizes about—well, it boggles the mind to think what could happen." Critics also took note. Evangelical theologian Harold O. J. Brown warned conservative readers of the *National Review* that they stood in danger of losing the born-again electorate.[8]

Despite such high expectations, the 1970s evangelical left amounted to less than the sum of its parts. From the start there were fundamental differences between Calvinist-oriented evangelicals, who promoted a reform agenda within the ordained political system, and Anabaptist-influenced evangelicals, who sought to build prophetic communities separate from the fallen order. Racial and gender divisions rattled the evangelical left no less than the political left as a whole. Some progressive black evangelicals, many of whom had emerged from white-dominated evangelical institutions, balked at being grouped with the similarly white-centered community of young evangelicals. Other progressive or moderate evangelicals remained wary of alienating their more conservative peers. In a host of books, they attempted to prod evangelicals from their wariness of political activism, while largely steering clear of policy specifics.[9]

Many voices on the evangelical left struck more strident notes. In a widely cited book, *Rich Christians in an Age of Hunger*, Ron Sider called for radical "structural" approaches to global poverty. "Famine is alive and well on planet earth," he wrote in an allusion to (and implicit dismissal of) end-times theologian Hal Lindsey's recent book, *Satan Is Alive and Well on Planet Earth*. Another prominent progressive evangelical, Jim Wallis, belonged to the Post-American community, which in 1975 relocated from suburban Chicago to Washington, DC, and changed its name to Sojourners. Contributors to the group's publication did not hesitate to brand the United States as a modern-day Babylon. Sojourners aspired to form "a new community which is a sign of the kingdom in history, an alien society of God's people," while the magazine that took the same name provided "a forum for the advocacy of new forms of discipleship, community, social action, and biblical political witness." Wallis made a point of grounding his arguments in biblical support even as he echoed New Left themes. What an early chronicler of the young evangelicals called their "revolution in orthodoxy" often pushed the limits of conventional evangelical readings of scripture. Leaders of a "biblical feminism" movement aspired to provide "organized opposition" to Marabel Morgan's Total Woman philosophy. The editors at the normally conservative *Christianity Today* shared their support for ratification of the Equal Rights Amendment. More controversially, two leading biblical feminists explicitly endorsed the *Roe v. Wade* decision, a minority position among evangelical leftists, many of whom initially hesitated to take a public stance on abortion. Still farther to the left were a nascent gay-support organization, Evangelicals Concerned, and an explicitly gay denomination, Metropolitan Community Church, the latter of which defied stereotypes with its Pentecostal roots and evangelical tones.[10]

By the mid-1970s, as "the expansive social policy of the sixties" yielded to "the more restrictive and hesitant social policy of the seventies," progressive evangelicals had few political victories to show for their efforts. Indeed, the subsequent history of the evangelical left practically begs for a tragic interpretation. Its initially hopeful rhetoric rested on an impassioned but inaccurate reading of the born-again terrain. Evangelicalism's "very survival in the 1970's may well depend on whether it can escape from the Unequal Yoke," Pierard wrote in 1970, on the cusp of a decade in which conservative and moderate forms of evangelicalism would generate unprecedented headlines. "If nothing is done, evangelicalism in the 1980's will be relegated to the status of a small and insignificant sect."[11]

Still, the broader evangelical left found sympathizers in surprisingly high places. Between the resolution of the Watergate crisis and the arrival of Jimmy Carter, a modest but thriving group of evangelical politicos came of age. An August 1974 *Time* profile called them "the God Network in Washington." Mark Hatfield, John Anderson, Iowa Democratic senator Harold Hughes, Minnesota Republican congressman Al Quie, and Mississippi Democratic senator John Stennis were among the most prominent names within a highly informal community that, on an even less formal level, also included Carter, Reubin Askew, and Alabama Republican congressman John Buchanan. The mid-1970s "God Network" contained liberals, moderates, and conservatives, although the loudest voices came from the left. Hughes, a recovered alcoholic whose proclivities for charismatic Christianity surfaced when he made a brief run for the 1972 Democratic presidential nomination, was "Hatfield's closest ally in the Senate on a spiritual, theological, personal, and political level," according to a longtime Hatfield aide. Many leading Washington evangelicals shared an attachment to Doug Coe, leader of the publicity-shy but well-connected Christian political outreach organization commonly known as "the Fellowship." Hughes retired from the Senate in 1974 in order to work with the Fellowship. Coe's ties to Hatfield dated back to Willamette University, where as an undergraduate Coe had ministered to the future senator, who was then the dean of students. Two decades later, Coe, Hatfield, and Hughes provided spiritual mentorship to Charles Colson, whose political beliefs remained decidedly to the right of the two senators. Colson described the Fellowship as comprising a "veritable underground of Christ's men all through government." Indeed, its work remained unclear even to some of the participants in its array of Beltway prayer groups. The organization, which had existed in various forms since the mid-1930s, brought together such an influential set of political actors that, then and more recently, critics wondered if its detachment from a specific ideology was merely cover for a power grab.[12]

Some mid-1970s evangelical politicos aspired to forge a new kind of politics. They spoke a bipartisan language of righteousness that straddled conventional political categories in an attempt to transcend them. John Anderson, who remains underappreciated as an evangelical political actor, epitomized the sometimes strained search for an evangelical political style. He started his congressional career in the early 1960s as a conventional Midwestern Republican. Faced with an early political challenge, he proposed amending the Constitution to formally declare the United States a "Christian nation." His move to the left began in the mid-1960s and led him to provide bipartisan cover for the landmark 1968 open housing legislation. Anderson's evangelical credentials remained intact, however. He held an honorary degree from Wheaton College, served on the board of the evangelistic group Youth for Christ, and earned the National Association of Evangelicals' Outstanding Layman of the Year honor in 1964. By the Nixon years, Anderson was on a mission to refashion evangelical politics. "To begin with, while I am essentially a religious conservative," he wrote in one of several books released by the evangelical publishing house Word, "I do not believe that religious conservatism must be equated with or regarded as synonymous with conservative solutions to all our political problems.... We need a more positive outlook toward government. As evangelicals, we have tended to have a negative attitude toward government." He quoted the Chicago Declaration when making the case for Christian political involvement.[13]

Mark Hatfield, though, was the true hero of the evangelical left. The Oregonian had long been a rising star in GOP circles and a fixture in evangelical ones. By 1972, his version of Republican liberalism made him appealing as a rumored running mate not for Nixon this time, but for McGovern. Hatfield's popularity within the evangelical left derived from his strident criticism of civil religion and his willingness to take the young evangelicals seriously. Hatfield's aide Wes Michaelson (who eventually became a *Sojourners* editor) introduced the senator to Wallis. Hatfield eagerly mentored the Post-American community and encouraged Wallis to relocate to Washington, DC. Wallis, by his own account, provided much of the language that Hatfield used when denouncing "civil religion" (and, by extension, Nixon) at the 1973 National Prayer Breakfast. Hatfield was hardly a thoroughgoing liberal, however, on many fiscal and social issues. He became a strong, if somewhat unconventional, opponent of abortion rights, and he cosponsored early legislation to amend the Constitution to overturn the 1973 *Roe v. Wade* decision (while permitting exceptions for rape and endangerment of pregnant women). Hatfield endured into the 1990s as a museum piece of the evangelical Seventies.[14]

Hatfield, Anderson, and their loose clique of evangelical statesmen carved out a unique political space in the mid-1970s. Before the moment was over, a politically moderate and explicitly evangelical candidate occupied the White House. Even many conservative evangelicals who could barely stomach Hatfield's politics celebrated Jimmy Carter's successful candidacy. "The post-Watergate evangelical recovery," observed the managing editor of *Christianity Today* in 1976, "brought out a feeling long latent that evangelicals should attempt to take a stronger hand in the affairs of the country, especially through political avenues."[15]

"J. C. CAN SAVE AMERICA!"

Jimmy Carter rode an evangelical wave into the White House. By the time he appeared on the national scene, born-again Christianity was ripe for a presidential run. Carter succeeded where Hatfield, Anderson, and Hughes did not because he shared their pious ways but not their iconoclastic proclivities. His firm Baptist belief in the separation of church and state gave him confidence that he could keep his identities as Christian and politician in tidy categories, even as he talked openly about his faith. Carter recalled disagreeing with Harold Hughes's skepticism about whether a good politician or businessmen could, in the end, also have a "full-time commitment to Christ." Commentators, including McGovern himself, noted the similarities between Carter's outsider strategy and McGovern's insurgent run, including their use of moralistic language. Yet Carter was a Sunday School teacher at heart. As a candidate, he preferred the extended hand of Christian fellowship to the pointed finger of pastoral rebuke.[16]

For all of these reasons, Carter attracted tepid support and, in some cases, fierce criticism from evangelical leftists. Their increasingly prophetic tone, combined with their dismissive take on civil religion, left them largely unwilling to embrace the retail side of presidential politics. Clearly, Carter was no McGovern. Wes Michaelson, the confidant of Hatfield and Wallis, cast a protest vote in 1976 for Donald Duck. Four years later, a journalist described evangelical left activists as "even more" upset with Carter than were their counterparts on the right.[17]

Still, Carter filled a role that Michaelson and his peers had helped to create. Carter was never intimate with most of the "God Network"—just as he lacked ties with the elite, largely Northern neoevangelical world. But he had deep links with progressive Southern Baptists, who in turn had connections to the growing evangelical left. Jimmy Allen, an influential Baptist pastor and Carter supporter, belonged to Sider's Evangelicals for Social Action, and leading Southern Baptist progressive Foy Valentine contributed an essay to the book version of the Chicago Declaration.[18]

Carter's religious identity was evident long before it became a cause célèbre during the 1976 Democratic primary season. In December 1974, when announcing his presidential candidacy at the National Press Club in Washington, DC, Carter described his run in biblical terms. "The Bible says: 'If the trumpet give an uncertain sound, who shall prepare himself to the battle? [1 Corinthians 14:8].' As a planner and a businessman, and a chief executive, I know from experience that uncertainty is a devastating affliction in private life and in government," said Carter. "It is time for us to reaffirm and to strengthen our ethical and spiritual and political beliefs." His audience included Presbyterian minister Richard Halverson, a longtime associate of the Fellowship and "Washington's best-known evangelical preacher." Halverson's Fourth Presbyterian Church in Bethesda, Maryland, served as a kind of gathered community for elite Beltway evangelicals, including Hatfield, Anderson, and Coe. Carter called himself "a born-again Christian" in a 1975 *Newsweek* article, while the *Los Angeles Times* titled its profile of him "Carter: The Religious Moralist Candidate for President." The candidate linked his faith with his political mission while campaigning that year in the critical primary state of New Hampshire. "I'm running for president because I am a deeply religious person," he told an audience in Manchester. "The most important thing in my life is my belief and my commitment in God." The *New York Times* columnist William Safire condescendingly declared Carter's subsequent victory in the New Hampshire primary "a triumph of evangelical pseudo-conservatism."[19]

Carter's faith made national news during the run-up to the important North Carolina primary. At a small gathering in Winston-Salem, Carter described "a deeply profound religious experience that changed my life dramatically." His personal transformation followed a brutal and unsuccessful 1966 run for the Georgia governorship. Carter continued talking about his faith during a press conference the next day. It was nothing new for an avowedly Christian candidate—and a Southern Baptist, at that—to seek major office. By the time of the late March primary, though, Carter commanded coverage as the clear front-runner for the presidential nomination. Moreover, to judge from the more restrained tone Carter had previously used to describe his Christian faith—even in *Why Not the Best?*, his campaign biography published by a Southern Baptist press—his new candidness appeared part of a larger strategy. Carter claimed that his decision to respond to questions about his faith followed "a great deal of prayerful thought" and was not intended "to get votes." At the same time, he told Houston television journalist Cal Thomas, "I think I'll be a better president because of my deep religious convictions."[20]

Carter's faith talk drew attention to born-again Christianity, as well as to his campaign. While Carter only occasionally used the phrase "born again," a journalistic establishment already primed by the Jesus Movement and other evangelical phenomena quickly fixated on the term. Charles Colson's memoir of the same title, released around the time of the North Carolina primary, reinforced the emphasis. By June 1976, Carter's Sunday School class at Plains Baptist Church attracted as many reporters as congregants. One network news celebrity introduced himself to the class as "Sam Donaldson of Great Falls, Virginia." Journalists sometimes stumbled over "born-again" jargon or used "evangelism" when they meant "evangelicalism." NBC news anchor John Chancellor assured viewers that Carter's "profound experience" was "described by other Baptists as a common experience, not something out of the ordinary." (To be sure, casual born-again talk was then unfamiliar even to many Christians, including Catholics and high church Protestants.) Carter also received some ribbing from the press corps. An Associated Press reporter taped to Carter's charter jet a poster featuring a bearded, Christ-like Carter above the caption "J. C. CAN SAVE AMERICA!" The slogan, which appeared on several items of campaign paraphernalia, straddled the line between satire and support. Generally, though, the coverage of Carter's religious background was polite and inquisitive. The evangelical press, of course, needed no primer on the meaning of born again, and Christian publishing houses quickly churned out ruminations on Carter's faith. Most such works had a boosterish quality that bordered on hagiography. Carter, two authors crowed, "was one of the best things to happen to American evangelical Christianity in this century."[21]

Ultimately, Carter crafted a winning brand of evangelical politics. In contrast to the Christian Right leaders who would soon oppose him, he linked his faith with personal integrity and political cleanliness, rather than with

Christian nationalism and social conservatism. He discussed his faith in deeply personal, character-based terms, combining the Protestant ethic with the therapeutic turn. Carter was, as journalist Robert Shogan argued, the first successful presidential candidate "to use his character, as expressed by his religious faith and accompanying morality, as a direct reason for voting for him and for supporting his stewardship." "As President," Carter stated in an interview released by the Baptist Press news service, "I would try to exemplify in every moment of my life the attitudes and actions of a Christian." "I believe God wants me to be the *best* politician I can possibly be," he declared.[22]

This approach allowed Carter to reach out to theologically conservative voters while also riding the post-Watergate reform wave. "If I ever tell a lie," he declared in a prominent campaign release, "make a misleading statement, avoid a controversial issue, or betray your trust, don't support me." When asked to describe his campaign in a word, Carter responded, "That word would be faith." Such casual—and, to judge from the reception, credible—faith talk enabled him to reach fellow evangelicals without resorting to Nixon-style paeans to civil religion. Instead, he could simply appeal to the widely held belief among evangelicals that good Christians make good leaders. During convention season, a "Citizens for Carter" advertisement appeared in *Christianity Today* asking, "Does a Dedicated Evangelical Belong in the White House?" The advertisement, paid for by an independent political action committee, made a nonideological pitch for Christian statesmanship. "In this post-Watergate era," the 1976 election presented "a unique opportunity for evangelicals to support good government" and to embrace "the cause of American Renewal." Carter was the perfect vessel for this mission. "Remember," the advertisement advised by way of quoting 2 Samuel 23:3, " 'He that rules over men must be just, ruling in the fear of God.' "[23]

The possibilities of born-again politics, four years removed from McGovern's landslide loss, were potent enough to defuse the occasionally hyperbolic concerns of liberal Democrats about "the implication that evangelical principles can solve social, economic, and international perplexities." Presidential candidate Henry "Scoop" Jackson, Carter's rival for the affection of moderate Democrats, complained that Carter was "wearing his religion on his sleeve." At the same time, Jackson hired evangelical author Lowell Streiker to advise him on religious voters. The revivalistic tone of the 1976 Democratic convention caused one evangelical Republican to wonder facetiously "whether God had indeed switched parties." Carter's faith also offered hope that the party could overcome its racial divisions. The convention climaxed with Carter and running mate Walter Mondale sharing the stage with civil rights legends Andrew Young, Coretta Scott King, and Martin Luther King Sr. Also present, along with other Democratic power brokers, was segregationist emblem George Wallace. "Surely the Lord is in this place," said the elder King when giving the benediction. "Surely the Lord has sent Jimmy Carter to come out and bring America back to where it belongs." Afterward, the convention crowd—journalists included—swayed to the civil rights anthem "We Shall Overcome."[24]

Evangelical politics did have inherent perils, especially for a Southern Baptist candidate from a Deep South state. Carter's civil rights allies proved helpful amid the late revelation that his home congregation had a policy of excluding "Negroes and other civil rights agitators" from the church. In late October, journalist Helen Thomas asked Carter about the absence of African Americans at Plains Baptist. Carter said that he thought blacks could join the church "if they wanted to." On the following Sunday, Clennon King, a local black minister known for creative forms of civil rights activism, attempted, unsuccessfully, to do so. Carter had to address the issue in his final preelection press conference, explaining why he would not resign his membership. He cast his stand as a matter of religious integrity. "I think my best approach is to stay within the church and to try to change the attitudes which I abhor," Carter said. "Now if it was a country club, I would have to quit. But this is not my church, it's God's church. And I can't quit my lifetime of worship habit and commitment because of a remnant of discrimination which has been alleviated a great deal in the last ten years." Despite the Plains Baptist flap, Carter's evangelical faith assisted his successful outreach to African American voters. Following the November election, his church voted to end its policy of excluding blacks from services. After Carter took office, though, the congregation fired embattled pastor Bruce Edwards.[25]

Carter's biggest evangelical problem lay with some of his fellow believers. Even before the Plains Baptist policy surfaced, the candidate caught flak for remarks he made in a widely covered (and presumably widely read) interview in *Playboy* magazine. In the 1970s, *Playboy* remained a respected venue, if not exactly a mainstream forum, for long-form print journalism. The publication took particular interest in the evangelical turn in American politics, a development that both threatened the Hefnerian worldview and provided it with a handy foil. Its monthly interviews routinely attracted figures of Carter's stature. The Carter campaign desired to reach out to the sophisticated, liberal-leaning readership of this self-styled gentleman's magazine—precisely the type of voters who might be put off by his Baptist piety. The candidate simply wanted to say, "I'm normal," insisted Carter media guru Gerald

Rafshoon a decade later. In keeping with the general tone of *Playboy* interviews, including an earlier one with George McGovern, Carter offered candid and detailed insights on a range of subjects. The controversial comments came toward the end of the interview. Almost as a postscript, and apparently without prompting from journalist Robert Scheer, Carter turned introspective and confessional. "I've looked on a lot of women with lust," the candidate admitted. "I've committed adultery in my heart many times," he added, before noting that Jesus warned against judging the "one guy [who] screws a whole bunch of women while the other guy is loyal to his wife." However awkward his choice of words, Carter surely was trying to humanize himself more to swing voters than to swingers. His closing lines echoed a recurrent campaign strategy of linking religious honesty with political integrity. "But I don't think I would *ever* take on the same frame of mind that Nixon or Johnson did— lying, cheating and distorting the truth," he stated. "Not taking into consideration my hope for my strength of character, I think that my religious beliefs alone would prevent that from happening to me. I have that confidence. I hope it's justified." Carter had already told Scheer that he did not anticipate criticism for granting an interview to *Playboy*.[26]

The prediction proved mistaken. Opponents deftly converted Barry Goldwater's failed 1964 campaign slogan, "In Your Heart, You Know He's Right," into a joke about Carter: "In his heart, he knows your wife." For many critics, Carter's decision to grant an interview to a soft-core pornographic magazine was problem enough. Carter tried to minimize the damage by describing the interview as "a good way to let the American people, particularly *Playboy* readers, know about my religious beliefs." His contemporaneous interview with libertine writer Norman Mailer (who produced a surprisingly favorable profile in the *New York Times*) did nothing to redeem his image in some quarters of the Bible Belt. The loudest reproaches came from conservative evangelicals who were already wary of Carter. "A lot of us are not convinced that Mr. Carter is truly in the evangelical Christian camp," stated a minister from Mobile, Alabama. Rising televangelist Jerry Falwell, who had already invited President Gerald Ford to visit his church in Lynchburg, Virginia, singled out Carter for criticism on his nationally syndicated *Old-Time Gospel Hour* program. Candidate Ford eagerly noted that he had turned down a *Playboy* interview request "with an emphatic no," and the Ford team soon began what one civil libertarian called "a massive smear campaign aimed at breaking down [Carter's] image of a deeply committed Christian." The effort reportedly entailed widespread distribution of a cartoon depicting Carter behind a pulpit wielding both a Bible and a *Playboy*. Leading conservative Southern Baptist W. A. Criswell, the pastor of First Baptist Church in Dallas, used the *Playboy* flap as a pretext to declare his support for Ford after a Sunday service that the president himself had attended. Ford believed that Carter's disparaging remarks about Lyndon Johnson in *Playboy* had put Texas in play. Carter made a point of attending church in nearby Fort Worth the Sunday before the election and ended up winning the state. In the final presidential debate, which Carter was widely credited with winning, he attempted some self-deprecating humor. "If I should ever decide in the future to discuss my deep Christian beliefs and condemnation and sinfulness," he declared, "I'll use another forum besides *Playboy*." In the end, most Southern Baptist leaders stood by Carter, whose pastor defended the candidate in a campaign letter mailed to all ministers in the Southern Baptist Convention (SBC) directory. Carter's equation of lust with adultery, after all, came directly from the Sermon on the Mount.[27]

The *Playboy* controversy revealed that Ford, too, had an evangelical strategy. His denial of that fact has shaped the subsequent conventional wisdom that the 1976 race "was a battle between two born-again Christians— but only one was willing to run as one." Ford's 1979 autobiography reinforced the myth of noble quietude in the face of Carter's pious pandering. "I have always felt a closeness to God and have looked to a higher being for guidance and support," he wrote, "but I didn't think it was appropriate to advertise my religious beliefs." Ford made similar comments during the campaign season. Clearly, Carter's faith overshadowed Ford's as the campaign entered the sum- mer—a fact that Ford backers resented. "I've broken bread and drunk the cup with Jerry Ford for over thirty years," one GOP convention delegate from Michigan reportedly griped, "and nobody's going to tell me he isn't as close to God as Jimmy Carter!" An editorial in *Christianity Today*, whose readership leaned heavily toward the GOP, framed the issue in a way that made neither candidate look fetching. It asked readers to consider whether "circumstances" might ever permit evangelicals "to try to elect a highly talented person who was known to lie, or to be an adulterer, or even to have cheated or stolen, rather than a devout Christian with very limited gifts."[28]

Despite Ford's purported reticence, he practiced an evangelical politics alongside his evangelical faith. He was easily the most active Christian to reside in the White House since Woodrow Wilson. While an Episcopalian and thus a member of a mainline Protestant denomination, Ford possessed a clear populist evangelical bent. Back in 1974, in fact, then-Governor Carter introduced then–Vice President Ford at a banquet during the annual meeting of the SBC. To judge from media reports, Ford's piety was a known quantity from the moment he occupied the White House. Well before the Carter campaign, journalists contrasted Nixon's religious posturing with Ford's "more believable" faith and noted the new president's involvement in a Capitol Hill prayer group. "There is nothing artificial about the President's public expressions of religion," declared historian Martin Marty. For Ford, averred James Reston of the *New York Times*, "religion is not a role but a reality; he doesn't fake it but lives by it." Ford had extensive evangelical connections. The president's son was enrolled at an evangelical seminary, and Ford had long been close to evangelical entrepreneur Billy Zeoli, who operated Gospel Films in Ford's home community of Grand Rapids, Michigan, a center of Northern evangelicalism. During his presidency, Ford received 146 typewritten devotional notes from Zeoli—one every Monday—that began with the slogan "God's Got a Better Idea" (taken from the popular Ford Motors mantra "Ford's Got a Better Idea").[29]

Ford made use of his evangelical connections during the campaign, even before Carter's "born-again" identity became a political issue. GOP primary challenger Ronald Reagan gave him good reason to do so. The two-term governor of California had a long-standing and growing evangelical base of support. Reagan's critics would later express wonder that a man of such seemingly milquetoast piety benefited from a "systematic effort on the part of evangelical conservatives to portray [him] as a man of faith." While by no means a model churchgoer, Reagan was comfortable in the sprawling world of Southern California evangelicalism. His deep personal interest in biblical eschatology led him to Hal Lindsey's *The Late Great Planet Earth*. Reagan usually steered a safe political course, though, and was fluent enough in the language of civil religion to quote 2 Chronicles 7:14 as his favorite Bible verse while campaigning in North Carolina ("If my people, which are called by my name, shall humble themselves, and pray, and seek my face, and turn from their wicked ways; then will I . . . heal their land"). Later in the primary season, Reagan spoke with a prominent Christian radio host in California and claimed a past "experience that could be described as 'born again.'"[30]

During the campaign year, Ford attempted to head off the born-again appeal of Carter and Reagan. He lined up speaking engagements at Wheaton College, a joint meeting of the National Association of Evangelicals and National Religious Broadcasters, and Carter's own SBC. The SBC appearance was the first ever by an incumbent president. Ford jokingly recalled the introduction Carter gave him during his previous address before a Southern Baptist audience. Many listeners, though, wished that Carter had also received an invitation. Future SBC president Bailey Smith quipped that the nation needed "a born-again man in the White House...and his initials are the same as our Lord's." Still, only superficial observers believed that Carter had evangelical voters in the bag. A Carter supporter within the Texas Baptist Christian Life Commission—known for its progressive leanings—wrote to the campaign at the end of the summer stressing the need to keep reminding sympathetic Protestant voters of the candidate's faith. "If that feeling is lost," he argued, "much of that support will inevitably swing to Ford who is more closely aligned with the conservative political posture of many of these people." The Ford team clearly hoped for such a scenario. While Carter parsed the theological implications of lust, Ford met with a group of evangelical leaders and released a transcript of their conversation. Ford's seminarian son appeared in a commercial touting the president's faith, and Billy Graham paid a visit to the White House.[31]

Standards for tabulating evangelical votes were far from uniform in the mid-1970s, but by most accounts Ford received more support from evangelicals than did Carter. This was hardly a surprising development. Outside of the traditionally Democratic South, the born-again electorate had long leaned Republican. But Ford's 51 percent of the evangelical vote in 1976 was down substantially from Nixon's 84 percent in 1972. Carter made critical inroads, which (along with numerous other factors, Watergate fatigue and a low turnout among them) swung a close election his way. While Carter's success in the South was the key to his electoral victory, he also picked up evangelical-heavy counties throughout the swing states of the Midwest.[32]

Carter clearly made an impression on a generation of evangelicals—so much so that disillusionment with his administration became the default explanation for the rise of the Christian Right. Yet Carter did not shed his born-again identity upon winning an electoral majority. His final Sunday School class before moving to the White House attracted journalists, tourists, and members of the Atlanta Braves. At the urging of his staff, Carter chose to quote Micah in his inaugural address, instead of his first choice, the ever-popular "If my people..." passage from 2 Chronicles (which, curiously, advisers thought might sound too harsh). Carter related the anecdote at the National Prayer Breakfast a week later. In an allusion to the latter verse, though, Carter thanked Ford at the inaugural "for all he has done to heal our land"—a gesture that impressed an ABC news reporter as "the final benediction on Watergate and Vietnam." Carter, whose Secret Service handle was "The Deacon," remained an active Baptist layman while in office. He occasionally taught a couples' class at First Baptist Church in Washington, DC (where his nine-year-old daughter, Amy, was baptized three Sundays into the president's term), "witnessed" to political leaders from South Korea and Poland, and prayed at a Baptist service in Lagos, Nigeria. The president also openly endorsed Southern Baptist missionary work. In a 1977 video address to the SBC, he pledged to support a volunteer missionary for two years. A year later, Carter hosted more than 200 Southern Baptist lay leaders to promote the Mission Service Corps, part of a larger SBC effort, as Carter put it in his address, "to carry the good news [of Jesus] throughout the world." He urged his well-heeled audience to "consider how you, led by the spirit of Christ, can join in this renewal...of the entire Southern Baptist Convention, indeed our whole nation, indeed perhaps all Christendom." The meeting sparked criticism even within normally friendly SBC circles. "We Baptists would lead a howling protest," wrote a Baptist editor in Georgia, "if a Roman Catholic President entertained Catholic officials in the White House and raised money for them; that's what we said John F. Kennedy would do." Unsurprisingly, though, the sharpest evangelical criticism of Carter came from the right.[33]

From Evangelical Chic to Evangelical Rage

In July 1979, President Carter canceled a scheduled speech and retreated to Camp David. There, Americans eventually learned, Carter held an extemporaneous ten-day summit to gauge what he and many Americans perceived to be a national crisis. The moment revealed how, as historian Kevin Mattson has argued, Carter was both a Christian "moralist" and a rational "technician." The guests at Camp David included a nine-person, interfaith "God Squad," of which only one participant (Southern Baptist pastor Jimmy Allen) clearly qualified as an evangelical. The meeting ended, at Carter's request, with the group holding hands during a prayer led by Rabbi Marc Tanenbaum. The outcome of the summit confirmed Carter's comfort with an explicitly evangelical tone, but not with specifically evangelical policies. As president, he attempted to finesse or avoid altogether many of the gender and family issues that would consume the Christian Right. Carter consistently indicated that he would defer to Supreme Court decisions permitting abortion and forbidding sanctioned prayer in public schools. His rhetoric, however, struck strongly religious chords. His famous "Crisis of Confidence" speech—the first fruit of the summit—spoke directly to a "crisis of the spirit" that Billy Graham and other prominent evangelicals had persistently cited as the nation's core problem. In the address, Carter repeatedly referred to God, "faith," and "the spirit." Initially well received, but soon ridiculed as the "malaise" speech (even though Carter never used that word), the sermonlike address did not fit comfortably within the evangelical left-evangelical right dichotomy. It deployed the civil religion that the former abhorred (Robert Bellah was a member of the "God Squad") to push an agenda that the latter rejected.[34]

By 1979, evangelical faith rested on the fault line of American political culture. A number of commentators already linked the renewed prominence of religion (especially evangelicalism) in the 1970s to a declining American sense of confidence. At the end of the decade, an almost glib sense of pessimism was pervasive. "It was the worst of times, it was the worst of times," one magazine declared in summation of 1979. In his crisis speech, Carter sought to address this anxiety, offering a kind of therapeutic jeremiad. In sharp contrast, Jerry Falwell and his peers in the Christian Right offered a more traditional jeremiad, one that was profoundly critical of American society but equally hopeful about the American nation itself. *America Can Be Saved!* and *Listen, America*! were two Falwell book titles during the run-up to the 1980 campaign.[35]

Falwell's dual senses of optimism and despair grew from the conundrum of an increasingly born-again society that, in his eyes, was also an increasingly immoral society. "Christianity Up—Morals Down" read the subsection of a 1979 book by Falwell ally Tim LaHaye. "Without a doubt," LaHaye wrote, "Christianity is on the rise in America—Gallup confirms that—yet we are daily confronted by the fact that our nation's morals are deteriorating rapidly." LaHaye possessed a Gallup-driven faith (as he told *The Wittenburg Door*) in "the 84 percent of the people in this country who still believe the Ten Commandments are valid." Yet the signs of the times suggested that the pious majority was losing its franchise. Such thinking motivated political action— and, with it, opposition to Carter.[36]

The triumph of the evangelical right over the evangelical left did not happen in a vacuum. Rather, it occurred while the eyes of more and more Americans were trained on the born-again world. A few years before Falwell became a fixture on the front page, right-wing fundamentalist politics appeared not to have weathered the 1960s. Cold War firebrand minister Billy James Hargis stood accused of engaging in the same type of lurid sexual behavior he had long denounced. Throughout most of the 1970s, the most vocal calls for evangelical engagement came from the center and left. That changed as a prominent group of evangelicals began to link calls for social engagement with calls for conservative activism. By the time Carter sought reelection, conservative organizers and a small but powerful group of fundamentalist kingmakers had combined to create a movement soon known as the Christian Right. It first became visible through a series of spectacles culminating with Reagan's election. Falwell's strident, if electorally unfocused, "I Love America" tours of the mid-1970s evolved by 1980 into the wheeling and dealing of his political organization, Moral Majority. Conservative evangelicals attacked not only Carter, but also evangelical left leaders like Jim Wallis, as well as the less controversial and more popular Ron Sider. The latter's landmark *Rich Christians in an Age of Hunger* garnered a book-length retort titled *Productive Christians in an Age of Guilt Manipulators* (dedicated to Pat Robertson). Gary North, a libertarian and evangelical economist, remembered believing that "Sider was preparing the way for evangelicals to get involved in social action and politics, but that my economic opinions, not Sider's, were representative of the broad mass of evangelical opinion." Conservative churches possessed a similar confidence. By the late 1970s, Lutheran Church—Missouri Synod conservatives had ousted the denomination's purportedly liberal leadership, and the SBC was in the midst of a similar regime change.[37] The national media were well primed to notice yet another evangelical phenomenon. The emergence of the Christian Right was the final chapter of the evangelical Seventies.

Evangelical thinker and activist Francis Schaeffer revealed how the evangelical left's simmering kettle became the evangelical right's roiling pot. Like the Jesus Movement ministers of the late 1960s and early 1970s, Schaeffer blended an open-door style with a case-closed dogmatism that betrayed his fundamentalist roots. He gained fame in evangelical circles after founding a Swiss retreat—L'Abri ("the shelter")—in the mid-1950s. During the following decade, he emerged as a guru to what passed for an evangelical youth movement. Schaeffer's relative eccentricities (longish hair, lederhosen), combined with his willingness to engage the cool and the avant-garde (the Beatles, New Wave films), gave young evangelicals a chance to encounter the times without surrendering to them. Those characteristics made him an exotic species within the globe-trotting counterculture. By the late 1960s, youthful drifters were finding their way to L'Abri, and Schaeffer's work was drawing interest from hip celebrities, including Bob Dylan, Eric Clapton, and Mick Jagger. Many evangelicals assumed that Schaeffer was something of a political progressive, if not an outright radical. However, while Schaeffer welcomed an eclectic crowd to L'Abri, he retained a fundamentalist's theological implacability. His aesthetics really were apologetics. In taking secular art and philosophy seriously, his overriding purpose was not to highlight their portraits of modern despair, but rather to decry their embodiment of it. Schaeffer was a reactionary, not a proto-postmodernist. Rather than attacking the recourse to reason, he upheld biblical revelation as the foundation for all true reason. Schaeffer's methodology was novel and his tone intense. Yet his essential message did not stray far from the evangelical conventional wisdom found in many sermons and Sunday School classes. At the core of his serious, if unsystematic, interpretation of art and philosophy was a sweeping denunciation of the drift of Western culture. Schaeffer thus had little trouble reaching the rank-and-file back home through published versions of his lecture notes. His profile among the American evangelical mainstream grew after his 1976 book and documentary, *How Should We Then Live? The Rise and Decline of Western Thought and Culture*. Billy Zeoli's Gospel Films produced the series. By then, Schaeffer was coming to be known less as a 1960s sage and more as a hard-line defender of biblical inerrancy. Within a few years, he was a thoroughgoing culture warrior.[38]

The abortion issue turned Schaeffer into a foundational influence on the Christian Right. The conduit was a second book and film series, *Whatever Happened to the Human Race*? Schaeffer cohosted the 1979 documentary with Dr. C. Everett Koop, who would go on to serve as surgeon general in the Reagan administration. The five episodes offered a comprehensive pro-life perspective. Schaeffer, introduced to viewers as "one of the world's most respected thinkers," was the documentary's guiding voice. He quickly linked his existing critique of "mechanistic" humanism with a full-fledged attack on "abortion, infanticide, euthanasia." Abortion clearly was the main subject at hand though. The documentary described in graphic, provocative detail various abortion procedures, drawing an explicit analogy between present times and the biblical wicked city of Sodom. Casting opposition to abortion as a matter of upholding "true freedom and true rights," Schaeffer summoned the collective memory of moral failings both national (e.g., the Supreme Court's *Dred Scott* decision) and global (e.g., Nazi Germany) in scale. While the film was sufficiently evangelistic to suit its producers, it included explicit appeals for faith-based and secular opponents of abortion to "stand up and be counted." Such activism, Schaeffer argued, was more necessary than ever to counter the Supreme Court's "arbitrary sociological law." The initial film tour met with a somewhat muted response among evangelicals not accustomed to militant activist language (never mind graphic discussions of human sexuality); the average audience numbered between 700 and 1,500. The documentary grew in influence, however, and had an outsize effect on its early viewers, including future antiabortion activist Randall Terry.[39]

Whatever Happened to the Human Race? cast a wide theological and philosophical net. It suggested—against Schaeffer's fundamentalist instincts—that there was more than one path to pro-life absolutism. "The issue of abortion," he declared, "is not one divided along religious lines, and it has nothing to do with the separation of church and state." Here, Schaeffer effectively gave conservative Protestants permission to align with Catholics against legalized abortion. The philosophy behind such a move, which he called "co-belligerency," helped Christian Right leaders to explain their willingness to cooperate not only with persons of different theological or religious persuasions, but also with secular conservatives. Falwell credited Schaeffer with inspiring his turn toward politics, and Tim LaHaye dedicated his first explicitly political book to "Dr. Francis Schaeffer, the renowned philosopher-prophet of the twentieth century." Moral Majority leader Ed Dobson later bragged that the organization welcomed "anyone who shares similar moral convictions," be they Jewish, Catholic, Mormon, or not religious at all. "The underlying ideology was that which was advocated by the late Francis Schaeffer—co-belligerency." The improbable transition of Schaeffer from maverick evangelical intellectual to hard-right evangelical political activist led subsequent observers to lament the lost opportunities of the early 1970s evangelical left. While Schaeffer the L'Abri host inspired a generation of moderate evangelicals with his love of knowledge and culture, Schaeffer the culture warrior very much qualified as an "intellectual guru" of the Christian Right.[40]

Schaeffer demonstrated the delayed but ultimately triumphant status of abortion politics in the Christian Right. Opposition to legalized abortion was by no means the most pressing concern of many evangelical conservatives. Other gender and family issues played an important role in the 1970s conservative turn—for example, debates over sex education and the ratification of the Equal Rights Amendment. The same was true for many progressive evangelicals, such as Ron Sider, who would later take strong stands against the procedure. Many critics of the Christian Right thus came to see abortion merely as a retroactively applied, and hence misleading, justification for political mobilization. Jerry Falwell did not make a statement in opposition to abortion until 1975, two years after *Roe v. Wade*. Even then, he and other future Christian Right luminaries were initially more outspoken about Internal Revenue Service (IRS) guidelines (formally announced in 1978, but rooted in previous court decisions and IRS policies against segregation) that threatened the tax-exempt status of exclusively or predominantly white religious schools in the South. "In some states it's easier to open a massage parlor than to open a Christian school," Falwell later alleged. His thinly desegregated Lynchburg Christian Academy was vulnerable to IRS intervention. When candidate Jimmy Carter clarified his stance on abortion—declaring his belief that abortion was "wrong" and should be minimized, but indicating he would work "within the framework" of *Roe v. Wade*—the strongest criticism came from Catholic leaders. As historian Seth Dowland has pointed out, evangelical Protestants were traditionally wary both of Catholic activism and government interference with private matters (including religion); both tendencies made them less likely to rally against *Roe.*[41]

Hesitancy to engage in pro-life activism usually did not amount to even a tacitly pro-choice position, however. While the early abortion stances of some evangelical leaders struck later observers as surprisingly moderate, they almost always involved medical exceptions concerning the health of the mother or probable birth defects. That is, the abortions in question could be labeled "therapeutic," not "elective." A 1971 SBC resolution on abortion urged Baptists "to work for legislation that will allow the possibility of abortion under such conditions as rape, incest, clear evidence of severe fetal deformity," and harm to the mother. It also endorsed "the belief that society has a responsibility to affirm through the laws of the state a high view of the sanctity of human life, including fetal life, in order to protect those who cannot protect themselves." These and similar statements almost never used the language of personal rights that would define American pro-choice politics. Billy Graham's initial comments on abortion reflected the SBC's views. Graham's pastor, W. A. Criswell, who was not known for his liberalism, appeared to go much further. "I have always felt that it was only after a child was born and had life separate from its mother, that it became an individual person," Criswell stated in response to *Roe v. Wade*, "and it has always, therefore, seemed to me that what is best for the mother and for the future should be allowed." More common were the views of progressive Southern Baptist Foy Valentine and his fundamentalist nemesis, Adrian Rogers, who in 1977 could "basically agree" that "all life is sacred including fetal life but that sometimes, such as in cases of rape, incest, manifest deformity to the life of the fetus, and clear danger to the life and health of the mother, abortion may be the lesser of the available evils."[42]

The evangelical or evangelical-friendly scholarly sources that informed such seemingly moderate stances on abortion were largely clinical in nature. Abortion was a threefold concern of the expectant mother, the doctor, and God. Abortion—again, more specifically, "therapeutic abortion"—thus represented one of many ethical conundrums that arose from human sinfulness.

"There's no doubt in my mind that in some cases abortion is justifiable," said evangelical political scientist Paul Henry, a moderate Republican who was close to John Anderson. "Killing is wrong, but in some cases war is justifiable. There is no difference. Our choices are all fallen."[43]

In the mid- to late 1970s, estimates of the abortions performed each year following *Roe* soared toward one million—and the tone began to shift. While the SBC did not explicitly embrace legal restrictions on abortion until 1980 (and even then backed a health exception), its language grew stronger each year after 1971. "Every decision for an abortion, for whatever reason," the Convention declared in 1976, "must necessarily involve the decision to terminate the life of an innocent human being." Meanwhile, pro-life activists ratcheted up their rhetoric. "The primary cause of death in the United States last year was abortion," contended evangelical theologian Harold O. J. Brown in 1976. A year earlier, Brown helped to found the anti-abortion group Christian Action Council, which sought to rally Protestants behind what was still seen as a Catholic cause. Many evangelicals eschewed such a hard-line stance. Still, as the policy implications of the *Roe v. Wade* decision became more apparent, it was not such a dramatic step for many others to move toward more explicit opposition to "abortion on demand." What occurred in most cases was the hardening of existing antiabortion stances. Conspicuously pro-choice evangelicals—such as John Anderson, who during the run-up to the 1980 election penned a fund-raising letter for National Abortion Rights Action League—had never been common. They were even rarer by the end of the 1970s.[44]

Moreover, the ambivalence of prominent evangelical leaders about abortion did not always reflect sentiment among grassroots activists. Conservative leader Paul Weyrich's oft-quoted opinion that the proposed IRS policy changes, "not abortion, school prayer, or the ERA," were "what galvanized the Christian community" represented the perspective of the organizer, not necessarily the base. It was easier to mobilize opposition to a single policy change than to create a broad movement against a Supreme Court decision. Yet abortion had more staying power. Evangelical activists in places like California, where abortion liberalization predated *Roe v. Wade* (having occurred under the watch of Governor Ronald Reagan), pioneered the transition from a clinical antiabortion position to an emotional pro-life stance. Abortion was well on its way to becoming a standard campaign issue. By 1978, both Christian Right activists and the Catholic-dominated Right to Life Committee received credit for defeating pro-choice incumbent Democratic senators in Iowa and New Hampshire.[45]

Abortion policy became one of many points of contention between Carter and conservative evangelicals. Born-again alternatives to Carter were not hard to find. Besides Ford and Reagan, there was John Conlan, the Republican congressman from Arizona. A fervent and charismatic speaker, the ubiquitous Conlan represented the more explicitly partisan wing of the "God Network." In the evangelical press, he made for an easy contrast with Mark Hatfield. Conlan had dreamed for decades about organizing a viable right-wing Christian political movement. His work intensified after he won election to Congress in 1972 and participated in a takeover of the Christian Freedom Foundation, a long-standing libertarian group. His wife, Irene, hosted an influential Bible study in their northern Virginia home, and she urged qualified Christian men and women alike to seek political office. Bill Bright, head of Campus Crusade for Christ, backed Conlan. Bright's growing involvement in Beltway politics included support for a Washington ministry called the Christian Embassy, a more explicitly conservative counterpart to the Fellowship. Conlan hit the evangelical circuit running during the mid-1970s. In 1975, he appeared at a special reception at the SBC's annual gathering (hosted by Criswell and Rogers) and addressed the Christian Booksellers Association to press the case for activism. "I know we are looking for the Lord to come again," he declared to the latter audience. Yet "we are also told to occupy until He comes." Tim LaHaye made the same point with more urgency. The end-times will indeed feature a period of tribulation, he believed. "But the pretribulation tribulation—that is, the tribulation that will engulf this country if liberal humanists are permitted to take total control of our government—is neither predestined nor necessary."[46]

A potential problem, as Conlan admitted behind closed doors, was that evangelical liberals and moderates were already making the case for political involvement. These evangelicals did not focus on the same issues as Conlan and his ally at Third Century Publishers, Rus Walton, who stressed strong defense, low taxes, and resistance to "secular humanist philosophy." According to an April 1976 exposé published in *Sojourners*, Conlan privately impugned the born-again credentials of Hatfield and Hughes. Authored by Jim Wallis and Wes Michaelson, the *Sojourners* piece was a preemptive strike against the coalescing Christian Right. It created enough of a stir to scare away both Bright and the even more controversy-averse Billy Graham. The election results in 1976 were less than encouraging for what Wallis and Michaelson termed the "alarming political initiative by the evangelical far right." Bright did help to organize a National Prayer Congress event two weeks before Election Day, but it drew a disappointing crowd of 1,000 to Dallas. Four years later, by contrast, the Bright-supported "Washington for Jesus" rally drew at least 200,000 to the National Mall.[47]

By 1978, Carter was in trouble even with many of the evangelicals who had supported him. Anita Bryant, newly famous for her anti-gay-rights activism, voiced representative sentiments in her own *Playboy* interview. After struggling to field devilish questions about why she was "obsessed with homosexuality," Bryant explained her beef with Carter. "I think the reason I'm so disillusioned," she explained, "is because I really looked at Jimmy Carter as a hero, as one who had caught the eye and the heartbeat of the grass roots of America. I really had great expectations of him, and I [have] found that in life, when you put different individuals on a pedestal, God very carefully takes them off the pedestal and shows us that we're to put *no one* there." The disenchantment sometimes came quickly, as was the case with Pat Robertson. Toward the end of the 1976 campaign, Robertson traveled to Carter's porch in Plains to interview the candidate for his television show, *The 700 Club*. It was a friendly conversation (which aired after the election), but Robertson pressed the issue of appointing godly Christians to executive positions. Carter hedged but hinted that Christian statesmen would be welcome in the executive branch. "I think it would be a mistake for me to define the qualifications of a public servant according to what kind of a church they attend or what their denomination is," Carter said. "Obviously, a commitment to the principles expressed to us by God would be an important prerequisite." According to one administration official, Robertson and other prominent evangelicals sent Carter a list of similarly minded Christians who were qualified for presidential appointments. When none of those names appeared on the federal payroll, Robertson accused Carter of appointing secular liberals and having "ignored the wishes of Evangelicals." Robertson's retreat from Carter subsequently became a key turning point in his political story. Later, Robertson even claimed to have switched his vote at the last moment to Gerald Ford.[48]

Carter was not caught off guard by the existence of an evangelical right, but he did underestimate the political consequences of its strident opposition to his presidency. Following the 1976 election, leading Southern Baptist minister Robert Maddox, a Georgian and pastor to one of Carter's sons, volunteered his services as a "lightning rod" between the president and conservative evangelical groups. Carter declined the offer. Of the many potentially disgruntled forces in his coalition, Carter felt he had more reason to fear his party's liberal wing. His preferred mode of religious politics involved gestures like inviting gospel and Jesus rock performers to the White House grounds for an afternoon "Old Fashioned Gospel Singin'." Finally, in 1979, the president hired Maddox as a speechwriter and religious liaison. Maddox's main task was to rebuild bridges with conservative Protestants. He reached out to Billy Graham and peppered Carter with memos urging the president to engage his growing critics in the evangelical community. Carter accepted an open invitation to speak before the National Religious Broadcasters. The president also hosted "A Breakfast for Evangelical Leaders" with Falwell, LaHaye, and other pastors (including a few, like Oral Roberts and Jim Bakker, who generally shied away from politics). The meeting provided a pretext for some of the ministers to highlight their complaints about Carter.[49]

By then, several Christian Right groups had emerged to mobilize a variety of conservative constituencies. The most important such organizations during the 1980 election season were Christian Voice, Religious Roundtable, and the one that captured the most media attention, Moral Majority. The successful effort to block the IRS policy on Christian schools gave them a taste of success. An energized Christian Right was firmly on display at an orchestrated walkout during Carter's long-promised 1980 White House Conference on Families (initially, as critics on the right noted, called the White House Conference on *the* Family). Carter retained the loyalty of many evangelicals, such as Bakker, who made a campaign appearance with the president. Still, most evangelical right leaders had turned against Carter by then, and many had never backed him in the first place. Their candidate of choice remained to be seen. But one obvious option existed: Ronald Reagan. Christian Voice established a Christians for Reagan group and took to publicizing his 1976 "born-again" interview.[50]

At the close of the 1970s, the modern evangelical right was rapidly coming of age. The evangelical left had been reduced to "stacking sandbags against a conservative flood," in the words of *Christianity Today*. Inspired by Francis Schaeffer, the spokespersons for the evangelical right cited the same evangelical heroes of yore—whether William Wilberforce or Charles Finney—as did the young evangelicals, but toward much different ends. Secular journalists continued to give a handful of progressive evangelicals attention; Jim Wallis made *Time*'s 1979 list of "50 Faces for America's Future." Yet their focus increasingly shifted toward prominent television ministers with conservative politics. Jerry Falwell was "the next Billy Graham," while Pat Robertson stood as "the Billy Graham of tomorrow." Both were still in their forties. Falwell and Robertson, not Wallis and not even Graham, defined public impressions of born-again Christianity for the coming generation. By 1980, the label "evangelical" had taken on the kind of explicitly conservative connotations that John Conlan had long desired.[51]

Conservative evangelicals capitalized on the residue of the 1970s born-again boom. In April 1979, just before the founding of Moral Majority, Jerry Falwell wrote an appeal to his supporters. The evangelical renaissance was all well and good, he argued, but they needed to translate prominence into political action. "I realize that it is 'popular' to be a born-again Christian," Falwell wrote in an obvious dig at the pious Carter. "But for some strange reason it is 'unpopular' to stand up and fight against the sins of our nation." Carter's invocation of Christian character influenced a generation of aspirants, Democrats and Republicans alike. But its most immediate effects, post-1976, benefited his opponents. Ron Sider later lamented that "we called for social and political action but instead we got eight years of Ronald Reagan." The conservative standard-bearer ran in a presidential election that featured not two but three avowedly born-again candidates. "Here's an election year prediction: the person who will occupy the White House next year will be a born-again Christian," wrote Marjorie Hyer in the *Washington Post*.[52] Reagan's version of evangelical politics, however, was clearly ascendant by 1980. His backers on the evangelical right were moving beyond the Christian statesman ideal and toward a more specific, more strident agenda. Theirs was no cry in the wilderness. Many politicos were listening; some were quaking.

3 THE POWER AND THE SPECTACLE

If 1976 was the Year of the Evangelical, then 1980 was the Year of the Evangelical Right. By that time, surprisingly few commentators noticed the difference. What would become known as the "Christian Right," or the "religious right," had largely coalesced by the end of the 1970s, but the presidential race of 1980 thrust it further into the national spotlight. That year witnessed a conclusive pivot in modern evangelical politics—a pivot, indeed, in the image of American evangelicalism as a whole. All three candidates in 1980—Democratic incumbent Jimmy Carter, Republican challenger Ronald Reagan, and independent Republican John Anderson—described themselves as born-again Christians. Yet Carter had lost his presumed base and Anderson had moved to the left in an effort to capture moderate Republicans and discontented Democrats. The energy resided on the right side of the evangelical spectrum. For the next three decades, the Christian Right—a movement propelled by evangelicals but also containing sympathetic Catholics, Mormons, and a handful of Jewish allies—occupied a distinct place in the imaginations of many Americans. The Christian Right's leaders received disproportionate media attention, not least because they served up a steady dish of spectacles. In the minds of many, they *were* the public expression of born-again Christianity. Politics, of course, hardly captured the full power of evangelicalism within American culture. But it influenced all impressions of that power.

The process happened very quickly. Less than four years after the rise of Jimmy Carter, journalists were unlikely to be caught off guard again by a proliferation of pious politics. The booming "electric church"—later rebranded the "electronic church" and ultimately labeled "televangelism"—had been a news media staple since at least 1978. Coverage naturally gravitated toward Lynchburg, Virginia, preacher Jerry Falwell, who had supported Anita Bryant's 1977 anti-gay-rights crusade, and Virginia Beach television mogul Pat Robertson, who was involved with the Washington for Jesus rally of

April 1980 (scheduled to coincide with the anniversary of the first landing at Jamestown). The rally, which attracted a crowd of around 200,000, confirmed that born-again politics was back and that it now threatened President Jimmy Carter's livelihood. "You have seen the great silent majority," declared Robertson to the Capitol Mall crowd, invoking Nixon's populist metaphor. Falwell was not among the rally's participants, perhaps because he feared a low turnout, perhaps because the Baptist fundamentalist was uncomfortable with the charismatic faith of Robertson and the conference co-organizer John Gimenez. Yet Robertson himself was wary of risking his kingdom for a campaign. Falwell, head of the Moral Majority (another nod to Nixon), was more eager to enter the political arena. He thus became the first anointed spokesperson of what was then commonly called the "Religious New Right."[1]

During the 1980 campaign, Ronald Reagan and the evangelical conservatives engaged in a very public courting ritual. Evangelicals had entertained possible GOP alternatives to Carter since at least 1979. Options abounded—ranging from right-wing purist Philip Crane of Illinois to early front-runner John Connally of Texas—but Reagan, long a darling of conservatives in general, was an especially compelling choice. By the time Moral Majority executive director Robert Billings signed on as a Reagan campaign adviser, the deal was pretty much sealed. The 1980 GOP convention gave journalists further reason to believe that the Moral Majority had muscles to flex. As national outlets duly reported, Moral Majority supporters controlled the Alaska Republican organization. Congressman Guy Vander Jagt of Michigan, an evangelical conservative, delivered the keynote address. Convention delegates approved the GOP's most socially conservative platform ever, as the party strengthened its antiabortion stance and reversed its historic support for the Equal Rights Amendment. On social issues, at least, the pew trumped the country club. "It's right down the line an evangelical platform," gushed one Republican at the Detroit convention. Reagan struck an explicitly religious note in his acceptance speech (whereas Carter made no direct mention of God in his), merging established modes of civil religion with a newer rhetoric of antisecularism: "I'll confess that I've been a little afraid to suggest what I'm going to suggest. I'm more afraid not to," declared the nominee. He then paused. "Can we begin our crusade joined together in a moment of silent prayer?" This gesture followed Falwell's decision to stomach (if not endorse) the vice presidential selection of George H. W. Bush, a long-standing social moderate who had only recently embraced the antiabortion cause. While Bush vacationed with Billy Graham after the convention, Reagan intensified his courtship of the evangelical right. His most important stop was in Dallas for the National Affairs Briefing, an event intended to consummate the relationship between a vote-hungry Reagan and an electoral base in the making. There, Reagan uttered perhaps the most famous lines of the Age of Evangelicalism. They received prominent play in an influential *Newsweek* cover story three weeks later. "I know you can't endorse *me*," he was quoted as saying. "But...I want you to know that I endorse *you*." The presence of Falwell in Detroit and Reagan in Dallas raised the profile of the Christian Right even further. Falwell soon appeared on daytime television shows debating liberal Protestant activist William Sloane Coffin.[2]

The romance between Reagan and the Christian Right quickly experienced prominent hiccups. Christian Right leaders were not inclined to strike the more inclusive tone required of a successful presidential campaign. Baptist minister and former Carter backer Bailey Smith, speaking at the Dallas gathering, saw fit to aver that "God Almighty does not hear the prayer of a Jew." Then, Falwell felt compelled to clarify that God did hear the prayers of any Jew or Gentile, provided that they were converts to Christianity. The topic of Jewish salvation predictably greeted Reagan during his October visit to Lynchburg, where Falwell hosted a gathering of the National Religious Broadcasters. Confronted by journalists at the airport, the candidate embraced a much more generous take on God's sense of hearing. Falwell—by then a political operative, as well as a fundamentalist minister—agreed with Reagan a few days later, reversing his position after consulting with the American Jewish Committee's liaison to Christians, Rabbi Marc Tanenbaum. God "hears the heart cry of any sincere person who calls on Him," Falwell now stated.[3]

The surge of attention given to the outspoken and provocative Falwell gave Carter an opening. Falwell, of course, did not speak for all evangelicals, not even for many of the televangelists who generally shared his theological outlook. "If I backed a Republican for President," wondered prominent televangelist Rex Humbard, "what about the Democrats in my audience?" A number of Reformed theologians criticized Falwell's politics as simplistic, while many members of the evangelical old guard—not least, Billy Graham— kept their distance from the Virginian. Carter and his religious liaison, Robert Maddox, were aware of these divisions. They reached out to relatively nonpartisan evangelists like Jim Bakker (who, to be sure, had interviewed Reagan on his television show earlier that year). The other side of Carter's strategy involved branding the Moral Majority and its crowd as unrepresentative of American society in general and American Christianity in particular. Carter came late to this approach. In October, he noted that "the Bible doesn't say how you balance the federal budget....It's never been done before, but certain religious groups are trying to say what the definition of a Christian is." Carter's tone was considerably more moderate than that of Secretary of Health and Human Services Patricia Roberts Harris. "I am beginning to fear that we could have an Ayatollah Khomeini in this country," she declared in a September speech. Harris's real problem, Falwell shot back, was with the "Judeo-Christian community" itself.[4]

Reagan won in a landslide, but the postelection sorting out of Moral Majority's role was much less conclusive. The initial verdict, buttressed by polling data that posited a near-equivalence between "evangelical" and "Moral Majority," saw Falwell as the new political kingmaker. The minister did little to discourage such analysis. On the night following the election, Falwell offered commentary on an award-winning episode of *Nightline*. Via satellite, he was connected with the defeated Democratic senators George McGovern, Birch Bayh, and Frank Church—Christian Right targets all. "George Gallup didn't get a chance to declare 1980 the 'Year of Born-Again Politics,' " two chroniclers wrote. "The evangelicals beat him to it." *Christian Century* listed the "ascendance of the New Religious Right" as the top religious news story of 1980. As more sophisticated number crunchers demonstrated, though, Reagan had not needed the Christian Right—however broadly defined—to win. Moreover, as Seymour Martin Lipset and Earl Raab argued, it was impossible to separate religious motivations from other reasons for choosing a particular candidate. An eclectic range of figures, including civil rights icon Ralph Abernathy and Watergate prosecutor Leon Jaworski, had backed Reagan. Perhaps evangelical voters simply reflected the broader momentum. Still, evangelicals unquestionably were an important force in the Reagan wave. They were "the major factor," Albert Menendez subsequently contended, "in twelve of the seventeen states that switched from Carter to Reagan."[5]

A second round of reconsiderations took the form of media criticism. Early reports vastly overestimated the audience size for televangelistic shows. *Playboy* reported a weekly television audience of thirty million for Falwell's *Old-Time Gospel Hour*. A better estimate for the average weekly audience for the top ten syndicated religious shows combined was seven to ten million. Even the higher-end estimates still trailed the weekly audience for the sitcom *M.A.S.H.* As such, Jerry Falwell remained less than a household name at the start of the Reagan Revolution. A *Washington Post*–ABC News poll published in June 1981 revealed that half of Americans had not heard of Moral Majority, while those who had were sharply divided in their evaluations of the organization. Moral Majority was better known in a Bible Belt locale like Dallas-Fort Worth, but it was far from popular even in that metropolitan area. Perhaps, argued journalist Tina Rosenberg, the media itself had "made the Moral Majority." Players on both ends of the political spectrum, Rosenberg wrote, had "a powerful interest in letting exaggeration and oversimplification pass for gospel truth." Still, she conceded, "what's described as powerful often ends up being powerful." Media construction or not, many Republican elites believed that they needed the Moral Majority—and the voters for whom it claimed to speak—to sustain a political majority.[6]

By the mid-1980s, the "new Christian Right" (or the Christian Right) and the "new Religious Right" (or the Religious Right) had become the preferred terms for an enduring American political phenomenon, replacing references to the "religious New Right" and largely subsuming allusions to a self-styled "pro-family movement." Indeed, the Christian Right outlasted its organizational parent—the conservative "New Right"—as a term with currency. Much of the print coverage acknowledged the diversity within American evangelicalism and used categories—"fundamentalist," "charismatic," and so on—that evangelicals themselves often employed. Billy Graham's statement that Moral Majority did not speak for him received prominent play.[7] Yet even Graham, who was a household name, was now framed in relation to the next big story. The joint meetings of the historically intertwined National Association of Evangelicals (NAE) and the National Religious Broadcasters during the late 1970s and early 1980s reinforced the impression that the new center of the evangelical world was the electronic church, especially its most politicized figures. Reagan's presence at three consecutive such meetings, from 1982 to 1984, contributed to that belief as well.

The Evangelical's President

Ronald Reagan was more an evangelical's president than an evangelical president. While lacking Jimmy Carter's Sunday School piety, Reagan was quite comfortable in his born-again skin (among many other skins). It was Reagan, not Carter, who inaugurated what scholars David Domke and Kevin Coe have called the "God strategy" in American presidential politics, as "religious communications increased to levels never before seen in the modern presidency." Since Reagan's two terms, "U.S. presidential candidates who want to be taken seriously by religious voters, particularly conservatives, now face a come-to-Jesus moment in which they must display public religiosity in a manner that is inevitably calculated and yet cannot appear overtly so." Perhaps the clearest evidence of the God strategy was Reagan's persistent use of the expression "God bless America" in his 1980 convention speech and throughout his two terms. A commonplace in presidential discourse at the start of the twenty-first century, "God bless America" appeared in a major presidential address precisely once before Reagan (in 1973, as Richard Nixon attempted to mitigate the Watergate scandal).[8] To a certain degree, the flourish was but a new spin on the all-American tradition of civil religion. Politicians had long proffered mere Christianity for political gain. Yet it was no coincidence that this newest rhetorical wrinkle appeared precisely as the Christian Right arose.

For the evangelical right, Reagan's presidency provided a lot of symbolism and a bit of substance, often blurring the line between the two. Reagan saw evangelical conservatives in much the same way that he viewed other major GOP constituencies (big business, defense hawks, etc.). Even as allegations swirled that White House aide Michael Deaver wanted Christian Right leaders to enter through the "back door," Falwell was among the first visitors to the Reagan White House. Reagan knew, though, that his new coalition partners wanted some clear victories. A few of the president's initial appointments offered hope. James Watt, a Pentecostal and a strong conservative, joined the cabinet as Secretary of the Interior, antiabortion activist C. Everett Koop became surgeon general, and Robert Billings landed a position in the Department of Education. In the GOP-majority Senate, Richard Halverson— the ministerial dean of Beltway evangelicals—served as chaplain. Morton Blackwell used his evangelical connections to massage relations with the Christian Right during his time as Reagan's liaison to conservatives. Faith Whittlesey, who took over Blackwell's outreach to religious conservatives, likewise kept out the welcome mat for evangelical leaders. Such contacts no doubt factored into Reagan's decision to declare 1983 the "Year of the Bible" and, that same year, to contribute an article to the antiabortion *Human Life Review*. At the start of the subsequent election year, the White House released an "Issue Alert" suggesting the "many ways" in which public school officials could encourage voluntary (i.e., constitutionally permissible) student prayers during the school day. These were mere gestures, no doubt, but Carter's lack of similar moves had cost him dearly.[9]

The Christian Right, to be sure, expected more substantive policy victories following the 1980 election. Moral Majority leader Ronald Goodwin was conscious of the need to move "from the media period to the organizational period." One critical effort was the formation in 1981 of the Council for National Policy (CNP), the "first successful umbrella organization on the right." Evangelical conservatives dominated CNP from the start. Tim LaHaye served as its first president, while other early members included James Dobson, Pat Robertson, Bill Bright, Jerry Falwell, and Robert Dugan of the NAE. CNP never attained the kind of gatekeeping authority to which it aspired. The first Reagan term did not produce decisive action on many of the social policies that Falwell had said mattered most, constitutional amendments concerning school prayer and abortion foremost among them. Falwell stuck to his line that Reagan was "the greatest thing that has happened to our country in my lifetime," but being a team player frequently required compromise. An early case was the selection of George H. W. Bush. Then came the Supreme Court nomination of Sandra Day O'Connor. Falwell stomached the choice even though her judicial record suggested an unwillingness to overturn *Roe v. Wade*.[10]

Almost from the start, then, most Christian Right leaders made a strategic decision to participate in the Reagan Revolution. Critics, such as liberal journalist Sidney Blumenthal, noted that the Reagan administration stood to benefit if evangelical conservatives remained just unsatisfied enough to be "in a state of perpetual mobilization." While this line of analysis contained some truth, it downplayed the obvious legislative barriers facing the Christian Right's agenda—namely, a Democratic-majority House of Representatives and a GOP-controlled Senate with many moderate Republicans. It also ignored the reality that conservative evangelicals had no place else to go in the two-party system. The national Democratic Party responded to the Christian Right by attempting to run against it. As historian Daniel K. Williams has argued, the Christian Right quickly became the most reliable component of the new GOP coalition (more reliable than, say, socially conservative Catholic bishops and less vocally critical than the secular wing of the New Right). Tellingly, then, Reagan delivered his famous address branding the Soviet Union an "evil empire" at the 1983 annual meeting of the NAE. He did so in no small part because the organization affirmed his resistance to the burgeoning nuclear-freeze movement, which had garnered support from many other religious leaders, including Catholic bishops. The evangelical right was not only part of Reagan's coalition; it was also one of its pillars.[11]

In 1984, Falwell and other Christian Right leaders offered an unrestrained endorsement of the incumbent presidential candidate. They were omnipresent at the Republican National Convention in Dallas. Firebrand social conservative James Robison opened the convention with a prayer, and Falwell delivered the closing benediction, calling Reagan and Bush "God's instruments in rebuilding America." Reagan published an election-year book titled *In God I Trust*, while both he and the vice president attended the 1984 launch of another Christian Right vehicle, the American Coalition for Traditional Values. Pat Robertson called Reagan "probably the most evangelical president we have had since the founding fathers." Reagan's faith received closer analysis in the media. Especially apropos in 1984 was his long-standing interest in scriptural prophecy. According to an election-year poll, nearly 40 percent of Americans linked the biblical end-times with a nuclear apocalypse. Unlike Hal Lindsey, though, they were not eager to ponder this prospect. During the second presidential debate, Reagan fielded a question about a possible "nuclear Armageddon." This was one of several areas where Reagan's ties to the Christian Right threatened to cost him votes.[12]

The campaign team of Democratic nominee Walter Mondale unsuccessfully tried to make the separation of church and state an issue. While conservative evangelicals, such as Carl F. H. Henry, complained that their input was not welcomed by the elites who controlled the Democratic platform committees, Mondale sought to cast Reagan as a tool of the Christian Right. "Both [party] platforms were prepared by Jerrys," Mondale asserted during a late September campaign speech, "ours under the leadership of [vice presidential nominee] Geraldine Ferraro and theirs by Jerry Falwell." A Mondale commercial began with the line "Ronald Reagan and Rev. Jerry Falwell cordially invite you to their party on November 6." The ad was one of Mondale's most effective spots, in the analysis of one Reagan aide; however, it did not appear until mid-October and ran sparingly.[13]

Reagan ruled the religion issue in 1984. That fact alienated some secular voters, but it cemented his popularity among most evangelicals. "Religion is honored when it is separated from party platforms and valued for the moral force of faith and hope," wrote columnist Colman McCarthy, a fierce critic of the president. "It is dishonored when it is Americanized and militarized. Earlier presidents have done one or the other. Reagan is the first to do both." Reagan positioned himself as the defender of all American believers. Speaking at a prayer breakfast during the GOP convention in Dallas, he affirmed the "positive role" of religion in American history, from the abolitionist movement through the Civil Rights Movement. Now, he suggested, religion itself was a worthy political cause. Previously, "the state was tolerant of religious belief, expression and practice. Society, too, was tolerant." This was the general context in which, back in 1960, John F. Kennedy famously stated that his Catholic faith would not determine his policies. That was a different America, Reagan argued. Now, the secularists and their political allies "refuse to tolerate [religion's] importance in our lives." Without explicitly saying so, Reagan spoke not of religion in general, but of a traditional—that is, conservative—faith in need of protection. Such a move did not require the religiously amorphous Reagan to consistently identify as an evangelical. Indeed, Reagan joined Mondale in offering a polite dodge in response to a presidential debate question about whether he considered himself "a born-again Christian." (The question came from *Baltimore Sun* reporter Fred Barnes, himself an evangelical.) As the front-runner, Reagan ignored matters of labeling and reiterated his reliance on prayer. Mondale stressed his "deep religious faith" before turning the question into an attack on Jerry Falwell's influence on judicial nominations. Labels aside, Reagan largely had born-again ballots in the bag. Eighty percent of evangelicals voted with the landslide majority that election year.[14]

November 1984, even more than November 1980, was Falwell's moment in the sun. Every national news network was on hand in Lynchburg to record his response to the election. A leading newsmagazine soon rated him the fourteenth most influential person in the nation (third in the private sector, behind businessman Lee Iacocca and newscaster Dan Rather). Falwell was a persistent and savvy media presence. He demonstrated how the Christian Right could shape public discussions even without achieving clear policy victories. With the help of speechwriter Cal Thomas, Falwell evinced a knack for quips that were simultaneously provocative and disarming. When confronted by gay-rights supporters, Falwell voiced the emerging conservative truism, "God created Adam and Eve, not Adam and Steve!" Those "mainline" Protestants who chafed at such lines were now on the "sidelines" of relevance. Critics wrote of the "Falwell Goosestep." "I think it's fair for the conservative goose to do what the liberal gander does," Falwell said in explaining his entry into the political arena. "People are saying to me," he declared during the 1980 campaign, "'You're trying to get born-again Christians elected to office.' That's ridiculous. We're trying to get rid of some." He and his supporters were "not trying to jam our moral philosophy down the throats of others. We're simply trying to keep others from jamming their amoral philosophies down our throats." Immediately following the 1980 election, Falwell frequented recording studios around the nation, granting interviews to nearly all comers, including *Los Angeles Times* reporter Robert Scheer (who had conducted Jimmy Carter's *Playboy* interview) and two independent journalists. The latter duo promptly sold their tapes to *Playboy*'s competitor, *Penthouse*. Falwell remained eminently quotable. No, he would not run for office. "That's the Khomeini approach. That's wrong." While increasingly artful in his public comments, Falwell's antics retained the qualities that had made him such a compelling public personality in the first place. For example, he unsuccessfully sued to prevent the sale of the *Penthouse* issue featuring his interview (in which he criticized Carter for granting an interview to *Playboy*). *Penthouse*'s lawyer, Norman Roy Grutman, toyed with Falwell during the court hearing, going so far as to include scriptural references in his remarks. "Where the spirit of liberty is," Grutman declared in a twisted paraphrase of 2 Corinthians 3:17, "there is the Lord. I don't think it should start retreating in Lynchburg." Falwell subsequently turned the flap into a fund-raising mailer headed, "I Did Not Give an Interview to *Penthouse* Magazine." A few years later, Falwell turned around and hired Grutman to bring suit against Larry Flynt, whose *Hustler* magazine ran a satirical liquor ad containing a facetious interview in which Falwell discussed how he lost his virginity (while drunk, in an outhouse, to his mother). The case went all the way to the Supreme Court. In 1988, Falwell lost that one, too.[15]

The rapid ascendance of evangelical conservatism unleashed political energy that a power broker like Jerry Falwell could not always control, however. Not everyone on the evangelical right was content to be a cheerleader for the Reagan Revolution. Francis Schaeffer, whose theory of co-belligerency had provided conceptual cover for Falwell's turn toward politics, sought to ensure it did not become a synonym for compromise. Schaeffer moved even farther to the right in the final years of his life. His 1981 *A Christian Manifesto* posited a kind of religious-political struggle between secular humanists and Christians. The former, Schaeffer deduced from the research of fundamentalist lawyer John Whitehead, were attempting to subvert the nation's Christian heritage. "As Christians," Schaeffer wrote in his call to arms, "we must stand absolutely and totally opposed to the whole humanist system, *whether it is controlled by conservative or liberal elements.*" The famous commandment of Jesus to "Give to Caesar what is Caesar's, and to God what is God's," Schaeffer argued by way of ideogram, did not render those spheres equivalent:

> GOD and CAESAR
It was, is, and it always will be:
> GOD
> and
> CAESAR.

To be sure, the recent "conservative swing" had left "an open window" for political solutions. Yet Christians also needed to ponder "what to do if the window closes," in which case civil disobedience might be necessary. Either way, argued Schaeffer's son and would-be heir, the times called for an "ecumenism of orthodoxy."[16]

One Schaeffer disciple became the most influential antiabortion activist of the late twentieth century. Randall Terry, a charismatic-fundamentalist Christian, played a major role in bringing Protestants into the pro-life movement. When his organization, Operation Rescue, began its work in 1987, antiabortion activism still was a predominantly Catholic affair. Over the next few years, Operation Rescue encouraged many evangelicals to express their pro-life sentiments in arenas beyond the voting booth. "If we believe that abortion is murder, then it is time for us to act like it is murder," stated Terry in what amounted to his organization's rallying cry. In advocating sit-down protests and other acts of civil disobedience, Terry and his group explicitly invoked the legacy of Martin Luther King Jr., sometimes singing "We Shall Overcome." Schaeffer was a more immediate influence, Terry told journalist Garry Wills. Despite Terry's often abrasive style, Operation Rescue gained the endorsement of numerous Christian Right leaders, including Falwell, Robertson, and James Dobson. By the 1990s, a scholar could claim that two-thirds of the antiabortion movement was evangelical.[17]

"Tax-Exempt Savonarolas"

Critics tended to overlook the tension between pragmatists and purists within the broader evangelical right. Political liberals, of course, had similar divisions within their own ranks. Moreover, they lacked a unifying figure like Reagan around whom to rally. The Christian Right gave liberalism an enduring foil, though—an opportunity, as well as a threat. Both dynamics surfaced in an advertisement for the American Civil Liberties Union (ACLU) that first appeared in the Sunday *New York Times* a few weeks after Reagan's victory in 1980. "IF THE MORAL MAJORITY HAS ITS WAY," blared the headline, "YOU'D BETTER START PRAYING." The officially nonpartisan ACLU attacked the Christian Right for subverting the founding principles of American politics. The "new evangelicals" were "not a conservative movement," as many might assume, but rather "a radical anti-Bill-of-Rights movement." The ACLU was necessary to ensure that the Constitution itself did not "become a casualty of the new order." The advertisement attracted the desired attention. Eventually, the Moral Majority responded with its own advertising slogan in the *New York Times* and other national publications: "They have labeled Moral Majority the Extreme Right because we speak out against Extreme Wrong!"[18]

A year later, Yale University president A. Bartlett Giamatti threw another high-profile rhetorical dagger. Giamatti, a former literature professor who later served briefly as commissioner of Major League Baseball, welcomed Yale's freshman class with a speech (distributed in written form to each student and subsequently published in the *New York Times*) celebrating the liberal arts tradition by way of ripping the Moral Majority. A moderate Republican and friend of George H. W. Bush, Giamatti was not exactly a man of the left. Nor was he the only high-profile academic leader to castigate Falwell's organization that fall. Yet his provocative flourishes echoed those of the ACLU ad. "A self-proclaimed 'Moral Majority,' and its satellite or client groups," he charged, "cunning in the use of a native blend of old intimidation and new technology, threaten the values" of liberal education. He branded these groups "tax-exempt Savonarolas who believe that they, and they alone, possess the truth." They confused "pluralism" with "relativism" and in doing so "licensed a new meanness of spirit in our land," a trend Giamatti linked with the recent growth of the Ku Klux Klan and other far-right groups. In this case, as well, the Moral Majority pushed back, with assistance from leading conservative William F. Buckley Jr. and others happy to take down the ivory tower a peg or two. The speech put Vice President Bush in a bind; he had Yale ties to Giamatti, but he wanted to protect his political ties to Falwell. The following year, Bush arranged a mostly conciliatory meeting between the scholar and the pastor.[19]

The Reagan-era prominence of the Christian Right sparked noisy debates about the place of faith in US public life. These debates resounded as pointedly on the Upper West Side as they did in Lynchburg. They represented a notable shift from the curious, if sometimes condescending, attitude many leading liberals had taken toward Jimmy Carter's born-again politics. Back in 1976, evangelicalism had not seemed to be on the verge of a sharp rightward shift. To be sure, the political work of Bill Bright and his man in Washington, Congressman John Conlan, raised alarms during that campaign year. But Carter's success helped to revitalize the Democratic coalition. By 1980, though, progressive activists had started connecting the dots between the nominally secular New Right and the suddenly growing Christian Right.[20] As the ACLU ad suggested, a full-fledged reaction commenced soon after the 1980 election. The result was an evangelical scare, the first of two during the Age of Evangelicalism. It shaped the tone and course of liberalism in the late twentieth century.

The evangelical scare of the 1980s rivaled the evangelical chic of the 1970s as a media event. Editors were inundated with submissions related to the Falwell phenomenon. Although much of the coverage was relatively balanced (if by no means sympathetic), an anti–Christian Right industry quickly arose. Works critical of the Christian Right tended to stress the label "fundamentalist" over "evangelical" (as did Falwell, to be sure, who sought to redeem the former term). *Playboy* and *Penthouse* expended particular energy covering their cultural bête noirs. Talk shows such as *The Phil Donahue Show* routinely pitted atheist activist Madalyn Murray O'Hair against fundamentalist adversaries. Books bore such titles as *The New Subversives*, *God's Bullies*, and *Holy Terror*. To a striking degree, these works embraced the zero-sum logic of their opponents, positing an American society divided between the religious and the worldly. One book, the product of two reporters who a few years earlier had authored an influential attack on religious cults, described "a tale of two cultures—one fundamentalist, one secular—and of a declared holy war for the soul of America being waged on a society that, for the most part, still refuses to acknowledge that it is being attacked." Hollywood translated the holy war into a generational conflict. The 1980s saw a renaissance of films, such as *Footloose* (1984) and *Dirty Dancing* (1987), which pitted youthful freedom against adult prudishness. While *Footloose* takes place in a small town with a Rocky Mountain backdrop, its antagonist is an authoritarian minister with a Falwell-esque Southern drawl.[21]

Critics debated how to gauge the threat represented by this "subculture that had become a *super*culture." Science fiction writer Isaac Asimov saw the villain as religion itself. Many others contended that the Christian Right was a "deviant" brand of evangelical Christianity. Still others saw a new form of fascism at work. An otherwise polite early portrait of Falwell pondered whether, "like Mussolini," he "could make the trains run on time." Columnist Nicholas von Hoffman managed allusions to the old ("round-heads"), the recent ("Christian Stalinists"), and the present ("born-again ayatollahs"). Unsurprisingly, the most durable charge was McCarthyism—although the Moral Majority found the allegation handy, too. George McGovern invoked historian Richard Hofstadter's influential "paranoid style" interpretation of American-style populism (by then almost exclusively applied to right-wing phenomena). *The Handmaid's Tale*, the Canadian novelist Margaret Atwood's influential dystopian novel, embraced nearly every available analogy in describing the fundamentalist Republic of Gilead (née New England), including apartheid South Africa and Khomeini's Iran. Besides being theocratic, Gilead is patriarchal, nativist, racist, and belligerent. Just as clearly, it is an offspring of the early 1980s Christian Right. More moderate observers noted that religion had played a role in debates about the Civil Rights Movement, too (on both sides). The more pressing task, they suggested, was to keep the political conversation civil. A scholar who had studied the early fundamentalist right warned against a new "Brown Scare." Others argued that, rather than obsessing over the Moral Majority "bogey man," Democrats should adjust their economic and foreign policy stances to better reach alienated voters.[22]

A more successful tactic was to defend the venerable American traditions of pluralism and inclusion against a new threat. "Call me a liberal, or a moderate, or a progressive—I think I'm a bleeding-heart conservative—but it's my flag too," television producer Norman Lear declared. Despite the barrage of historical analogies, the 1980s evangelical scare rested on the assumption that the Christian Right was at heart a novel phenomenon. "This is apparently an American first," said one longtime watchdog of the right. Such rhetoric discounted the prominent (if not always named) role that religious interests had long played in American politics. Selective amnesia served a useful rhetorical purpose, not least because Christian Right leaders wanted to paint the exaltation of tolerance as the real historic aberration. They were misusing American ideals, progressive critics argued. "In the past few years," two such critics wrote, "a small group of preachers and political strategists has begun to use religion and all that Americans hold sacred to seize power across a broad spectrum of our lives." They were "exploiting…our most intimate values and individual beliefs…in a concerted effort to transform our culture into one altogether different from the one we have known." Already, wrote one liberal theologian in 1982, "the Christian Right can lay claim to being a complete culture."[23]

To be sure, a liberal counterattack was to be expected. McGovern and fellow Senate liberal Birch Bayh pushed back against religious conservatives toward the end of their losing reelection campaigns in 1980. McGovern minced no words. "I regard them as a menace to the American political process," he stated on *Nightline* after his defeat. Elsewhere, he spoke of "irrational forces in American politics that are a threat to both liberals and conservatives." McGovern started a political action committee, Americans for Common Sense, designed to halt the rightward shift. Similar organizations boomed in 1981.[24]

The threat of the Christian Right made civil and social libertarianism even more central to the identity of the national Democratic Party. This trend was a long time coming, but it became more striking after 1980. Americans

United for Separation of Church and State (Americans United, for short) emerged as one of the strongest critics of the Christian Right. A generation earlier, the organization—known until 1972 as Protestants and Other Americans United for Separation of Church and State—shared with evangelical elites an anxiety about Catholic political power. Now, Moral Majority was the stomach churner. Skeptics charged that the ACLU was changing, as well, calling its attack on the Moral Majority "a rather significant departure" from its history of defending controversial groups, such as neo-Nazis. The ACLU received a membership bump in the 1980s, eventually exceeding its Watergate-era peak.[25]

A new organization, People for the American Way, revealed how the Christian Right gave liberals a new cause. Embryonic at the tail end of the 1980 campaign and officially founded in 1981, it was the most consequential organizational outgrowth of the first evangelical scare. The group (then abbreviated as PAW and soon colloquially known as "People For") was the brainchild of Norman Lear, whose landmark sitcoms—most memorably *All in the Family*—humorously navigated what pundits later termed the culture wars of post-1960s America. Lear was a well-known supporter of both the ACLU and progressive crusader Ralph Nader. It was not surprising, then, that Lear turned his cameras on the Christian Right. During the 1980 campaign year, Lear considered making a film about televangelists. The project evolved instead into a series of television spots. The ads linked political with religious freedom, upholding church-state separation and condemning pastoral interference in politics. In one ad, a Southern-accented woman counters the notion that "television preachers" speak for Christians such as herself. "If my preacher and I don't tell anyone how to vote," she declares, "then nobody will tell me how to worship. After all, that's the American way, isn't it?" In the words of *Saturday Review* editor Norman Cousins, a supporter of People For, Moral Majority was "on a collision course with the American tradition that draws a line between religious influence and religious control."[26]

Disgruntled evangelicals played a prominent role in resisting the Christian Right. The most influential examples were not evangelical left activists, but Jimmy Carter–style moderates not clearly linked with a particular policy agenda. John Anderson's unsuccessful presidential run portended this trend. As the campaign wore on, Anderson turned leftward, although he periodically reaffirmed his strong faith and occasionally faced fallout over his past ties to the evangelical right. His defense of abortion rights rested uneasily beside his affiliation with the theologically conservative Evangelical Free

Church. "The political marriage of the Moral Majority and the New Right is not ordained in heaven," he declared to fellow evangelicals at the National Religious Broadcasters meeting in 1980. A month before the election, Anderson chided Carter for not standing up to the same religious voters "that helped elect him four years ago." Anderson attracted the support of Norman Lear. Former congressman John Buchanan of Alabama offered another strong attack on the early Christian Right. Buchanan, an ordained Southern Baptist minister who began his political career as a Goldwater Republican, lost to a more conservative challenger in the 1980 primary. "They beat my brains out with Christian love," he said of the Moral Majority. Buchanan went on to chair the board of People For. Other evangelicals involved in founding the organization included Ruth Carter Stapleton, Harold Hughes, and Southern Baptist activist James Dunn. "They want a theocracy," Dunn said in an address to Americans United. "And if you listen very carefully...you'll realize they not only want a theocracy, but every one of them wants to be Theo." Fellow Southern Baptists Jimmy Allen and Robert Maddox, who were both associates of President Carter, voiced similar sentiments. Allen blasted the "total capitulation of a segment of the evangelical Christian movement to right-wing politics and sword-rattling jingoism." Maddox went on to serve as executive director of Americans United. The spirit of the counterassault, however, was rooted in mainline Protestantism. One journalist described Lear's initial effort as "a newly formed coalition of church leaders and laymen." People For's founders included William Howard, president of the National Council of Churches, and Barry Lynn, a United Church of Christ staffer who also went on to head Americans United.[27]

People for the American Way grew into one of the best-funded nonlabor organizations on the left, with an annual budget of $8 million by 1986 and a membership of around 300,000 into the 1990s. Its tone was sometimes shrill; one letter from Lear referred to "fascism masquerading as Christianity" and called Christian Right activism "the ultimate obscenity, the spiritual pornography of a debased religiosity." People For soon adopted a more calculated approach, casting a second round of television spots in 1981 as "public service announcements." While still quite strident in opposition to "moral authoritarians," "moral monopolists," and the "radical right," it took pains to avoid attacking faith-informed politics as a whole. The organization was not, as televangelist Jimmy Swaggart asserted, "People for the Atheist Way." Perhaps befitting its early constituency, People For explicitly embraced "mainline" over "ultra-fundamentalist" Protestants, while noting that not all evangelicals fit the latter category. It envisioned the public sphere as a safe space for pluralism, a zone wherein citizenship trumps sectarian desires to legislate morality. On the issue of homosexuality, a 1982 report declared: "To some Americans homosexuality is a sin; to others it is a sickness; to others it is simply a matter of preference. But, the debate about homosexuality should be irrelevant when it comes to constitutional rights; all Americans are entitled to equal protection under the law." The organization cast the Christian Right as at once a serious threat and a demographic outlier. Lear initially numbered the electronic church's weekly audience at a whopping 130 million; People For soon lowered the count to around 20 million.[28]

People for the American Way established a model for how liberals could handle the Christian Right: by positioning themselves as the new modern mainstream. While clearly progressive, it sought to define itself as bipartisan, at times even nonpartisan. In 1986, People For released a list of guidelines for how politicians and their backers should address matters of faith. They should not claim that their faith made them or their chosen candidate uniquely qualified or that it specifically sanctioned a particular position. Likewise, they should not attack their opponent's faith (or lack thereof). Such sentiments rested uncomfortably beside a People For position paper from that same year, titled *Pat Robertson: Extremist*.[29]

As the GOP and the evangelical right grew increasingly entwined, People For and other anti–Christian Right organizations also felt the pull of partisan politics. Portions of the GOP remained hostile to the Christian Right, to be sure. But those groups most invested in countering Falwell and friends gravitated toward the Democratic Party. Starting in the 1980s, the pro-choice movement and the National Organization for Women pursued an "electoral strategy," which likewise aligned them more clearly with Democrats. In the new political era, as historian David Courtwright has written, ideological "consistency counted for less than temperament." Democratic liberals and exiled moderate Republicans could find common ground in their shared aversion to the Christian Right.[30]

That resistance could take many forms. During the 1984 campaign, for example, the Democratic Party offered a number of responses to the Reagan-era evangelical right. Insurgent candidate Jesse Jackson, an ordained minister, provided an explicitly Christian alternative to Reagan-style civil religion. At the Democratic National Convention (by which time his long-shot candidacy was teetering but technically still alive), Jackson opened with an appeal to "faith in a mighty God" before delivering a passionate jeremiad that upheld Jesus as a political model for treating "the least of these." "Jesse Jackson held church in the Democratic National Convention," declared a veteran civil rights activist. Conservatives complained bitterly about those progressives who swooned over Jackson's God talk, but fretted about Reagan's. "Can you imagine the protests of the media should a Fundamentalist minister run for a major public office?" asked a professor at Falwell's Liberty University. Indeed, Jackson (who ran again in 1988) was the closest thing to a bona fide evangelical left presidential candidate as had yet appeared, and his presidential campaigns garnered enthusiasm among progressive evangelicals. The moral authority of the Civil Rights Movement thoroughly enveloped modern liberalism and, increasingly, American politics as a whole. The evangelical right could claim no such mandate. At the same time, as a product of the activist black church tradition of Martin Luther King Jr., Jackson had few personal ties to progressive evangelicals. Moreover, even he felt the pull of his party's platform. In 1977, his byline appeared in the *National Right to Life News*. A decade later, he ran as a supporter of abortion rights. The party politics of abortion continued to leave the evangelical left in an awkward place.[31]

The 1984 Democratic nominee, Walter Mondale, voiced a perspective similar to that of People For. In a fall 1984 address to the Jewish organization B'nai B'rith, Mondale expressed shock that he—the son of a minister, married to the daughter of a minister—would have "to defend my faith in a political campaign." Unlike Reagan, Mondale explicitly embraced John F. Kennedy's separation of faith and policy. "Today, I follow his example," the challenger declared. This was Mondale's American way. The alternative, he argued, was "an extreme fringe poised to capture the Republican Party and tear it from its roots in Lincoln."[32]

Despite Mondale's electoral failure, the Christian Right ultimately gave the Democratic Party an opening. In 1980, polls showed that an avowedly evangelical candidate had a better-than-average chance of winning the presidency. Eight years later, when Pat Robertson sought the GOP presidential nomination, polls suggested the opposite. The overarching dynamic, in the words of social scientists Robert Putnam and David Campbell, was that "religion itself and conservatism (theological, social, moral, and political) became increasingly symbiotic and identified, especially in the public eye, as the Religious Right." The risk for Democrats was that an attack on the Christian Right might appear to be an attack on religion itself. The potential reward lay in the fact that the Christian Right in and of itself was not very popular. It and much of the political right remained vulnerable to charges of extremism. People for the American Way led the successful opposition to Robert Bork's 1987 nomination to the Supreme Court by making that very claim about the conservative jurist.[33] The televangelism scandals of the same year further fueled negative impressions of the Christian Right—and evangelicalism as a whole.

Panics and Politics

Just as the 1980s was not the sole property of Ronald Reagan, so the public impact of evangelicalism during those years was not strictly political. The "satanic panic" of the mid- and late 1980s and the televangelistic "holy war" of 1987 were cases in point. They revealed the breadth of evangelical templates—how evangelical anxieties and spectacles were American anxieties and spectacles, too.

The satanism scare was a genuine "moral panic," popularly known as the "satanic panic." The previous decade had seen widespread worries about personality and religious cults, such as Jim Jones's Peoples Temple. But the satanic panic took such fears to a new level. For a brief moment in the late 1980s, Americans routinely heard reports that 50,000 or more children were sacrificed each year, victims of an occult underground. Such allegations permeated the world of daytime talk shows (especially *Geraldo* and *The Oprah Winfrey Show*), but they also received play in more mainstream journalistic venues, such as ABC's *20/20* and National Public Radio's *Morning Edition*. Stories of sadistic abuse—ritualistic torture, for example, and even secret births for the purpose of sacrifice—gained credibility for a host of reasons. A portion of the increasingly deregulated therapy industry had begun using recovered memories to treat patients suffering from a new diagnosis, Multiple Personality Disorder. At the same time, the expansion of childcare outside of the home raised anxieties about children's safety. Two religious developments helped to connect the above trends with satanism. The expansion of charismatic Christianity in both Protestant and Catholic circles introduced more Americans to the idea of spiritual warfare over individual souls. The related "deliverance ministry," which experienced a comeback in the 1960s and 1970s, linked victory over sin with release from demonic influences. A Judeo-Catholic tradition of exorcism already existed, of course. The newer charismatic demonology, though, put more emphasis on the power of prayer to conquer and cast out Satan's minions. Lawrence Pazder, the Canadian psychiatrist who publicized his client's recovered memories of childhood abuse in a highly influential 1980 book, *Michelle Remembers*, had close ties to the conservative wing of the Catholic charismatic movement. Meanwhile, movies such as *Rosemary's Baby* (1968) and especially *The Exorcist* (1973) had raised the profile of satanic and demonic forces for popular audiences. The singular specter of convicted cult murderer Charles Manson—whom journalists regularly described as a satanist—alone lent credibility to the connection between Satan and sadism. The evolving mental health field and a scandal-hungry media ultimately were the most critical factors connecting satanism with child abuse. Pazder and Michelle Smith, his client and eventual spouse, served as consultants in the 1983–1984 McMartin preschool case in California, in which seven childcare employees were indicted on charges of molesting 360 children as part of what many parents came to see as a conspiratorial cult. (The expensive and drawn-out case resulted in no convictions when it finally ended in 1990.)[34]

The 1980s satanic panic was a product of the collective imagination. The media's composite satanism was an ahistorical and generally inaccurate amalgam of the established Church of Satan, cinematic representations of Satan worship, various eclectic occult traditions, the aesthetics of punk and heavy metal music, and isolated examples of genuinely sociopathic behavior, which sometimes involved satanic symbols or claims. Yet a powerful coalition emerged to support accounts of ritual abuse, even in the face of little corroborating evidence. By one count, that coalition consisted of "social workers, therapists, physicians, victimology researchers, police, criminal prosecutors, fundamentalist Christians, ambitious politicians, antipornography activists, feminists, and the media." Satanic ritual abuse even acquired the imprimatur of an acronym, SRA.[35]

The satanic panic overlapped with evangelical prerogatives in significant ways. Evangelical readers had been purchasing anti-satanism books since the 1970s. Hal Lindsey's 1972 follow-up to *The Late Great Planet Earth* was called *Satan Is Alive and Well on Planet Earth*. The most influential such work was by Mike Warnke, a professed ex-satanist who was active in the Jesus Movement before becoming a celebrity Christian comedian in the 1980s. One analyst called him the first "confessing witch" of the satanism scare. His 1972 book, *The Satan Seller*, foreshadowed the type of tales that a decade later received attention in the secular media (although it did not feature ritual child abuse). Warnke's story was widely cited during the satanic panic, and the governor of Tennessee even declared a day in his honor. The satanism scare echoed evangelical concerns about popular culture. A 1985 *20/20* story, which featured Warnke, warned parents about the number 666 (associated with the biblical Antichrist and hence a popular symbol in satanic circles), while other stories highlighted the pervasive occult symbolism of the heavy metal scene. Led Zeppelin founder Jimmy Page was an avowed admirer of

British occultist Aleister Crowley, for example, while "death metal" bands, such as Slayer, made a point of striking satanic poses, often in a blatantly parodic fashion. Celebrity television journalist Geraldo Rivera broadcast a controversial but highly rated NBC documentary on satanism during the Halloween season of 1988. It featured teenager Sean Sellers, a confessed ex-satanist then on death row for murdering his parents. Sellers appeared alongside fundamentalist and anti-satanism activist Tom Wedge. Rivera later wrote the foreword to a book on satanism, published by an evangelical press and dedicated to Sellers.[36]

The viewers of Geraldo Rivera's documentary included members of the Ingram family from Olympia, Washington. A month later, police officer and local GOP leader Paul Ingram confessed to sexually abusing his two daughters. Ingram claimed that his own recovered memories confirmed those of his children. The horrific recoveries soon escalated among the Ingrams, leading to allegations of an SRA cult involving not only Paul and his wife, but also other members of the police department. All sides had reasons to assume the worst: the investigators, who were predisposed to link abuse allegations with SRA; professional satanism watchers, who saw Olympia as another McMartin; and apparently Paul Ingram himself, a charismatic Christian who believed in a personified Satan. A former FBI agent led a search team, flanked by television-news helicopters, on a failed hunt for satanic burial grounds. Amid the shifting and increasingly implausible charges, the case eventually exhausted itself, but not before Paul Ingram pleaded guilty to charges of third-degree rape. His attempts to withdraw the plea were unsuccessful. "At no time," wrote New Yorker journalist Lawrence Wright, "did the detectives ever consider the possibility that the source of the memories was the investigation itself—there was no other reality."[37]

In response to such outrageous cases, which critics likened to the Salem witch trials, Wright and other journalists launched a backlash in the early 1990s. The targets included Warnke, whose stories of past service as a satanic high priest failed basic tests of chronological plausibility. The stakes were much higher in the case of the "West Memphis Three," teenagers convicted in 1994 of the grisly murders of three young boys one year earlier. Prosecutors did not produce any physical evidence linking the accused to the slayings, which the state claimed were part of a satanic ritual. They did, however, highlight alleged ringleader Damien Echols's interest in witchcraft and other forms of occult practice. On the stand, the emotionally troubled Echols fielded questions about his interest in Crowley's writings and adherence to the neo-pagan Wicca religion. At this late stage of the satanic panic, one defense attorney employed that very term during his closing argument. An award-winning 1996 cable television documentary brought attention to the case, sparking a grassroots movement to free the three convicts. Echols, sentenced to death row, proved especially sympathetic to viewers who identified with the alienated, caustic youth's embrace of black clothing and heavy metal music. Metallica, one of his favorite metal bands, provided the soundtrack for the documentary and its sequels. Other celebrities took up the cause as well. Seventeen years after their conviction, the West Memphis Three accepted a surprise release plea in the face of new forensic evidence casting severe doubt on their guilt.[38]

Satanism's moment in the mainstream waned, but the satanic panic survived in evangelical circles as part of a broader reaction against the New Age movement. The New Age agenda ranged, according to its critics, from spiritualism to the occult and outright Satan worship. Evangelical novelist Frank Peretti's 1986 best seller *This Present Darkness* chronicled the parallel temporal and spiritual battles to save the town of Ashton (and, with it, humanity) from the clutches of Omni Corporation, a front for the demon-powered Universal Consciousness Society. The novel celebrated spiritual warfare against a vast, seductive New Age conspiracy. The popular conflation of the New Age with satanism undoubtedly contributed to the conviction of Damien Echols. To the public at large, though, crystals and lotus positions seemed decidedly less worrisome than the goat heads and sundry forms of sacrilege dotting their children's album covers.[39]

The televangelism scandals of 1987 focused attention more specifically on evangelical actors. If Jerry Falwell increasingly seemed a sophisticated but bombastic political operative, the older Elmer Gantry–Marjoe stereotype resurfaced with a vengeance in the form of Jim and Tammy Faye Bakker of PTL Ministries in Charlotte, North Carolina. The PTL scandal was the dominant evangelical story of the late 1980s. The Bakkers came from an exuberant wing of Pentecostalism that evangelical elites had long sought to cast as a marginal sideshow but that gained increasing prominence in the era of televangelism. "It's not listed in the Bible," Jim Bakker stated in a 1979 interview with *Christianity Today*, "but my spiritual gift, my specific calling from God, is to be a television-show host." PTL stood for both "Praise the Lord" and "People That Love." Critics called the ministry "Pass the Loot." Rising stars up to the moment of their fall, the Bakkers epitomized the collection plate–powered highlife. They had expensive cars, multiple homes, and even an air-conditioned doghouse. Unsurprisingly, suspicions of financial malfeasance nipped at their heels. Their lavish amusement park and resort-in-progress,

Heritage Village, USA, garnered numerous profiles in 1986. It featured water-slides, high-rise hotels, and Billy Graham's actual childhood home (rescued from a developer's wrecking ball). There were plans to build "the largest Wendy's in the world." Heritage Village drew upward of six million visitors a year at its peak. Modeled in part on Disneyland and Walt Disney World (the only theme parks with higher rates of attendance), it brashly blended consumerism and spirituality; hot tubs doubled as baptismal tanks. The Bakkers' popularity and comparatively conciliatory tone made them attractive to politicians seeking to widen their base. With the encouragement of mutual associate Doug Wead, Vice President George H. W. Bush courted the Bakkers during the mid-1980s, visiting with Jim in Charlotte while Barbara Bush hosted Tammy Faye for lunch in Washington, DC. The vice president even told reporters that he tuned into the Bakkers' flagship *PTL Club* show "from time to time."[40]

Their empire fell apart in early 1987 amid charges of adultery against Jim Bakker. The *Charlotte Observer*, which had spent years on the trail of PTL, garnered a Pulitzer Prize for its coverage of the resulting scandal. But the story was tailor-made for television. A rival Pentecostal televangelist, Jimmy Swaggart of Louisiana, followed the *Observer*'s leads and fanned the flames. What surfaced was a pattern of sexual indiscretions with men and an awkward sexual encounter arranged in 1980 between Bakker and a young woman named Jessica Hahn. A few years later, $265,000 of hush money was dispensed to Hahn and her wildcat legal representatives, neither of whom was actually a licensed attorney. Stripped of his ministerial credentials by the Assemblies of God denomination, Bakker abruptly resigned from PTL. In an even more startling move, Jerry Falwell then assumed directorship of the PTL board. The prospect of Falwell—a fundamentalist Baptist whose theology disavowed the spiritual gifts intrinsic to the Pentecostal faith—associating with Bakker struck one journalist as, "on the face of it, the strangest thing in Christendom." Theological differences aside, many Americans likely conflated the two Southern-based television ministers. Their ensuing rift was, in the words of *Newsweek*, an "irresistible spectacle." The Bakkers soon accused Falwell and their shared attorney (none other than Norman Roy Grutman, who had both contested and represented Falwell in court) of engineering a hostile takeover. Most likely, Falwell saw an opportunity to enhance his status as an evangelical statesman and, with a little luck, to broaden his own television ministry. Perhaps he also sought to shield the televangelism community from any additional embarrassment the Bakkers might cause it. Whatever the case, Falwell inherited a fiscal and organizational mess. CNN broadcast, live, a PTL board press conference addressing allegations of loose bookkeeping and tax evasion by the Bakkers. Falwell called the affair "probably the greatest scab and cancer on the face of Christianity in two thousand years of church history," and he and his board appointees stepped down by the end of the year. Meanwhile, the Bakkers plotted a comeback. Their tearful appearance on ABC's *Nightline* in May—the second installment of a three-night special on televangelism—was the highest-rated episode in show history, garnering an audience of twenty-three million and thus giving the Bakkers a viewership they never had achieved with their own program.[41]

The televangelism scandals exposed the eager news media as no less a creature of spectacle than PTL. The "Holy War," known also as "Gospelgate," "Heavengate," and "Pearlygate," was one of the major news stories of the year. *Newsweek* twice featured the Bakkers on its cover, while *Nightline* aired sixteen episodes on the topic. Attention quickly shifted from the gilded corruption of the Bakkers to the intra-televangelist battle royale. Additional fodder came from pioneering televangelist Oral Roberts, who early in 1987 retreated to a prayer tower and warned that God might "call me home" if not enough donations were forthcoming. A year later, Swaggart tearfully confessed to his own sexual sins involving a New Orleans prostitute. Jim Bakker ended up in a federal penitentiary for his financial transgressions, while Hahn twice appeared on the cover of *Playboy*. In the aftermath of the televangelism wars, the remarried Tammy Faye Messner evolved from an Imelda Marcos prototype to a minor camp icon. Drag queen RuPaul narrated a sympathetic 2000 documentary titled *The Eyes of Tammy Faye*. Tammy Faye and her trademark lashes subsequently became a regular at gay-pride parades.[42]

The spectacle quality of evangelicalism did not dissipate with the televangelism scandals. While many evangelical leaders cringed at such attention, others welcomed it for their own purposes. One particularly macabre episode starred evangelical child psychologist James Dobson and convicted serial rapist and murderer Ted Bundy. In January 1989, Dobson conducted an exclusive interview with Bundy from death row. The execution-eve interview came at the initiative of Bundy. He might still have hoped for a reprieve, or perhaps he had a psychopathic desire to manipulate the conversation all the way to the electric chair. Regardless, Bundy patiently answered James Dobson's inquiries about his youthful obsession with hard-core pornography. That line of questioning revealed Dobson's stake in the encounter. He previously had served on the Meese Commission on Pornography, which produced a controversial 1986 report suggesting a connection between pornography and crime. Bundy and Dobson skillfully pushed the moral panic button during their widely publicized videotaped conversation. "What I hope will come of our discussion," Bundy offered, "is that I think society deserves to be protected from itself." Dobson had played a prominent role in an earlier spectacle, the boycott of the 1988 film *The Last Temptation of Christ*, which explored the sexual imagination of Jesus. The Bundy interview brought him new attention. The footage appeared on local cable stations and was marketed to churches as a videotape called *Fatal Addiction*.[43]

The televangelism scandals tainted the evangelical right just as the 1988 presidential campaign year approached. Before and immediately after that election, the conventional wisdom saw the Christian Right as a declining force. The two most evangelical-friendly Republican candidates, Pat Robertson and New York congressman Jack Kemp, failed to catch front-runner George H. W. Bush. In reality, the campaign confirmed the Christian Right's status as a pillar of the Reagan-era GOP. Four years earlier, Sidney Blumenthal had observed that, in offering "insincere gestures of support" to evangelical conservatives, the Reagan administration "served as an incubator for the movement it was trying to contain." The striking fact of the 1988 GOP presidential race, historian Preston Shires has argued, "was not that Robertson and Kemp failed, but that no Republican candidate dared offend the Christian Right."[44]

Pat Robertson launched the first presidential campaign by a recognized Christian Right leader. Like the Bakkers, Robertson signaled the growing prominence of Pentecostal modes within the broader evangelical world. He could reach an audience much less accessible to a fundamentalist like Falwell. More specifically, Robertson could reach socially conservative minorities; his *700 Club* long had featured an African American cohost, Ben Kinchlow. J. O. Patterson, president of the Pentecostal, predominantly black Church of God in Christ, supported Robertson's campaign. Yet Robertson risked alienating noncharismatic evangelicals, who echoed the discomfort of more secular voters with many of his antics. Especially problematic was Robertson's widely publicized claim that, through the power of his prayers, God had steered a hurricane away from his Virginia base.[45]

Pat Robertson's unsurprising failure indicated the limits of the Christian Right as a discrete entity, even while the election year as a whole pointed to its ongoing influence in the GOP. Robertson was an easy target for the left. He formally announced his presidential run in Brooklyn's Bedford-Stuyvesant neighborhood, where he had done missionary and service work as a young adult, only to have activists from the AIDS awareness group ACT UP and other organizations disrupt the event. Already, he had taken steps to gain more respectability, going so far as to embrace the label "evangelical" over Pentecostal or charismatic. In trying to reach a broader audience, he awkwardly resigned his Southern Baptist ordination and took to describing himself as a "religious broadcaster," rather than a "television evangelist." A few media outlets, including *The Saturday Evening Post*, facilitated Robertson's rebranding. Yet many influential evangelical politicos endorsed other Republican candidates, namely Kemp (who attended Richard Halverson's Fourth Presbyterian Church) and Vice President Bush (the presumed favorite). As early as 1985, Falwell publicly signaled his support for Bush, who later also gained the backing of influential NAE operative Robert Dugan. For Falwell and Dugan, 1988 was a chance to flex their muscles as political power brokers.[46]

Clearly, Bush believed that he needed conservative evangelical voters to win the presidency. Campaign aide Doug Wead was not about to allow the candidate to think otherwise. Wead, a founder of the evangelical relief ministry Mercy Corps, demonstrated how far the reach of the evangelical right extended. Wead believed that Bush could successfully court evangelical voters even though the candidate resisted describing himself as "born again." For example, Bush could declare that "Jesus Christ is my personal savior," associate more with Billy Graham, and write an endorsement for "my friend" Jerry Falwell's autobiography. He also could select Indiana senator Dan Quayle as his vice presidential nominee. Although Quayle's reputation was as a conservative stalwart, rather than a Christian Right icon, he had numerous connections to the evangelical world. Quayle, like Kemp, attended Fourth Presbyterian. For good reasons, though, observers in the know did not see Bush as personally sympathetic to the Christian Right. Bush privately distinguished between the respectable Graham and, in the words of a 1982 letter from Bush to Bartlett Giamatti, the "flamboyant money-mad, teary temple builders." The socially conservative and somewhat impolitic Wead did not long survive in a Bush White House filled with establishment Republicans. In 1988, however, Bush did not need to be a Christian Right partisan in order to hold evangelical support for his candidacy roughly at Reagan's levels. He brashly followed Reagan's model of playing up the threat of secularism. Bush's Democratic opponent inadvertently helped him make the case. Garry Wills famously described Michael Dukakis as "the first truly secular candidate we had ever had for the presidency." Dukakis was not a "secularist," Wills wrote, so much as "someone entirely free *from* religion." The Democratic nominee took pains to note his Greek Orthodox background. Yet Dukakis was no son of a minister; he was, as Bush declared, "a card-carrying member" of the

ACLU, which, even as it struck back against the right, remained a handy punching bag.[47]

As the political intensity of the Reagan years subsided, numerous analysts cast the Christian Right as a spent force, "something of a summer flower only." Another political scientist agreed, but added that "being co-opted by the GOP may be seen as a victory in that it gives status to [Christian Right] activists and hence legitimacy to their positions."[48] The latter analysis proved correct. American evangelicals continued to enter the mainstream in fitful, variegated, and influential ways.

FIGURE 1 Evangelist Billy Graham (left) and pollster George Gallup Jr. (right) converse at a press luncheon. Gallup pronounced 1976 the "Year of the Evangelical," giving popular resonance to a phenomenon that Graham had long epitomized. © AP Photo/Barbara Walton.

FIGURE 2 Marabel Morgan holds her best-selling 1973 advice book for wives, *The Total Woman*. Morgan's brand of therapeutic antifeminism appealed to a readership well beyond her initial evangelical audience. © Ray Fisher/Getty Images.

FIGURE 3 This novelty poster from the 1976 presidential campaign both satirized and celebrated Democratic nominee Jimmy Carter's status as a born-again alternative to the political status quo. © AP Photo.

FIGURE 4 The rise of the Christian Right sparked a vigorous counteroffensive celebrating the American traditions of pluralism and tolerance. People for the American Way led the charge with television spots in the early 1980s. Reprinted with permission.

FIGURE 5 The affordable housing charity Habitat for Humanity demonstrated evangelicalism's vitality in civil society. Habitat gave an opportunity for Democrats, such as 1992 running mates Bill Clinton and Al Gore, to show their support for faith-based activities. © Timothy Clary/Getty Images.

AR✝HUR BLESSITT

COMING TO MIDLAND

APRIL 1-6
7 pm

CHAPARRAL CENTER

A MISSION OF LOVE AND JOY TO THE PERMIAN BASIN

HEAR ARTHUR BLESSITT, world evangelist who has carried a twelve foot cross in 60 countries on six continents.
In Christian unity many churches, organizations and individuals support "Decision '84" with the sincere prayer that we might experience the love of God, the grace of the Lord Jesus Christ, and the fellowship of the Holy Spirit.

DECISION '84

FIGURE 6 In 1984, roving evangelist Arthur Blessitt—an icon of the Jesus Movement—met with George W. Bush—a scion of the Republican establishment—while holding a crusade in Midland, Texas. Their encounter was an important part of Bush's journey into evangelical Christianity and, with it, evangelical politics. Reprinted courtesy of Arthur Blessitt.

"And may the Lord in his wisdom see to it that we get our hands on some of that government scratch."

FIGURE 7 President George W. Bush's advocacy of "compassionate conservatism" included federal funding for religious charities. Critics branded his faith-based agenda a cynical move to court and reward conservative Christian supporters. © Mick Stevens/The New Yorker Collection/www.cartoonbank.com.

FIGURE 8 Democratic presidential hopeful Barack Obama courted progressive evangelicals as part of his effort to address the alleged "God gap" between his party and the GOP. In 2007, Obama took part in a CNN candidates' forum hosted by longtime evangelical left leader Jim Wallis. © Chip Somodevilla/Getty Images.

4 THE PARADOX OF INFLUENCE

In spite of the televangelism scandals and the failed presidential run of Pat Robertson, the evangelical right remained the political and cultural baseline for measuring the status of religion in American public life. The emergence of groups like Moral Majority, wrote theologian Richard John Neuhaus in the mid-1980s, "kicked a tripwire" in the ongoing church-state debate.[1] Perhaps, as wise minds across the political spectrum once again argued, religion was vital to the health of American democracy. In the Age of Evangelicalism, "religion" was often translated, however inaccurately, as "evangelical Christianity." Yet many evangelical elites saw themselves as an embattled minority even as they sought—and gained—public influence. In the 1990s, the audacious Christian Coalition and other born-again banes of President Bill Clinton shared the stage with a disproportionately prominent group of moderate evangelical scholars and public intellectuals. They, in turn, coexisted with (and chafed at) the booming evangelical music and entertainment market.

Two metaphors profoundly informed discussions of faith and public life in the fin de siècle United States: the "naked public square" and the "culture war." Neuhaus, who coined the first term, and James Davison Hunter, who popularized the second, each wrote in the shadow of the 1980s evangelical scare. Both Neuhaus, a formerly radical Lutheran minister well on his way to becoming a Catholic traditionalist, and Hunter, a sociologist who first made his name as a careful student of American evangelicals, positioned themselves as civic-minded referees of the public discourse. They echoed the belief of Os Guinness—one of many moderate evangelicals who admired their work—that the nation had an "urgent need to clarify the role of religion in public life."[2] Much of the impetus for clarification came from evangelicals themselves. Hunter and Neuhaus possessed, respectively, established and expanding connections to the evangelical world, and they had a shared distaste for aggressive secularism posing as judicious neutrality. They demonstrated the extent to which evangelicalism established the terms for debates that extended well beyond its presumed turf. Evangelicalism was woven into the interpretative metaphors of the times, and many who shaped those symbols were themselves believers or fellow-travelers. Late twentieth-century evangelicalism was paradigmatic in ways both obvious and subtle.

Learning from the Christian Right

In *The Naked Public Square: Religion and Democracy in America*—first published in 1984, then revised in 1986—Richard John Neuhaus argued that secular elites had "systematically excluded from policy consideration the operative values of the American people, values that are overwhelmingly grounded in religious belief." The result was a "naked public square," which Neuhaus defined elsewhere as "the enforced privatization of religion and religiously informed morality." The artificial divorce of religion from American public life, he contended, imperiled American democracy, not to mention the liberties of the faithful majority of Americans. At this transitional stage in his career, Neuhaus did not yet write as a full-fledged conservative—and certainly not as an evangelical. If anything, he wanted to tame what he saw as the potential for excess among those "evangelicals and fundamentalists who have lately come in from the cold of their sixty-year exile." However, he reserved the hottest irons for his fellow mainline Protestants, who presumed to speak on behalf of all believers even as they kowtowed to a secular moral agenda. Neuhaus thus positioned himself as a hostile critic of the religious left, even while he offered "critical sympathy" for the evangelical right. He sought to create a kind of vital religious center, adding the ingredient of faith to the spirit of moderate postwar liberalism. Neuhaus wondered why his project might seem extraordinary. "How strange is this historical moment," he declared, "in which talk about the public role of religion is thought to be conservative."[3] In fact, Neuhaus reinforced this very trend. Two tendencies worked against his mediating impulses: a strong presumption that the populace at large shared his moral perspective and a tendency to downplay matters of economic justice. The increasingly conservative Neuhaus contributed to the growth of a more vital evangelical right.

By the time *The Naked Public Square* appeared, Neuhaus had traveled far from his days as a progressive supporter of the Civil Rights Movement and a strident opponent of the Vietnam War. He began his rightward drift as an in-house critic of liberalism. In the mid-1970s, he echoed Dean Kelley's *Why Conservative Churches Are Growing*, chiding mainline Protestants for committing "theological abdication" by endorsing progressive activism wholesale and "celebrating its loss of confidence as a sign of renewal." Like many public intellectuals who garnered the label "neoconservative," Neuhaus downplayed evidence of discontinuity. He delighted in the assertion that Martin Luther King Jr. and Jerry Falwell—obvious differences aside—were "similar" in their efforts to "disrupt the business of secular America by an appeal to religiously based public values." Just as provocatively, he toyed with an analogy between the *Dred Scott* and *Roe v. Wade* decisions.[4]

Neuhaus came to see liberal elites as unduly detached from the fabric of American society. In particular, he attacked the emerging "new class" of information workers, many of them associated with educational and governmental bureaucracies. His friend and fellow Lutheran, sociologist Peter Berger, branded the new class a "spectre... haunting the Western world." In an influential 1977 American Enterprise Institute study, Berger and Neuhaus upheld nongovernmental "mediating structures" as necessary supplements of (perhaps even alternatives to) the modern welfare state. Their analysis contributed to a rediscovery of "civil society" that extended across the ideological spectrum. In everyday parlance, Berger and Neuhaus's mediating structures became known as the "nonprofit" sector. Churches were among the most important mediating structures, and the authors criticized efforts to exclude them from matters of public policy. During the 1976 presidential campaign, Neuhaus backed Jimmy Carter, whom he celebrated as "an embarrassment to the press because he prays for his campaign in public." Not surprisingly, then, Neuhaus also took an interest in the early Christian Right, which sought to claim the space liberal Protestants had supposedly abdicated. Consulted for *Newsweek*'s 1980 cover story on the Christian Right, Neuhaus characterized Jerry Falwell and Pat Robertson as "profoundly immature." He saw their antics as the logical outcome of attempts to exclude them from the public square.[5]

While Neuhaus set out to explain the Christian Right, he ultimately became entangled in it. *The Naked Public Square* was published by the respected evangelical press, Eerdmans, and its argument resonated profoundly in evangelical circles. Charles Colson went so far as to liken the book to Augustine's *City of God*. In 2005, *Time* magazine included Neuhaus—by then a Catholic priest—on a list of "The 25 Most Influential Evangelicals in America." His faith in the moral bearings of the American majority grew notably shakier in the 1990s after a plurality of voters twice elected Democrat Bill Clinton as president. Neuhaus had already posed a rhetorical question that was anything but civil: "Can Atheists Be Good Citizens?" The tone of his journal, *First Things*, grew increasingly reactionary. In 1996, a controversial *First Things* symposium called "The End of Democracy?" appeared to question the legitimacy of the American government. An article in *The New Republic* soon branded Neuhaus and his peers "theocons," contrasting them with the predominantly Jewish and comparatively secular "neocons."[6]

At the time of its appearance, though, *The Naked Public Square* tapped into a discourse that extended well beyond specifically evangelical readers or even generally conservative ones. The book received extensive and largely favorable reviews in prominent outlets. Neuhaus's embrace of civil society complemented the tone (if not the politics) of communitarian thinkers, such as sociologist Robert Bellah. Communitarians sought to recover the principles of civic virtue and the public good—the core, many of them argued, of the "republican" values that underlay the nation's founding. They saw these values as an essential alternative to both the liberal insistence on individual rights and the conservative acquiescence to an impersonal market. Bellah was the lead author of a 1985 book, *Habits of the Heart: Individualism and Commitment in American Life*, the most influential sociological study associated with American communitarianism. *Habits of the Heart* did not put particular stress on religion. It did, though, criticize the rise of a therapeutic sense of "cosmic selfhood." In fact, "Sheilaism," the label that one research subject gave her faith, quickly became the most famous anecdote from the book. "Sheilaism" was eponymous in brand and solipsistic in practice; Sheila Larson described her faith as a matter of following "my own little voice." Even though Larson embraced principles of self-respect, tolerance, and decency, her seemingly unmoored individualism worried communitarian theorists. Yet Bellah, whose scholarly reputation derived from his influential work on civil religion, clearly agreed with Neuhaus that religion ultimately was a socially constructive thing, at heart. Speaking to a group of moderate Southern Baptists in the early 1980s, Bellah had called for a "spiritual awakening" to combat the "amoral majority" and the Moral Majority alike.[7]

The communitarian movement was especially attractive to religion-friendly liberals, and Neuhaus's book held similar appeal. Battered by the success of Reagan and the failed 1988 campaign of Michael Dukakis, these liberals sought to promote viable religious alternatives to the Christian Right. They found inspiration in Yale law professor Stephen Carter's 1993 book, *The Culture of Disbelief: How American Law and Politics Trivialize Religious Devotion*. Carter resisted easy political categorization but was eager to show liberals the error of their ways. An Episcopalian, he called himself "an evangelical Christian who is hardly a movement conservative." He shared Neuhaus's annoyance that anyone might consider religion to be an outlier in American public life when it was, in fact, the statistical norm in society as a whole. Writing in a much more measured tone than did Neuhaus, Carter downplayed the impact of the newly popularized bête noir of political correctness, contending that, "nowadays, religion is treated more as a hobby than as an object of hostility." Carter argued for a "clothed public square" that would accommodate religion within the norms of liberal, pluralistic democracy. He also had a pointed message for Democrats: They should criticize policy positions, not religious worldviews, and they should avoid conflating the Christian Right with religion as a whole. If the Christian Right was "wrong for America," he wrote, "it must be because its message is wrong on the issues, not because its message is religious." One prominent Democrat who wanted to refashion his party as faith-friendly took Carter's argument to heart. President Clinton included *The Culture of Disbelief* in his summer reading and echoed Carter at an interfaith breakfast in 1993. "Sometimes I think the environment in which we operate is entirely too secular," Clinton declared. "The fact that we have freedom *of* religion doesn't mean we need to try to have freedom *from* religion. It doesn't mean that those of us who have faith shouldn't frankly admit that we are animated by that faith." According to conservative journalist Fred Barnes, the president "ostentatiously left a copy of Carter's book on his Oval Office desk for weeks."[8]

The Naked Public Square, which appeared nearly a decade before Carter's book, offered one of the earliest and most enduring efforts to learn something from the Christian Right and the issues that it had brought to the fore. "Of course it would be an irony of the first class," Neuhaus had mused in the book, "were the moral majoritarians to turn out to be the instrument of democratic renewal." For Neuhaus, the Christian Right was a catalyst, opening up for discussion a subject normally avoided in polite company. His book gave journalists a way to explore the larger meaning of the Christian Right for American society. Some scholars resisted Neuhaus's version of "religious correctness," but his metaphor triumphed in academia, too. A 2007 special issue of *The American Quarterly* asked, "Is the Public Square Still Naked?"[9]

Yet the "naked public square" paled in comparison to the "culture war" as a term for the times. The phrase (which harkened back to the *Kulturkampf* in late nineteenth-century Germany) surfaced occasionally during the late 1980s and early 1990s; Neuhaus titled a 1991 *First Things* column "Notes on the Culture Wars." The term went viral at the end of that year with the arrival of James Davison Hunter's book, *Culture Wars: The Struggle to Define America*. Hunter, a sociologist at the University of Virginia, described a conflict between "progressive" and "orthodox" forces in post-1960s America. For Hunter, the fundamental divisions now concerned matters of morality, lifestyle, and values. Journalists, interest groups, and political parties perpetuated "different systems of moral understanding," and these culture-based cleavages overrode traditional religious and ethnic divides. A nation that once thought in terms of Catholics or Protestants (or, more specifically, Polish Catholics or German Lutherans) had become a society of pro-lifers and pro-choicers. A conservative Southern Baptist now might have more in common with a traditionalist Catholic than with, say, Jimmy Carter. The new coordinates were easily politicized. Such divisions threatened to tear apart American society.[10]

While Hunter ambitiously sought to describe the reorganization of American society as a whole, his thesis derived from a particular interpretation of American religious history. "At the heart of the new cultural realignment," Hunter wrote, "are the pragmatic alliances being formed across faith traditions." For this reason, prominent scholars of American religion were often assigned to review the book. Hunter's thesis appeared in the aftermath of a paradigm-shaping 1988 book by Princeton sociologist Robert Wuthnow, who saw a post–World War II "restructuring" of American religion—especially, American Protestantism—along lines similar to Hunter's subsequent categories. Wuthnow offered a somewhat less stark interpretation. Rather than a war, he posited competing conservative and liberal "civil religions"— with evangelicals epitomizing the former and mainline Protestants the latter. Yet he, too, offered little sense that a rapprochement was on the horizon, especially since religious divisions tended to parallel political ones. In *Culture Wars*, Hunter went much further. Of the book's many bold arguments, perhaps the most startling was his suggestion that "the practical effects of the birth of Christianity and the Reformation have, at least in the U.S. context, become both politically and culturally defunct." The progressive-orthodox divide (which many Americans described as a split between "liberals" and "conservatives") now overrode Protestant-Catholic differences, not to mention Christian and Jewish ones. The polarizing Christian Right was an obvious contributor to these trends. Hunter conceded that "Evangelical and Fundamentalist Protestants are the most vocal and visible actors on the orthodox side of the new cultural divide," but he stressed that he was not writing only about the Christian Right and its opponents. Still, his argument would not have captured the popular imagination without those very forces.[11]

"Few descriptions of American society," wrote two scholars six years after the publication of Hunter's book, "have made a quicker transition from jargon to cliché than the phrase 'culture war.'" It provided a handy framework for describing any number of divisive political issues, and scholars even applied it to earlier periods of American history. Conservative Supreme Court justice Antonin Scalia accused the court majority of "tak[ing] sides in the culture wars" in one of his famously acerbic dissents. Hunter quickly faced pushback from scholars armed with mounds of evidence that his thesis ignored the great American middle that lay between the progressive and orthodox camps. Most observers, though, conceded that the thesis worked as a description of the elites who drove public rhetoric.[12]

Lost in the response to Hunter's book was its profound connection to evangelicalism. In the pages of *Culture Wars* and after his subsequent rise to fame, Hunter positioned himself as an impartial, if gravely concerned, chronicler of American public life. If he had an obvious bias, it was toward Bellah-style communitarianism. Yet Hunter's scholarly background deeply informed his analysis. A graduate of the evangelical Gordon College, Hunter's initial claim to academic fame was a series of sophisticated studies of American evangelicals. Reflecting the influence of his graduate mentor, Peter Berger, Hunter saw the new class intelligentsia as a force in American society. Even though the evangelical right garnered most of the headlines, Hunter linked the evangelical left with ascendant new class values. At the same time, he took pains to argue that the televangelism scandals and other spectacles hardly imperiled the survival of such a durable and diverse faith tradition as evangelical Christianity.[13]

Hunter's public position on "secular humanism"—a favorite rhetorical barb of the evangelical right—made him a minor participant in the very culture wars he gained fame for announcing. Like Neuhaus, Hunter believed that strident secularism was a historical novelty misleadingly posing as the best friend of pluralism. Like Stephen Carter, Hunter argued for a more accommodationist interpretation of the First Amendment's religion clauses. In court testimony and scholarly publications during the 1980s, Hunter argued that secular humanism—although "a relatively diffuse moral ethos"—had the sociological characteristics of a religion. He likened its cultural power to that of "nondenominational Protestantism in the nineteenth century." In 1987, Hunter testified as an expert witness on behalf of Alabama plaintiffs who were challenging the use of public school textbooks that, they claimed, advocated secular humanism to the exclusion of traditional forms of religion. In a creative twist on the usual course of First Amendment jurisprudence, they contended that use of the textbooks violated the Establishment Clause. In his testimony, Hunter stated that secular humanism, as the "dominant ideology of public school textbooks," was the "functional equivalent" of a religion. "Because of its specific role in the contemporary public school curricula," he wrote elsewhere, "it actually enjoys the status of a quasi establishment."[14]

As if to confirm Hunter's thesis, the phrase "culture war" itself became a political weapon. Both Colson and Neuhaus eagerly embraced Hunter's arguments. More famously, right-wing Republican Pat Buchanan spoke at the 1992 GOP convention of a "cultural war, as critical to the kind of nation we shall be as the Cold War itself, for this war is for the soul of America." Party chairman Richard N. Bond similarly averred that Republicans were in the midst of a "cultural war" with Democrats. Such militant declarations eventually gave liberals a chance to brand the term as an extremist chant. Buchanan's speech fed a media narrative of a GOP held captive by its evangelical wing. President Clinton, under fire from conservative Republicans during the summer of 1994, accused his adversaries of waging a "cultural war" over certain moral issues and soon after invited Hunter to a breakfast meeting with himself and Vice President Al Gore. While some conservatives viewed the culture wars as a useful summons to struggle, many progressives saw the value of identifying themselves as the targets of Buchanan and his charges.[15]

Although neither *The Naked Public Square* nor *Culture Wars* exclusively concerned evangelicalism, the Age of Evangelicalism was the source and origin of their arguments. It stood to reason, then, that attention would increasingly turn to moderate evangelicals who could offer an insider's interpretation to the larger public. Two years before the arrival of Hunter's book, Robert Wuthnow urged evangelical scholars to "play a vital role…in mediating between their own domain of special understanding and the interests of the wider public."[16] Wuthnow's call was already being heeded.

The Thoughtful Evangelicals

The 1990s saw the public emergence of what might be described as the conscience wing of modern American evangelicalism. As evangelicals and evangelical sympathizers gained renewed influence in the academy, a number of evangelical intellectuals attempted to interpret their tradition in a more nuanced way and to prod their fellow believers toward responsible intellectual engagement with secular society. Some of them embraced postmodernism in order to gain leverage within the scholarly community. Most, however, were methodological traditionalists at heart. They saw the new spotlight on American evangelicalism as an opportunity, but also as a potential pitfall. They found much to fret about even as they also found a surprisingly sympathetic audience outside their ranks. The rise of the thoughtful evangelicals demonstrated yet another way in which evangelicalism was thoroughly integrated into the cultural, political, and intellectual currents of late twentieth-century America.

To a remarkable degree, the thoughtful evangelicals followed a script of their own devising. As the naked public square metaphor continued to take hold, journalists proved increasingly receptive to evangelical voices of moderation. To be sure, the political coverage of evangelicalism continued to reflect what liberal journalist Joe Conason termed a "cycle of neglect followed by sensationalism and then more neglect."[17] The problem was not lack of aggregate attention, but lack of sustained focus. Each portrait of a new "wave" of Christian Right activism—whether the year was 1980, 1988, or 1994—confused persistence with recurrence. Still, the seeming novelty of the Christian Right ultimately drove interest in what the thoughtful evangelicals had to say.

Much of that interest concerned the concept of "fundamentalism." To many observers, the Christian Right was one expression of the global growth of "fundamentalism," a word that reentered popular and scholarly parlance in the late 1970s and early 1980s. An essentially Protestant term—first employed by conservative evangelicals themselves amid the doctrinal controversies of the 1910s and 1920s—now expanded to include militant Muslims, Jews, Hindus, and even certain Buddhist groups. The trigger for interest in "global fundamentalism" was not the creation of the Moral Majority in 1979, but the Iranian Revolution of that same year. Still, the two begged for comparison. The Iran hostage crisis and the Christian Right both were campaign issues in 1980. Influential observers of American religion—especially University of Chicago Divinity School historian Martin Marty, perhaps the most influential of them all—could not help but notice that the original fundamentalists were making a comeback in the United States.[18]

Marty helped to pioneer the trans-religious interpretation of fundamentalism. Along with his former student, Scott Appleby, he directed the decade-long Fundamentalism Project. Chartered in 1987 by the American Academy of Arts and Sciences and generously funded by the MacArthur Foundation, the endeavor gave scholarly legitimacy to the concept of global fundamentalism. Between 1991 and 1995, the Fundamentalism Project produced five dense volumes, which applied Wittgenstein's concept of "family resemblance" to analyze "generic fundamentalism" alongside localized expressions of the phenomenon. While most case studies concerned foreign examples, the

American Christian Right received prominent attention. Marty and Appleby produced a documentary series for public television that began with an overview of American Protestant fundamentalists (including Bob Jones II and Randall Terry) before addressing their Muslim counterparts in Egypt and Jewish counterparts in Israel. Such methodological ecumenism, as the authors recognized, rested uncomfortably beside American fundamentalists' proud claims to be the rightful owners of that label.[19]

A wealth of similar case studies coincided with the work of the Fundamentalism Project. Almost all of them challenged the already-battered secularization thesis. Gilles Kepel, a prominent French intellectual, saw the late 1970s rise of the Christian Right, the Iranian Revolution, the ascendance of the Israeli Likud Party, and the election of Pope John Paul II as signaling a wholesale "reversal" of modern secularization. Harvard political scientist Samuel Huntington incorporated Kepel's arguments into a monumental and controversial 1996 study titled *The Clash of Civilization and the Remaking of World Order* (although Huntington put little emphasis on American Christianity). Fundamentalism seemed a fundamental part of the post–Cold War order.[20]

A generation of prominent evangelical academics came of age amid this growing scholarly and journalistic interest in religion. They were united in their concern about the extent to which the Christian Right dominated perceptions of evangelicalism. To them, Francis Schaeffer's sharp turn to the right toward the close of his life was particularly disconcerting. A small group of evangelical historians chafed at Schaeffer's wholesale embrace of the Christian America thesis—most pointedly in his 1981 screed, *A Christian Manifesto*. The dogmatic Schaeffer was a logical foil, if also an ironic one, since he had inspired a generation of aspiring evangelical intellectuals during an earlier phase of his career. Historians George Marsden and Mark Noll, two evangelical scholars who acknowledged Schaeffer's past contributions, separately wrote to him in the early 1980s. They politely chided Schaeffer for ignoring scholarly studies that complicated his portrait of pious Founding Fathers now betrayed by liberal secularists. In response, Schaeffer questioned their fidelity to scripture. A 1982 *Newsweek* profile of Schaeffer greatly hindered the prospects for civil discourse. "The danger is that people will take [Schaeffer] for a scholar, which he is not," Noll told *Newsweek*'s Kenneth Woodward. Marsden also caught flak for his decision to testify as an expert witness for the plaintiffs in a 1981 court case—dubbed Scopes II—challenging an Arkansas law that required "creation science" to be taught alongside evolution in public schools. Unaccustomed to siding with the American Civil Liberties Union,

Marsden believed (as did the numerous prominent Protestants and Catholics who also supported the challenge) that the law "was based on a false dichotomy between creation and evolution." His evangelical critics had little patience for such nuance. "With friends like these," Schaeffer's son later wrote, "who needs enemies?" In 1983, Marsden, Noll, and a third historian—Nathan Hatch—published *The Search for Christian America*, a scholarly response to the Christian Right's spin on American history, particularly the works of Schaeffer and popular Christian historian Peter Marshall. Written from an evangelical perspective, the book sought "to introduce a note of realism to tone down a romanticized view of America's Christian heritage." The authors hoped to demonstrate that one could be faithful to the past while remaining faithful in the present.[21]

Marsden, Noll, and Hatch came to compose the core of the thoughtful evangelical community. They moved with increasing comfort in broader scholarly circles but dedicated significant energy to addressing their fellow evangelicals. Other thoughtful evangelicals—such as historian and documentarian Randall Balmer, who early in his career wrote the bibliographical essay for *The Search for Christian America*—positioned themselves as modern academics wrestling with emotional ties to their faith tradition. Still others, such as political scientist John Green, rarely showed their evangelical cards. A final group of secular scholars who hailed from evangelical backgrounds sought to parlay their childhood beliefs into empathetic portraits of an American faith community.[22]

If a manifesto for thoughtful evangelicalism existed, it was Mark Noll's 1994 book, *The Scandal of the Evangelical Mind*. Known as a careful intellectual historian, Noll came out swinging in this influential book. "The scandal of the evangelical mind is that there is not much of an evangelical mind," he declared. Noll concluded that postwar historian Richard Hofstadter's famous dismissal of the "evangelical spirit" in *Anti-Intellectualism in American Life* was "too simple" but not entirely unfounded. Evangelicalism had produced innumerable successful crusaders for the faith, but, as Canadian scholar N. K. Clifford once wrote, it "always tended toward an over-simplification of issues and the substitution of inspiration and zeal for critical analysis and serious reflection." For Noll, early twentieth-century fundamentalism had been an "intellectual disaster." Its unyielding biblical literalism and superficial dismissal of evolution represented an "uncritical adoption of intellectual habits from the nineteenth century." Noll cited many examples of influential evangelical minds, but they tended to produce popularized apologetics, rather than rigorous scholarship. Schaeffer was an obvious case, although Noll chose to spare him. Another example was the late British professor, novelist, and Christian apologist C. S. Lewis, who—while neither an evangelical nor an admirer of American Protestantism—contributed "the single most important body of Christian thinking for American evangelicals in the twentieth century." Noll tried to close on a hopeful note, yet his book was a call to introspection intended to counter the traditional evangelical call to arms. A professor at Wheaton College in Illinois, Noll later admitted that the book "came very close to being my letter of resignation from the evangelical movement." *The Scandal of the Evangelical Mind* was the most notable of several similar publications. Combined, they amounted to a period of great intellectual productivity in evangelical circles—an irony that outsiders were best positioned to notice. As Noll's increasing prominence suggested, the parties interested in his argument extended well beyond the usual evangelical suspects.[23]

In the acknowledgments section of *The Scandal of the Evangelical Mind*, Noll thanked the Pew Charitable Trusts, one of two wealthy American foundations that subsidized a generation of evangelical scholarship, effectively making thoughtful evangelicalism a going concern. The other foundation, the Lilly Endowment, passed the Ford Foundation to momentarily become the wealthiest foundation in the United States (thanks to the success of Eli Lilly and Company's drug Prozac). Indiana-based Lilly had a history of funding Protestant institutions of all varieties. While Lilly did not specifically target evangelical organizations, it was a major donor to Wheaton College's Institute for the Study of American Evangelicals (ISAE), and it showered resources on evangelical-friendly fellowship programs and seminars. Pew, which also grew to rank among the ten wealthiest American foundations, took a more direct funding route. The Pew Charitable Trusts represented the financial legacy of the offspring of turn-of-the-century oil baron Joseph N. Pew. The most prosperous heir, J. Howard Pew, became the most important financial backer of evangelical causes in the mid-twentieth century. Like the MacArthur Foundation and other trusts, the Pew funds moved sharply to the left after the passing of their initial benefactors. Yet Pew's ties to evangelicalism remained and underwent a revival in the 1990s.[24]

In 1990, Pew implemented the Evangelical Scholars Program, a decade-long effort to support and improve evangelical scholarship. Directed by historian Joel Carpenter (formerly of ISAE), the Christian Scholars Program (as the effort tellingly was renamed) poured a whopping $24 million into research projects, seminars, and fellowships during the 1990s, all toward the end of "increasing the number of evangelical Christian scholars contributing to academic discourse." In a 1990 report outlining religious grant-making efforts, Carpenter argued that "evangelicalism's new salience" necessitated "increased responsibility" in a public arena that too often was devoid of thoughtful religious input. He followed Neuhaus in hoping to create a new "vital center" in American religion, with evangelicals being the essential ingredient. "Ironically," Carpenter wrote, "it is the evangelicals, the religious group most marginal to intellectual life, who show the most promise in reasserting religious thought." His verdict on "politicized fundamentalism" was harsher than Neuhaus's, though, no doubt because the Christian Right's prominence diminished the intellectual reputation of evangelicalism. The Pew program increasingly focused on "mainstreaming" evangelical academics, "interpreted broadly, so as to include Catholics, Orthodox, and mainline Protestants who can affirm that term." Nearly every scholar who might be classified as a thoughtful evangelical (including Marsden, Noll, historian Grant Wacker, and sociologist Christian Smith) received significant funding from Pew or Lilly, as did such influential evangelical-friendly scholars as Hunter, Wuthnow, and Charles Marsh. Pew also supported centers for the study of religion at prestigious universities, such as Yale and Emory. "It is not an overstatement," wrote one sociologist who himself received funding from Lilly, "to say that the contemporary field of American religion was created largely thanks to the support of Pew and Lilly." Pew offered a similar self-evaluation as it wound down funding for the Christian Scholars Program in the early 2000s.[25]

Thoughtful evangelical scholarship thrived in a number of forums. The University of Notre Dame became its most important academic incubator. Notre Dame's role was curious only at first glance. It was America's flagship Catholic school, to be sure, but it was also the most culturally conservative major research university in the nation. As Noll and his peers were well aware, no evangelical institution approached its status. By the 1990s, Notre Dame employed Marsden, who held an endowed chair, and Hatch, who eventually served as provost, along with Reformed evangelical scholars Alvin Plantinga, a philosopher, and John Van Engen, a medievalist. It also housed the Evangelical/Christian Scholars Program, as well as Fundamentalism Project director Scott Appleby. The thoughtful evangelicals found another venue in the Catholic-oriented *First Things*, an eclectic journal founded in 1990 by Neuhaus, who formally aligned with the Vatican that same year. Five years later, the publishers of *Christianity Today* started *Books & Culture*. Calling itself a "Christian review," the smart journal overtly emulated the elite *New York Review of Books*. Both *Books & Culture* and the significantly more influential *First Things* demonstrated the periodic overlap between the thoughtful evangelicals, the evangelical right, and Catholic traditionalists. The grandest indication along those lines was the birth of Evangelicals and Catholics Together (ECT) in 1994. The brainchild of Neuhaus and one of his biggest evangelical supporters, Charles Colson, the organization was a striking confirmation of the Wuthnow-Hunter interpretation of recent American religion. ECT attempted to provide theological grounding for an alliance that had taken shape around the issue of abortion. Indeed, ECT's founding statement noted that the impetus for cooperation was, "in large part, a result of common effort to protect human life, especially the lives of the most vulnerable among us." Its endorsers included evangelical right figures Bill Bright and Pat Robertson, as well as leading evangelical intellectuals Noll, Hatch, and theologian Richard Mouw. By the late 1990s, prominent magazines began to profile the new wave of evangelical scholarship. Political scientist Alan Wolfe heralded "The Opening of the Evangelical Mind," even while noting that the largesse of Pew and Lilly had failed to produce an evangelical institution on par with the Catholic Notre Dame or the Jewish Brandeis.[26]

The influence of evangelical scholarship was most evident in the humanities and social sciences, especially the field of American religious history. There, the thoughtful evangelicals pulled off an artful maneuver; they countered evangelical shibboleths while also forcing American historians to take account of evangelicalism. In some respects, they took up issues first raised by the 1970s evangelical left—civil religion and the role of evangelical reformers foremost among them—and wrote them into mainstream American history. Marsden, Noll, and Hatch could not be described as progressives. However, their scholarly influence transcended their moral and political outlooks, which generally lay to the right of academia's left-facing center.

The impact of the thoughtful evangelicals far exceeded their numbers. Marsden's 1980 magnum opus, *Fundamentalism and American Culture*, quickly became the standard study of modern fundamentalism. Marsden linked the mind of American fundamentalism not with otherworldly supernaturalism but with Scottish Common Sense Realism, a philosophy popular in the nineteenth century. Marsden's fundamentalists were intellectuals of a different sort. Nathan Hatch authored arguably the most influential late twentieth-century study of religion in the Early Republic. Published in 1989, Hatch's book described how disestablishment resulted in the "democratization of American Christianity." The resulting free market in American religion—a sometimes chaotic environment in which populist versions of the faith tended to flourish most—helped to explain why the United States never experienced European-style secularization. The "odd combination of modernity and religion" during the early Republic, Hatch surmised, put the present "resurgence of Fundamentalism" and the "vengeance with which religious issues have again entered the public arena" in historical perspective. Evangelical scholarship thus thrived alongside evangelical politics. A church historian described the rise of Marsden, Hatch, Noll, and other historians who moved in an evangelical orbit (such as Wacker and Harry Stout) as "one of the most arresting phenomena in American religious scholarship today." Yale historian Jon Butler identified the "evangelical paradigm" as "the single most powerful explanatory device adopted by academic historians to account for the distinctive features of American society, culture, and identity." That paradigm saw evangelical Christianity as central to the course of American society and culture, if hardly vital to the vision of the Founding Fathers themselves. In exposing perhaps fatal flaws in the secularization thesis, it stressed the need to interpret religious ideas as critical historical agents in their own right, even if social, economic, and other secular forces had, of course, shaped those ideas. Evangelical-friendly scholars made similar contentions in the field of political science. There, the so-called gang of four—John Green, James Guth, Lyman Kellstedt, and Corwin Smidt—relentlessly highlighted the religion factor in American politics. They made their way into the Rolodexes of journalists, receiving more than 500 references in newspapers and magazines during the 1980s and 1990s. By the end of the 1990s, the dominant scholarly narratives about evangelicalism past and present had largely been authored by evangelicals themselves.[27]

Most of these scholars and public intellectuals aspired toward some notion of specifically Christian intellectual engagement. Marsden was the most dogged proponent of this goal, as in his mind the modern research university had become the most denuded of all public squares. He made his case in a monumental, Pew-funded study of the decline of Christian influence in modern universities. Marsden argued that the leading American universities—most of which had religious origins—had exiled their founders' spiritual heirs. He expressed "puzzlement as to how the dominant American academic life came to be defined in a way that such viewpoints, including their counterparts in other Christian or other religious heritages, have been largely excluded." In *The Soul of the American University* and related works, he acknowledged "that the century-long process of dismantling the old Protestant establishment was...an understandable way of addressing problems of equity in an increasingly pluralistic society." Yet Marsden saw a more insidious form of secularization at work by the 1990s. In response, he provocatively proposed that religious viewpoints be granted the same amount of space that, say, feminist theory already had acquired. Marsden thus endorsed postmodern pluralism, albeit largely for strategic ends. Noll sounded a similar, if more tentative note about the limits of secular objectivity.[28]

Other thoughtful evangelicals, especially those in the theological community, went much further by embracing theologian Stanley Hauerwas, who taught at Notre Dame before moving to Duke Divinity School in the mid-1980s. In contrast to Richard John Neuhaus, the famously provocative Hauerwas celebrated the suggestion that American Christianity had lost its cultural hegemony. A post-Christian America just might free the church to be itself—that is, to focus not on transforming or guiding society, but on forming a community of Christ's disciples. Hauerwas's biblicism, friendliness toward Anabaptism, and deliberately profane disdain for civil religion made him the closest thing to a Francis Schaeffer in evangelical left circles. As a nonevangelical, however, Hauerwas (whose oeuvre far surpassed Schaeffer's in quality, depth, and duration) did not desire to play that role. In relation to the evangelical mainstream, he was both a radical (who, under the influence of Anabaptism, became a pacifist) and a useful skeptic of liberal Protestant trendiness. The nontheologian Marsden, by contrast, was a traditional intellectual historian who cared very much about the church's stature in academia.[29]

Marsden's arguments received wide coverage within academia and the elite press. If he expected a sympathetic audience among postmodern pluralists, it was not forthcoming. Writing in *First Things*, which frequently opened its pages to contrarian viewpoints, theorist Stanley Fish saw Marsden's proposal for religious equal time as a "self-defeating argument because it amounts to saying that when it comes to proof, religious perspectives are no worse off than any other." Fish might also have noted that Marsden and his peers were already among the more influential American historians then writing.[30]

Subculture as Pop Culture

The thoughtful evangelicals were very aware of their lack of sway in evangelical popular culture. Their scholarly interventions bore little resemblance to the ongoing commoditization of born-again Christianity. The booming "Christian lifestyle" phenomenon took many forms, ranging from contemporary Christian music to megachurches and the rise of such Christian-friendly citadels as Colorado Springs and Branson, Missouri.[31] At the center of the evangelical-entertainment cash nexus lay a lucrative martyrdom complex. Feelings of marginalization begat a marketing strategy. Yet here, as well, many avowed evangelicals did not grasp the full scale of their relevance. Evangelical publishing and recording houses cultivated highly profitable expressions of popular culture, which they billed instead as alternatives to popular culture. The posture of subculture remained even as the product went mainstream.

The commercial bridges between evangelical culture and pop culture evolved into bonds. This was true even for Christian bookstores, which ostensibly existed to minimize such intermingling. By the mid-1990s, there numbered more than 2,500 Christian bookstores—including a self-styled "Christian superstore" in Birmingham, Alabama—with total sales growing from more than $3 billion in the early 1990s to $4 billion by 2000. These unabashedly sectarian spaces featured plenty of "God's Gym" tee-shirts along with an ever-proliferating variety of Christian-themed books, although the latter increasingly also found their way into Waldenbooks, Barnes & Noble, and especially Wal-Mart.[32]

Something similar had already happened to a small number of Christian music stars, such as the 1980s pop phenomenon, Amy Grant. She was the flagship "crossover" artist. Grant launched her career performing catchy gospel-pop titles like "Sing Your Praise to the Lord" and "I Have Decided," part of a 1982 album that went platinum. Her significantly more secular 1991 album, *Heart in Motion*, sold five times as many copies; its hit titles were "Baby, Baby" and "Every Heartbeat." Much more flamboyant was the Orange County heavy metal band Stryper, which offered a crossover gloss on a Satan-saturated genre. Stryper titled its 1986 platinum album *To Hell with the Devil* and gained notoriety for heaving copies of the New Testament into concert crowds. A few fundamentalists still questioned the propriety of such pulsating music, and observers of all types lamented its uneven quality. "You aren't making Christianity better, you're just making rock and roll worse," the cartoon character Hank Hill complained of his son's Christian rock band. By the late 1990s, some Christian bands, such as Jars of Clay and Sixpence None the Richer, largely bypassed the Christian market altogether. Most Christian artists did not aspire to such heights, though, and they did not need to in order to find a sizable market. Christian music revenues rose to around $1 billion annually by the mid-1990s, or about one-tenth of the total music market. By then, pop- and rock-driven "praise and worship" tunes had traveled far from their charismatic roots and onto the projection walls of many traditionally subdued evangelical congregations.[33]

Megachurches were especially amenable to catchy hymnody. Typically defined as congregations averaging 2,000 or more attendees per weekend, megachurches gained increasing prominence during the 1990s. By 1995, around 400 churches met this criterion. Many were "seeker churches"—

designed for the purpose of reaching prospective worshippers who otherwise shied away from organized religion. The stereotypical seeker church, wrote one chronicler, "tailors its programs and services to attract people who are not church attenders." The seeker approach to evangelism derived from the Church Growth Movement, which began at Fuller Theological Seminary in the 1960s. While the hallmark of seeker churches was their relative absence of identifiable religious symbols—even crosses, in some cases—almost all of them were unmistakably evangelical.[34]

The paradigmatic megachurch was Willow Creek Community Church of South Barrington, Illinois, a far northwestern suburb of Chicago. One scholar described Willow Creek's style as "born-again modernism." As with many innovative forms of evangelical outreach, the roots of Willow Creek extended back to the Jesus Movement. At Willow Creek, however, pastor Bill Hybels targeted a yuppie type: the "Unchurched Harry," who sought a worship experience that was a seamless expression of suburban living. Hybels founded Willow Creek in 1975. Two decades later, its annual budget had surpassed $12 million, about 63 percent of which covered its 260 employees. By the close of the 1990s, Hybels's church drew more than 15,000 persons each weekend to four services on its sprawling campus. His Willow Creek Association, a network of megachurches, grew to more than 5,000 members by 2000. Willow Creek was especially known for its ability to attract lapsed Catholics. In 1984, its success prompted Joseph Cardinal Bernardin to found a Catholic megachurch—the first of its kind—in an adjacent suburb.[35]

By the early 1990s, the megachurch phenomenon was "the hottest thing in Protestantism." Journalists and scholars often interpreted the growth of megachurches through the lens (rarely acknowledged) of sociologist Robert Wuthnow's emphasis on the declining power of American denominations. Although many megachurches held some sort of formal affiliation (usually an evangelical one), they largely functioned as their own brands within the spiritual marketplace. Critics derided the full-service nature of megachurches— which, in some cases, included McDonald's and Starbucks franchises—as "the religious version of the gated community." Management guru Peter Drucker influentially argued otherwise. In the pages of *Forbes* magazine and elsewhere, Drucker celebrated megachurches as "surely the most important phenomenon in American society in the last 30 years." Hybels and other megachurch pastors had identified a market need: "The greatest value for the thousands who now throng the megachurches—both weekdays and Sundays—is a spiritual experience rather than a ritual." Drucker personally advised both Hybels and the most famous megachurch pastor of the 2000s, Rick Warren of Southern

California. A poster outside of Hybels's office quoted three of Drucker's core questions: "What is our business? Who is our customer? What does the customer consider value?" Drucker saw megachurches as civil society in action. Megachurches were a "third force" in society, one that could meet social needs that the public sector could not handle and the private sector would not touch. In other words, megachurches supplied the "social capital" that sociologist Robert Putnam and others touted as a binding force in American society.[36]

The born-again boomtown of Colorado Springs, Colorado, contained perhaps the densest concentration of American evangelical social capital. Nothing captured the subculture paradox of late twentieth-century American evangelicalism better than the rapid emergence of Colorado Springs as the headquarters of numerous high-profile evangelical parachurch organizations, which existed outside of denominational structures. Colorado Springs was alternately branded the "Wheaton of the West" and, more ambitiously, the "evangelical Vatican." Its transformation was more akin to that of the postmodern desert flower of Dubai, which grew from an oil-dependent state into a global financial and transportation powerhouse. Colorado Springs's significantly more modest renaissance came just as suddenly. By 1995, the East Range city of 300,000 housed more than seventy parachurch organizations. From the youth ministry Young Life to the relief agency Compassion International, they collectively generated 2,400 jobs and pumped $36 million into the local economy. The new Colorado Springs was the product of a civic strategy to help the city survive the decline of its military and aerospace industries. The state of Colorado had recently liberalized its tax code for religious groups, and Alice Worrell—an evangelical who worked for a Colorado Springs economic development agency—argued that the city could use the policy change to lure evangelical groups. The strategy quickly paid dividends, bolstered, in part, by the rising cost of doing business in Southern California, long home to many evangelical organizations. James Dobson's Focus on the Family, the biggest born-again fish in Colorado Springs, relocated in 1991 from Pomona, California, constructing a $35 million headquarters with the assistance of a local foundation. The move raised the profile of both Colorado Springs and Dobson, whose presence linked the city indelibly with the Christian Right. Dobson was becoming more of a political presence, even though fans of his radio show—by 1995, the third most popular show in the nation, behind Paul Harvey's and Rush Limbaugh's—did not always interpret him that way. Dobson declared Colorado Springs the "Gettysburg" of the American culture war. A 1995 cover of Focus on the Family magazine featured the caption "June & Ward Were Right." Retrograde analogies aside, Colorado Springs was very much "a city of the future, not the past," as a contributor to *The Nation* unhappily conceded.[37]

Something similar could be said of another traditionalist startup: Branson, Missouri, which cast itself as the straight-edged alternative to Las Vegas, Nashville, or just about any tourist haven with a nightlife. As Branson revealed, the market for specifically Christian culture and entertainment overlapped greatly with down-home American kitsch. The combination proved quite lucrative. By 1996, Branson housed a gallery selling works by the sentimentalist evangelical artist Thomas Kinkade, a self-described "Painter of Light." The Kinkade brand garnered $120 million in sales by 2000 through a vast array of enterprises that extended well beyond the Christian lifestyle scene. Branson, an established but modest Ozarks tourist town, began drawing crowds to its proliferating stand-alone theaters, which showcased legendary country artists, such as Roy Clark and Glen Campbell, and decidedly clean comedians, such as Ray Stevens and Yakov Smirnoff. By 1989, around four million vacationers visited Branson annually. An even larger boom followed between 1991 and 1994, when the town added nearly 10,000 hotel rooms and restaurant seats and the annual guest rate rose to 5.8 million. The television news magazine *60 Minutes* celebrated Branson as "the country music capital of the universe." More accurately, it straddled the line between Nashville's country and Christian music scenes. Branson was a place where talk of crossover artists was unnecessary. "If you're not a born-again Christian…," groused country legend Merle Haggard after his brief turn in Branson in the early 1990s, "they won't even loan you money to build a place." Like Colorado Springs, Branson was part and parcel of the postindustrial service-sector economy. Wal-Mart, the ultimate symbol of that new service economy, was just an afternoon's drive across the Ozarks, and a growing number of Branson visitors took a day trip to the Bentonville, Arkansas, Wal-Mart Visitor Center. The company soon made a conscious move to reach out to evangelical shoppers. Media mogul Rupert Murdoch made a similar investment with his 1997 purchase of Pat Robertson's International Family Entertainment, which included cable television's Family Channel.[38]

Civil and Uncivil Society

The pull of the culture wars was so strong that even the most sympathetic observers of Colorado Springs and Branson struggled to resist interpreting them through a political lens. The rise, first, of the Christian Coalition, and second, of the Promise Keepers movement helped to explain why this was so. A third faith-based organization, Habitat for Humanity, benefited from the hope that it might mitigate the influence of the other two organizations. The obituaries for the Christian Right written after Pat Robertson's failed 1988 campaign were misguided for two primary reasons. First, many evangelicals already were part of the GOP establishment. Throughout the 1990s and into the next decade, the evangelical right was the most powerful noncorporate interest group in the Republican Party. The second reason had to do with shifting evangelical expectations. On the whole, conservative evangelicals were more attuned to the issues and better aware of how to go about winning through the political process. Political scientist Matthew Moen argued that the Christian Right was transitioning "from revolution to evolution."[39] In other words, it was becoming a fixture in the American political system. Something similar was true of evangelicalism's profile in American civil society, and this latter development gave the Christian Right's opponents a strategic opening.

The Christian Coalition grew from the warm ashes of Pat Robertson's 1988 campaign. Robertson had become the highest-profile Christian Right leader at a time when there was a momentary thinning of the ranks. Jerry Falwell stepped away from overt political activism, formally shuttering the moribund Moral Majority in 1989, one decade after it had crashed the political scene. Liberated from the constraints of political brokerage, Falwell generated new headlines as a conspiracy-prone critic of President Bill Clinton before closing out the decade on the debate circuit with newfound "friend" Larry Flynt (whose popularity was riding high in the aftermath of a feature film that celebrated him as a First Amendment crusader). James Dobson was not yet wholly invested in electoral politics, and antiabortion activist Randall Terry was too radical even for the most reactionary wing of the GOP. During the 1988 campaign, Robertson played the good Republican and supported his party's nominee, yet—in a replay of the Carter years—he quickly grew disgruntled with the George H. W. Bush administration's lack of specifically evangelical nominations and appointments. Looking to transform his campaign apparatus into an activist organization, Robertson stumbled upon young Ralph Reed, then an Emory University Ph.D. candidate in History. In Reed, Robertson found the evangelical counterpart to Bush campaign operative Lee Atwater, who had gained notoriety for his hardball tactics. While Reed desired a more inclusive name for the proposed organization, Robertson insisted on the unashamed moniker Christian Coalition. Many figures on the evangelical right, such as Dobson, were initially cool to the Tidewater, Virginia–based organization when it debuted in 1990. Reed's ambition quickly turned heads though.[40]

Unlike the founding fathers of the Christian Right, Reed came of age at the polls, rather than in the pews. He was, first and foremost, a politico steeped in the aggressive College Republicans culture that also produced future GOP power brokers Karl Rove and Jack Abramoff. After a religious conversion as a young adult, Reed graduated from partying to churchgoing. Still, as a former college classmate quipped, Reed "didn't change his views" on politics, so much as he "found out that God agreed with him." Reed's tone sometimes betrayed his brash background, most memorably when he exclaimed to an unfriendly local newspaper in 1991, "I do guerilla warfare. I paint my face and travel at night. You don't know it's over until you're in a body bag."[41] Generally, though, Reed was a smooth operator in selling his organization and himself. He was significantly more knowledgeable about the oft-demonized world of liberal politics—its strengths as well as its vulnerabilities—than the earlier generation of Christian Right leaders, who had less exposure to Beltway mores, had been. Overall, Reed had a firm grasp of interest-group politics in a modern democracy.

Reed positioned himself as the savvy chaperone for an evangelical political community on the cusp of adulthood. His style contrasted favorably with his boss's embrace of conspiracy theories and propensity for rhetorical extremism. Understandably, Reed differentiated himself more explicitly from Falwell. The Christian Right, Reed argued, needed to move beyond the misleading "moral majority" motif of its early years. Rather than imagining that they spoke for a majority in waiting, conservative Christians should aspire to be the "most effective" of the many "citizen movements" that were the modern heirs of the "factions" that James Madison had famously defended. "Unlike fundamentalist political movements in the Middle East," he stressed, "religious conservatives in the United States are properly understood as an interest group within a democratic order." Reed was candid about the barriers to success, namely the legacy of white evangelical racism. This history was "one of the main reasons why the pro-family movement's message of protecting innocent human life and religious freedom had had a difficult time achieving moral resonance in the broader society." In 1996, following a spate of arsons targeting black churches in the South, the Christian Coalition raised $750,000 for rebuilding efforts. Reed's use of the terms "religious freedom" and "pro-family movement" was no less calculated than his efforts to defuse charges of racism. Support for "religious freedom" pointed to a critical rhetorical shift, as Reed sought to move away from a narrower focus on issues like school prayer and toward a broader embrace of the naked public square thesis. Heeding the guidance of Stephen Carter's *The Culture of Disbelief*, which he cited approvingly, Reed explained his opposition to gay rights as "a matter of sound public policy, not an attempt to impose Judeo-Christian theology through the power of the state." Likewise, Reed followed other anti-abortion activists in putting special emphasis on banning late-term procedures, which they labeled "partial birth" abortions. Reed's talk of a "pro-family movement"—a term that had been in circulation since the late 1970s—reflected his ecumenical, even interfaith ambitions. Robertson and Reed made a point of reaching out to socially conservative Catholics and hiring conservative Jews, although the core of the Christian Coalition remained largely Baptist and charismatic.[42]

Reed's pretensions to sophistication often stood in tension with his everyday tactics. He knew how to play the culture wars card. The Christian Coalition made its first national splash with June 1990 full-page advertisements in *USA Today* and *Washington Post* attacking funding for the National Endowment for the Arts. Reed was poised to pounce on perceived slights against his constituency. Perhaps the most important such incident came in 1993, when the *Washington Post* published an article on conservative Christian pushback against President Clinton's proposal to end the ban on openly gay soldiers in the armed forces. The piece, written by the well-known journalist Michael Weisskopf, crudely and inaccurately characterized the grassroots Christian Right as "largely poor, uneducated and easy to command." Even though the *Washington Post* ran an immediate correction and its ombudsman savaged the lack of editorial oversight, the Christian Coalition and other conservative groups took full advantage of what a staff member of the National Association of Evangelicals called "a perfect example of the arrogant condescension that characterizes the media elite." They organized a barrage of faxes to the newspaper, and the Christian Coalition distributed buttons that said "poor, uneducated and easy to command" to Capitol Hill politicos who wished to express solidarity. Pat Robertson cited the Weisskopf article in an address to the National Religious Broadcasters, linking the slur with a "cultural war." "No other episode from the early Clinton administration so heartened and awakened our supporters," Reed later wrote. The Christian Right would feast on the quote for years to come.[43]

Ultimately, Reed sought to balance the evangelical right's desire to take back America with the tactical maneuvering necessary for success in the modern political system. At times, he posed as a "politically incorrect"

Christian seeking to move his fellow believers up from the "back of the bus." Yet he was hardly an edgy insurgent. The Christian Coalition received an early boost not just from Pat Robertson's mailing list, but also from a $64,000 grant from the Republican Senatorial Campaign Committee. When it suited him, though, Reed promoted an ecumenical civil religion that cut across party lines. Reed went out of his way to praise Pennsylvania's Democratic governor Bob Casey, who vocally opposed abortion rights and was denied a speaking slot at the 1992 Democratic National Convention.[44]

While Reed occasionally mouthed the language of bipartisanship, he tightened the alignment of the Christian Right with the GOP and the larger conservative movement. Responding to the Supreme Court's move toward a federalist approach to issues like abortion, the Christian Coalition put particular emphasis on state and local governments. Grassroots efforts could make a particular splash in school board and precinct elections. "Think like Jesus. Lead like Moses. Fight like David. Run like Lincoln," went a slogan used in Christian Coalition seminars. Most members knew which party Lincoln chose. At the organization's 1991 national conference, not a single soul showed up for a session on how to become a delegate to the Democratic National Convention. "The organized Christian vote is roughly to the Republican Party today what organized labor was to the Democrats," declared a leading congressional aide in 1994.[45]

The Christian Coalition's tactics paralleled trends in conservative evangelical legal advocacy. The 1990s saw the emergence of such public law organizations as the American Center for Law and Justice (ACLJ) and the Alliance Defense Fund (ADF). The ACLJ was another outgrowth of Robertson's failed presidential run. Founded in 1990 and modeled after the similarly abbreviated American Civil Liberties Union, it was led by Jay Sekulow, who shared Reed's charisma and media skills. The ADF, founded in 1994, drew support from many other powerful organizations on the evangelical right. A decade later, the two organizations ranked among the four best-funded conservative legal advocacy groups.[46]

The Christian Coalition enjoyed a steady run of political successes during Clinton's first term. Reed rightly saw Bush's defeat in 1992 as a huge opportunity for the Christian Right to return the Republicans to power. Evangelical support for the GOP was critical during the turnout-driven midterms of 1994, when the Republicans stunningly took control of both houses of Congress. Reed pressed his luck during that campaign, acquiescing to the insistence of Newt Gingrich, the prospective Speaker of the House, that the Republicans leave social issues out of their Contract with America platform and save those matters for after the election. In 1995, the Christian Coalition released a similarly structured and poll-tested Contract with the American Family, which, in keeping with the original pledge, embraced issues of broad appeal, such as restrictions on Internet pornography, a ban on "partial birth" abortions, and protections for religious freedom. The religious freedom issue was particularly promising. Congress had already passed the Religious Freedom Restoration Act in 1993, and advocates now began to frame the issue in terms of global human rights. Five years later, under Republican control, Congress also passed the International Religious Freedom Act, formalizing religious freedom as a federal priority. Other provisions of the Contract with the American Family also stood a good chance of passage. The Christian Coalition grew precipitously from a claimed 950,000 members in 1994 to 1.6 million by the fall of 1995. Contributions a year later approached $25 million. Boosted by glowing profiles in *Time*, *Fortune*, and other venues, Reed continued to press his pragmatic, state-by-state strategy. By 1996, the Christian Coalition was said to control as many as eighteen state Republican parties and to exert major influence on thirteen others.[47]

Reed's big-tent approach garnered pushback within some Christian Right circles. Especially controversial was his willingness to tolerate otherwise conservative candidates who supported abortion rights under certain conditions. Randall Terry took to the *Washington Post* to call the Christian Coalition "the mistress of the Republican Party." James Dobson emerged as the most influential critic of Reed, who responded by making sure that the GOP kept its 1996 platform strongly antiabortion. Still, Dobson had positioned himself as a powerful purist. After Reed left in 1997 to pursue a consulting and lobbying career, the popular but volatile Dobson became the most powerful figure in the Christian Right. The Christian Coalition quickly rose and fell as a political force, but Reed's dream of a more seasoned, tactical born-again politics lived to see a new century.[48]

While the Christian Coalition worked the precincts, another new organization, Promise Keepers, took the nation's stadiums by storm. The evangelical men's group was the brainchild of Bill McCartney, best known as the improbably successful coach of the long-moribund University of Colorado football team. McCartney also was a Christian and a recent convert to the charismatic brand of the faith. He was involved with the network of Vineyard churches, a Jesus Movement phenomenon that evolved into an influential force within the church growth scene. Vineyard churches stressed the "indwell[ing]" of the Holy Spirit accompanied by dreams, visions, and prophecies. McCartney founded Promise Keepers in 1990 while he was still coaching. Having experienced his own struggles with alcohol abuse and marital infidelity, he saw the need for an organization devoted to Christian husbands and fathers. Promise Keepers retained its athletic roots. During its trademark stadium rallies, men chanted "Jee-zus" to the rhythm of "Dee-fense." Promise Keepers was headquartered in ultra-liberal Boulder, but its organization was very much within the orbit of Colorado Springs, located a hundred miles to the south.[49]

Several trends combined to raise the profile of Promise Keepers. First, the politics of masculinity received much attention in the early and mid-1990s. The 1994 election results prompted talk of "angry white males" and what an influential book already had termed a "backlash" against feminism. The following year saw the Million Man March, organized by Louis Farrakhan of the Nation of Islam and supported by former National Association for the Advancement of Colored People head Benjamin Chavis, as well as many other prominent African American leaders. Promise Keepers was a mostly white organization largely removed from the social justice agenda of the Million Man March, although the two movements did share a traditionalist focus on male responsibility. What made Promise Keepers appealing to many would-be skeptics, though, was its embrace of therapeutic emotionalism—a characteristic of the emerging men's movement as a whole. The organization defined masculine responsibility as sensitive family leadership, sometimes rebranded as "servanthood" (following the evangelical and business fad of "servant leadership"). Leader was still the operative word, however. Perhaps the most-quoted statement by any Promise Keepers supporter came from pastor Tony Evans. "Sit down with your wife," Evans advised husbands, "and say something like this: 'Honey, I've made a terrible mistake. I've given you my role. I gave up leading this family, and I forced you to take my place. Now I must reclaim that role.'" Complicating nonevangelical responses to Promise Keepers was the organization's move to embrace "racial reconciliation." Evans was one of many African American speakers at Promise Keepers rallies. The organization exposed white audiences to a theology of reconciliation that had first emerged in the 1970s among black activists associated with the evangelical left. As invoked at Promise Keepers rallies, reconciliation tended to mean racial color blindness rather than social justice—and even then, white audiences were not always receptive to the message. Still, the organization made a concerted effort to diversify its hiring practices. The final trend sweeping Promise Keepers into the spotlight was a revitalized Christian Right. While McCartney pitched Promise Keepers as apolitical, his own actions suggested otherwise. He publicly supported Operation Rescue and was a prominent backer of Colorado's controversial anti–gay rights initiative in

1992. His organization's strident opposition to abortion and emphasis on the biblically sanctioned position of husbands as family heads put it firmly in James Davison Hunter's orthodox camp. To progressive critics, Promise Keepers was "crypto-Religious Right."[50]

Promise Keepers moved to the forefront of the culture wars debates during the run-up to its high-profile 1997 gathering on the Capitol Mall, "Stand in the Gap: A Sacred Assembly of Men." The National Organization for Women (NOW) used the event to launch a "No Surrender" campaign against the antifeminist backlash. NOW head Patricia Ireland called Promise Keepers the "hottest-religious-right marketing tool since televangelism" and summoned the dystopian specter of the Republic of Gilead in *The Handmaid's Tale*, "which is in the hands of the religious right." NOW's rhetorical overreach (one anti–Promise Keepers chant went "Racist, Sexist, Antigay/Born Again Bigots Go Away!") helped Promise Keepers to garner sympathetic media coverage, even as McCartney continued to complain of hostility from the press. The organization had a compelling racial reconciliation agenda and an adept public relations strategy. Moreover, it appeared by 1997 to have tempered the "angry white male" phenomenon of a few years before. Promise Keepers both epitomized and transcended the tradition of evangelical spectacle.[51]

The legacy of the 1970s evangelical left, sublimated in the Promise Keepers' talk of racial reconciliation, persisted in more obvious form through Habitat for Humanity, the wildly popular housing charity. The organization's success lay in its apparent distance from partisan politics. Instead, it demonstrated the civic good of faith in action. The evangelical left thus fared much better in civil society than in electoral politics. By the 1980s and 1990s, the two-party system was simply too strong for the evangelical left to have any discernible electoral impact. For example, a 1980s effort to create a JustLife political action committee to support pro-life liberals collapsed in the face of the partisan divide on abortion.[52] Civil society, by contrast, promised a path around such polarization. Habitat for Humanity caught the imagination of politicians and celebrities of all stripes during the 1990s.

Georgia businessman Millard Fuller founded Habitat for Humanity in 1976. The ambitious organization (popularly known as Habitat) specialized in using highly organized volunteer labor (combined with the "sweat equity" of recipients) to efficiently construct low-income housing. Fuller was a wealthy, hard-charging attorney and businessman in Alabama before a mid-1960s change of heart led him and his wife to give away their wealth. Under the mentorship of legendary progressive Southern minister Clarence Jordan,

Fuller created his own brand of entrepreneurial charity. Habitat was an explicitly "Christian organization," in the words of its mission statement, which sought "to demonstrate the love and teachings of Jesus Christ to all people." The organization became a national phenomenon after fellow Georgian Jimmy Carter embraced it in 1984. The sometimes prickly Carter, who had not responded to Fuller's overtures while he was president, soon began to hold an annual "Jimmy Carter Work Project." He was the first of many major political backers. Democratic centrists like Bill Clinton and Al Gore saw the value of volunteering for an organization that embraced a progressive mission but declined direct government funds. They volunteered for Habitat during the 1992 campaign. Habitat likewise offered an opportunity for leading conservatives, such as Jack Kemp and Newt Gingrich, to demonstrate their support for forms of compassionate volunteerism comfortably removed from the public sector. Celebrity endorsers spanned the cultural spectrum, ranging from Amy Grant to Paul Newman to Oprah Winfrey.[53]

Habitat was perfectly situated to become a communitarian antidote to the naked public square, the culture of disbelief, and the culture wars alike. One paean to the organization was titled "Habitats of the Heart." It was an explicitly faith-based organization that appealed to growing numbers of nonbelievers. In an age of divided government, Habitat attracted conservative money even as its corps of volunteers was disproportionately liberal. According to its mission statement, the organization "does not seek and will not accept government funds for the construction of homes." However, "funds to help set the stage" for such construction, such as land donations and grants to cover administrative costs, were permitted. Clinton honored Fuller with the Presidential Medal of Freedom in 1996. "This is the nature of Millard Fuller's accomplishment," wrote a *Christianity Today* journalist in 1999. "He has taken a radical Christian vision (building homes for poor people), inspired in the midst of a radical Christian community (Clarence Jordan's Koinonia Farm), and sold it to corporate and mainstream America. And they bought it."[54]

Yet when politics and culture collided during the Clinton years, the early rounds generally went to politics. Tactical debates aside, the evangelical right shared a distinct distaste for President Clinton. If the culture wars had a climax, it was the 1998–1999 impeachment saga, which began with the January 1998 revelation of the president's extramarital affair with onetime White House intern Monica Lewinsky. As Clinton's embrace of Habitat for Humanity suggested, he positioned himself as a faith-friendly candidate and president. During the 1992 campaign, Clinton spoke of a "new covenant" and made a point of targeting Catholic voters. A Southern Baptist comfortable with evangelical worship styles, Clinton was conspicuous in his church attendance as president. He was especially at home in predominantly African American churches, and he became the first president to visit a historically black congregation on Inauguration Day. Clinton cultivated relationships with progressive evangelicals, most importantly the activist sociologist and minister Tony Campolo, who at one point organized a group of moderate evangelicals, including Mark Noll, to talk to the president about evangelical hostility toward his administration. In 1995, Campolo and another progressive evangelical, Jim Wallis, founded Call to Renewal to counter the prominence of the Christian Coalition. The president also made friends with the irenic Bill Hybels, who, along with many of his seeker-friendly peers, was eager to distinguish himself from divisive figures such as Reed and Dobson. Clinton's outreach set the stage for the return of the evangelical left a decade later to some level of public prominence. At the same time, his unpopularity among conservative evangelicals could hardly have been higher. In 1996, his unfavorable rating among politically active conservative evangelicals stood at 87 percent. His innumerable evangelical critics branded the Arkansan an opportunist, at best, and a fraud, at worst. During the 1992 campaign, Pat Robertson blasted Clinton's "pseudo-Christianity." The politics of anti-Clinton was such that the evangelical-heavy Council for National Policy discussed working for Clinton's impeachment as early as June 1997, seven months before Monica Lewinsky became a household name.[55]

The stage was set, then, for the Lewinsky scandal to unfold as a kind of evangelical drama. Clinton's nemesis, independent counsel Kenneth Starr, was a committed evangelical Christian from a strict Church of Christ background. A Republican insider known for his agreeable but ambitious style, Starr suggested the commonplace nature of evangelical-GOP ties, to the point where they were not always noticed. His dogged pursuit of Clinton—well beyond the initial investigation into the Whitewater real estate deal—was unquestionably rooted in his moral distaste for Clinton's lifestyle. Just as importantly, Starr had many evangelical allies in the House of Representatives. The 1994 election had brought to Congress numerous self-styled Christian Republicans, including Sam Brownback, Todd Tiahrt, Mark Sanford, Mark Souder, Joe Pitts, and Tom Coburn. Majority Whip Tom DeLay, perhaps the most zealous Clinton-hater in a Clinton-loathing body, traced his born-again conversion from a hard-drinking lifestyle to a James Dobson video he viewed in 1985.[56]

Clinton had durable religious allies, too. During the height of the crisis, he turned to a core of ministers, including J. Philip Wogaman, a pastor at the

Foundry Methodist Church, which Bill and Hillary Clinton attended. He also confided in two liberal evangelicals, Campolo and Massachusetts pastor Gordon MacDonald. Years before, MacDonald survived a scandal surrounding his own extramarital affair. Campolo's involvement riled many alums of his academic home, Eastern College; under fire, he offered to step down from his professorship. Many clerical defenders of Clinton came from the broader black church and mainline Protestant traditions, although a few conservative ministers—such as Rex Horne, the pastor of Clinton's home church in Little Rock—separated "indefensible, but not unforgiveable" sins from the question of impeachment and removal. Such sentiments only grew when Clinton chose the September 11, 1998, White House prayer breakfast to make a public confession of his transgressions. The Starr Report was released that same day.[57]

As the impeachment crisis revealed, the evangelical right held more power in the House of Representatives than in society as a whole. Public distaste for the impeachment process was a pointed reminder that, while evangelicals might occasionally form a moral plurality, a true majority was out of reach. That distinction became particularly important a few years later, by which time the Christian Right again was the talk of the Beltway. "We are going to have to invent a presidential candidate for the year 2000," Ralph Reed declared after Clinton's reelection victory in 1996.[58] Four years later, Reed found his man.

5 SECOND COMINGS

In 1987, Charles Colson published a short story about a born-again Texan in the White House. Colson had progressed quickly from poster convert of the evangelical Seventies to pillar member of the evangelical establishment. His numerous books and regular column in *Christianity Today* reached a vast audience of fellow believers. The protagonist of his story was named Shelby Hopkins. A former history professor and dean at Baylor University, Hopkins "had entered the political arena in the eighties when evangelical Christians came out of nowhere to become a major force in national politics." A turn as Texas governor prepped Hopkins for a successful presidential campaign during which he united the Republican Party's establishment and its Christian Right insurgency. In the Hopkins White House, the rooms are prayer-filled, not smoke-filled.

Fourteen months into his term, in 1998, a foreign policy crisis sends the president back to the Bible. The Israeli Likud Party, on the cusp of taking power, is about to endorse a plot to blow up the Dome of the Rock and replace it with a rebuilt Jewish temple. While the electoral impetus for the effort comes from an ultra-religious party and likely Likud coalition partner, financial backing comes from a group of Christian fundamentalists in Hopkins's home state. Conveniently on hand in the Oval Office is Attorney General Hyman Levin, a Jewish convert to Christianity who is well versed in biblical prophecy. A move to rebuild the temple is sure to aggravate Israel's Arab neighbors, as even casual observers could deduce. But it also "will signal Armageddon," Levin reminds the president and informs the incredulous nonevangelicals who hold other cabinet positions. In other words, it "will pave the way for Christ's triumphant return." President Hopkins offers little comfort to those Americans who do not see the Bible as a weather vane. "Obviously, while these reports are frightening," he declares, "there's some excitement that comes with them too. You can't help but wonder if these could be events we've all waited for."

Still, the governing complexities of the moment do not escape the God-fearing president. When running for office on the slogan "Return America to God," Hopkins promised the best of times, not the end of time. He was elected to protect the safety of the citizenry (and to protest court challenges that forced name changes for Bethlehem, Pennsylvania, and Corpus Christi, Texas). Yet what is any world leader to do in the face of fulfilled prophesy? "Let's keep in mind while we make our plans that God has already made His," the president declares. His chief of staff sees matters differently: "The end of the world is His business. Our business here in the White House is to *prevent* the end of the world." The Dome of the Rock explodes as the president weighs just how to intervene in the escalating conflict. Colson left his readers hanging. Will President Hopkins be a cog, or a clog, in Armageddon's assembly line? One thing is clear: His existential decision will occur on prophetic terms.[1]

The story was the prologue to Colson's otherwise nonfiction meditation on the dilemmas of Christian political engagement. *Kingdoms in Conflict* appeared toward the end of the Reagan administration, as Pat Robertson went on a Hopkins-like quest for the White House. Colson, who noted that his story drew from "actual public statements" by Israelis and Americans, warned against "equating the gospel with a particular partisan agenda." After all, the former Nixon aide knew just how worldly a game politics could be.[2]

At the end of the twentieth century, a number of religious conservatives seemed to be taking Colson's ambiguous tale to heart. The survival of Bill Clinton put conservative evangelical stalwarts in a pensive mood, leading to another round of premature obituaries for the Christian Right. Cal Thomas and Ed Dobson, two veterans of the Moral Majority, warned that their former colleagues had been "blinded by might." Longtime conservative activist Paul Weyrich, who had helped to recruit Falwell for political activism, declared defeat in the culture wars, urging withdrawal from the institutions of secular society (if not from politics itself).[3]

That moment quickly faded when a variety of evangelical forces converged to support, influence, and, in some cases, oppose a real-life born-again Texan president. In 2007, Colson released a revised version of *Kingdoms in Conflict*, now titled *God and Government*. The plot of the prologue story remained largely intact, although a few changes put distance between Hopkins and the current president. President Hopkins now hails from Oklahoma and does not run as a Christian Right candidate. He converts after the 2012 election.[4]

George W. Bush spoke to the fullness of evangelical relevance at the start of the twenty-first century. His political success held profound significance for American evangelicalism. Bush was born into the East Coast elite, but his adult life intersected with the many varieties of late twentieth-century evangelicalism. He drew or borrowed from the therapeutic notes of evangelical popular culture, the moral agenda of the evangelical right, and even facets of the evangelical left. His was the evangelicalism of Billy Graham's warm invitation, but also of Graham's blessing of ordained authority; of James Dobson as family counselor, but also of Dobson as culture warrior. The evangelical right, Bush's base, had become diffuse enough to absorb all such elements and to blur the increasingly academic distinctions between "evangelical" and "fundamentalist."

Bush took the politicization of American evangelicalism to a new level. As candidate and president, he broadened the electoral imprint of evangelicalism. What characterized evangelical political culture during the Bush years was excess, a tendency to overreach reflected in the readiness to invoke evil in the face of Saddam Hussein and Michael Schiavo alike. Emboldened by Bush's disputed first-term victory and egged on by adviser Karl Rove, the Christian Right entered its baroque period. Evangelical popular culture followed a similar trajectory, as the two spheres continued to converge. A backlash loomed both outside evangelical circles and within them. The result was a period of second comings—first, of the evangelical presidency, then of the evangelical left.

Faith-Based

George W. Bush was a product of the very evangelical renaissance that worked to his political advantage. His religious "walk"—a term he preferred to "born again"—started with a spiritual awakening in the mid-1980s, when he was a struggling and hard-drinking (if hardly down-and-out) oilman in Midland, Texas. A cradle Episcopalian who attended a Presbyterian church as a child and who followed his wife into the Methodist church, Bush gravitated toward a nondenominational Bible study program following encounters with evangelists Arthur Blessitt and Billy Graham. Blessitt was best known as a pioneer of the Jesus Movement in California. By 1984, the former Sunset Strip evangelist was an itinerant minister passing through Midland on a quest to carry a twelve-foot cross throughout the world. Bush was no Hollywood hippie, but he proved receptive to Blessitt's message during an extended meeting in a Midland Holiday Inn. Bush remained a spiritual work in progress in the summer of 1985, when he conversed with his parents' friend Billy Graham at the family compound in Kennebunkport, Maine. Somewhere between a lush and an alcoholic, Bush recalled having several drinks in him during a walk and talk with the evangelist. A year later, at the age of forty, Bush decided to give up the bottle.[5]

While abandoning drink eased Bush's subsequent entry into the family business of politics, embracing faith enhanced his electoral potential in a Republican Party for which megachurches were the new country clubs. Graham appealed to both sets, and it was he—not the obscure and eccentric Blessitt—whom Bush credited in his campaign autobiography with having "planted a mustard seed in my soul," leading to "a new walk where I would recommit my heart to Jesus Christ." Bush's personal faith tilted toward what one skeptical biographer called "Self-help Methodism," the kind of piety commonly found in a professional athlete's postgame news conference.[6]

In the category of celebrity converts, though, Bush was much more Charles Colson than Eldridge Cleaver. His political application of evangelicalism was deft. He served as his father's evangelical liaison during the 1988 campaign and cultivated similar connections as governor of Texas in the latter half of the 1990s. Bush claimed that a sermon given during a private church service on the day of his second gubernatorial inauguration cemented his decision to seek the presidency. He soon relayed the calling to televangelist James Robison, a former Christian Right firebrand whose tone had cooled considerably since the early 1980s. Bush began his pursuit for the White House on an evangelical note. On the same weekend that he launched his presidential campaign exploratory committee, he gave two sermons at a prominent Southern Baptist congregation in Houston.[7]

Bush's ambitions benefited from the seemingly boundless political potential of evangelicalism in the years since the Carter and Reagan presidencies. Nothing demonstrated those possibilities better than the rise of "compassionate conservatism." Straddling the line between slogan and ideology, compassionate conservatism was the product of two converging trends: the civil society consensus and the mainstreaming of Richard John Neuhaus's "naked public square" metaphor. That combination yielded an effervescent thesis about the virtues of religion in public life. It was often reduced to a simple modifier: "faith-based." Promoters of that term proffered one central argument: Religion was a net positive in American society. A more controversial corollary held that religious social agencies deserved a place—perhaps a special place— in domestic policy considerations. Many evangelicals helped to promote this line of reasoning and, with Bush, they stood to reap its political rewards.

The faith-based tent was potentially quite big. By the mid-1990s, a bipartisan group of pundits and politicians touted faith-based institutions as vital components of civil society. As the widespread lauding of Habitat for

Humanity indicated, this sentiment was by no means the sole property of the political right. A similar coalition took shape around certain global human rights issues, especially religious freedom. Conservatives and liberals generally approached civil society from different angles, however. Conservatives saw faith-based civil society as an alternative to the modern welfare state. Liberals saw civil society as a vital space—perhaps even a countervailing force—between government and the market. On the right wing of the conversation stood Marvin Olasky, a journalism professor at the University of Texas. Olasky's biography paralleled the rise of both neoconservatism and the evangelical right. He grew up Jewish, became a student leftist and atheist in the 1960s, and then traded Marx for Christ during the 1970s. He also took up Francis Schaeffer. By far the most influential popularizer of compassionate conservatism, Olasky saw government support for charitable agencies as preferable to "compulsory [i.e., state-run] philanthropy." He hewed to a classical type of evangelical reform, but he attempted to update it for the modern era of big government. Olasky, whose work complemented the arguments of Myron Magnet and other well-connected conservative pundits, was a rising star on the right by the time Bush entered Texas politics. Their left-of-center counterparts included Boston Church of God in Christ minister Eugene Rivers and Ivy League political scientist John DiIulio, deeply religious men who saw the church as the most effective force for addressing the social problems of needy Americans. Rivers's and DiIulio's frames of reference were impoverished, crime-ridden urban neighborhoods, and on economic matters they generally leaned liberal. Rivers in particular attracted numerous sympathetic media profiles. He and other faith-based progressives backed the progressive evangelical group Call to Renewal.[8]

The faith-based agenda always had much better prospects on the political right, however. A key opening came with the landmark Welfare Reform Act of 1996. The contentious piece of legislation included a "charitable choice" provision stating that the federal government would consider all faith-based organizations, irrespective of the nature of their missions, for relevant government funds. Agencies like Catholic Charities and Lutheran Social Services had long received such support. The new provision—reinforced by additional legislation in 1998 and 2000—promised to engage a much wider range of religious organizations. Originally introduced by Missouri senator John Ashcroft, an outspoken evangelical, "charitable choice" represented a significant victory for advocates of faith-based civil society.[9]

Bush became the political face of compassionate conservatism. During his two terms as governor of Texas, he linked evangelical social concern with an otherwise predictably conservative business agenda. Bush gained attention for working with InnerChange Freedom Initiative, an extension of Charles Colson's prison-reform enterprise. During a visit to a Texas prison in 1997, the governor sang "Amazing Grace" with Colson and an inmate choir.[10]

In surprising ways, the residue of the 1970s evangelical left surfaced in the 2000 presidential campaign of a conservative Republican. Politically, compassionate conservatism promised the GOP a way to move beyond but not alienate its white evangelical base. To be sure, Bush's political pedigree biased him toward Olasky's perspective. Indeed, the words "compassionate conservatism" had circulated in conservative circles for at least two decades before Bush first wielded the term. Its users ranged from Southern strategist turned lay minister Harry Dent to New Right organizer Paul Weyrich and evangelical political entrepreneur Doug Wead (who tried to link the term with George H. W. Bush), as well as numerous GOP politicians looking for a fresh angle. "Compassionate" also resembled the 1980s and 1990s conservative byword "empowerment." Both were ways of linking conservatism with positive reform. On both a political and a policy level, though, the faith-based language of compassion dovetailed with enduring evangelical social priorities. Its leading legislative promoters tended to be evangelical Christians. Besides Ashcroft, champions of charitable choice included Senator Dan Coats of Indiana, Senator Sam Brownback of Kansas, and Congressman J. C. Watts of Oklahoma, Republicans all. More strikingly, numerous veterans of the evangelical left—Jim Wallis, Ron Sider, Tony Campolo, and especially James Skillen of the Center for Public Justice—joined conservative evangelicals like Colson in supporting the general thrust of Bush's faith-based vision. Sider even voted for Bush in 2000, despite the fact that their economic outlooks could not have been more different. Former Ohio congressman Tony Hall, a pro-life Democrat who became his party's version of Mark Hatfield during his tenure in the House of Representatives, served in the Bush administration as ambassador to the United Nations Agencies for Food and Agriculture.[11]

Bush's embrace of faith-based compassionate conservatism had the potential to heal evangelical political wounds still raw from the Carter and Reagan years. Despite strong differences over issues such as national defense and tax policy, evangelical activists across the political spectrum harkened back to the nineteenth-century spirit of Anglo-American reform. William Wilberforce, the British parliamentarian who led a successful crusade to end his nation's involvement in the slave trade, was the most popular shared point of reference by the 2000s. A Christian paternalist who was most decidedly not a social or economic radical, Wilberforce (or rather, Wilberforce as invoked by modern evangelicals) suggested the ideological parameters within which compassionate conservatism might operate.[12]

Michael Gerson, the GOP's "evangelical wunderkind," defined those parameters. A childhood supporter of Jimmy Carter, Gerson left the Democratic Party largely because of abortion. Along the way, he adopted his party's shibboleths about tax cuts and economic growth, but he never came to share its aversion to big government as such. While a student at Wheaton College, Gerson was recruited by Charles Colson. He served as a research assistant and ghostwriter for *Kingdoms in Conflict*, then moved into GOP politics, working for Dan Coats, a fellow Wheaton alum, as well as for Jack Kemp, Steve Forbes, and Bob Dole. More than a few conservative pundits wondered if the idealistic Gerson, who in the late 1990s wrote for *US News and World Report*, had chosen the wrong party for his ambitions. Still, he was a logical person for presumptive candidate George W. Bush to woo for the role of lead speechwriter. Gerson became a graceful advocate for compassionate conservatism, setting the tone for a faith-based campaign that preferred uplift to jeremiads.[13]

However, Gerson's brand of social concern risked disarming the very issues that continued to deliver evangelical votes to the GOP. Its communitarian notes often glossed over the culture wars that raged on in the minds of many grassroots activists. These two different sides of faith-based politics were a basic point of tension within the Bush administration. As the issue of Intelligent Design (ID) revealed, evangelical status anxiety over matters of educational and scientific authority continued to fuel political activism. ID emerged during the mid-1990s as a new alternative to evolution. It was politically sharp but scientifically dull. Advocates of ID did not base their arguments on scientific empiricism, but rather on the skepticism about scientific authority that had become a generic part of postmodern discourse by the close of the twentieth century. Seeking an alternative to the reigning paradigm of "scientific materialism," they argued that the existence of a higher power was a viable scientific hypothesis, one that did not depend on recourse to faith. Technically, adherence to ID did not require belief in the biblical creation story or even in the Christian God. If ID was not precisely " 'Creation Science' 2.0," as one prominent critic alleged, it was clearly intended to counter the "methodological naturalism" of the mainstream sciences. Phillip Johnson, a Berkeley law school professor and an evangelical convert, was the leading theorist of ID. Overall, ID had few scholarly supporters outside of the increasingly deep pockets of the Seattle-based Discovery Institute. At the same time, it had plenty of political backers. In 1999, the Kansas State Board of Education voted to delete evolution from the state's science standards. The short-lived decision portended a new round of conflicts (not to mention political opportunities) to come.[14]

The 2000 Bush campaign successfully balanced the inclusive language of compassion with the polarizing politics of the Christian Right. Bush's first major address on domestic policy, delivered in Indianapolis (home of Mayor Steve Goldsmith, a campaign adviser and supporter of faith-based policies), was a paean to compassionate conservatism. "A rising tide lifts many boats, but not all," Bush declared, wielding Gerson's words. The candidate called for a "government that serves those who are serving their neighbors." "It's not enough for conservatives like me...to call for volunteerism," Bush added. "Without more support and resources, both private and public, we are asking them to make bricks without straw." While Bush echoed the traditional Republican line in favor of tax cuts, he also proposed an $8 billion federal investment to assist the "armies of compassion." His faith-based message read like a doctrine: "In every instance where my administration sees a responsibility to help people, we will look first to faith-based organizations, charities and community groups that have shown their ability to save and change lives." As his campaign for the GOP nomination progressed, Bush strengthened his ties to the organized Christian Right. The ever resourceful Ralph Reed, whose big-tent approach to coalition building dovetailed with Bush's political style, vouched for the candidate's conservative bona fides. In October 1999, Bush met secretly with members of the Council for National Policy, a network of evangelical right elites dating back to the early Reagan years. Above ground, the candidate declared in an Iowa GOP candidates' debate that "Christ" was his favorite political philosopher, "because he changed my heart." He soon took a much greater political risk by speaking at South Carolina's Bob Jones University, a fundamentalist bastion known for its anti-Catholicism and prohibition on interracial dating. Amid the fallout, Bush apologized to John Cardinal O'Connor, Bob Jones lifted its ban, and opponent John McCain summoned the spirit of Bart Giamatti in a widely covered speech, which he delivered in Tidewater, Virginia, no less. McCain attacked Pat Robertson and Jerry Falwell as "agents of intolerance," tantamount to "union bosses." The speech burnished McCain's reputation as a maverick, but it smacked of political desperation. It came less than two weeks after Christian Right stalwart Gary Bauer, until recently a presidential contender himself, had endorsed McCain.[15]

Democratic nominee Al Gore understood faith-based politics better than did McCain. A Southern Baptist and former divinity school student, Gore absorbed the strategic upshot of Stephen Carter's thesis in *The Culture of Disbelief*: Faith should matter in politics because it matters to most Americans. A campaign adviser bragged in 1999 that Democrats were "going to take back God this time." Gore came out in support of faith-based organizations two months before Bush's Indianapolis speech. The Democratic front-runner's primary challenger, New Jersey senator Bill Bradley, felt similarly; he was a booster of Jim Wallis. Days before Bush called Jesus his favorite philosopher, Gore told *60 Minutes* that he was a born-again Christian. His selection of Joseph Lieberman as a running mate had much to do with Lieberman's "Holy Joe" piety as a Modern Orthodox Jew. Lieberman's frequent references to his faith promised to appeal to moderate evangelical voters. Yet candidate Gore was up against two decades of political momentum, and Bush and the Republicans were still much better positioned to profit from the political moment. Bush secured 74 percent of evangelical voters.[16]

Faith-based policies and faith-based politics overlapped awkwardly in the new administration. Political adviser Karl Rove made evangelical voters central to his analysis of the president's prospects. In a late 2001 appearance at the conservative American Enterprise Institute, Rove argued that low evangelical turnout contributed to Bush's defeat in the popular vote count. Contra Gerson, Rove understood that compassion was not necessarily what the conservative evangelical base expected from a Christian statesman. Rove knew better, though, than to explicitly counter someone so close to the president. Besides, Bush had sent more inclusive signals as president-elect when he met in Austin with a wide-ranging, bipartisan group of religious leaders. Such overtures were hardly unprecedented, of course; Clinton had done something similar after his first election victory. Still, Bush's compassion agenda struck even an unlikely ally like Jim Wallis as transcending conventional politics. Language along those lines found its way into Bush's highly regarded inaugural address. "Church and charity, synagogue and mosque, lend our communities their humanity, and they will have an honored place in our plans and laws," he declared.[17]

The president quickly delivered on his words. His first two executive orders created the White House Office of Faith-Based and Community Initiatives (WHOFBCI) and established faith-based centers within five executive departments. John DiIulio served as the inaugural director of WHOFBCI. DiIulio epitomized its bipartisan promise. Although a Democrat, DiIulio advised both Bush and Gore during the 2000 campaign. A self-described "born-again Catholic" and social conservative who called for Clinton's removal during the Monica Lewinsky scandal, DiIulio retained a progressive's faith in data-driven action. "Our goal is to energize civil society and rebuild social capital," read "Rallying the Armies of Compassion," the policy paper accompanying the rollout of WHOFBCI. While Bush failed to gain congressional support for most of the faith-based agenda, he expanded charitable choice through executive orders and departmental budget prerogatives. One order protected the ability of religious organizations to retain doctrine-based hiring-and-firing practices even if they received federal funds.[18] The confinement of the faith-based program to the executive branch enhanced the likelihood that it would become a political tool. So did Bush's ongoing outreach to evangelical conservatives.

The Bush presidency politicized evangelical elites to a degree not seen since the early 1980s. Partly this was a product of the sheer number of evangelicals who moved in elite Republican and conservative circles. The Bush White House's chief public liaison, Timothy Goeglein, had a mandate to engage both social and economic conservatives; after the president left office, Goeglein took a position with Focus on the Family. Florida secretary of state Katherine Harris—an indefatigable ally in GOP efforts to prevent a recount in that closely contested state—was a veteran of Francis Schaeffer's L'Abri. The Bush administration also pulled in evangelicals who had earlier positioned themselves as skeptics or friendly critics of the Christian Right. More than a few evangelical elites still considered the Christian Right to be a band of upstarts. In 2000, Charles Colson and Franklin Graham (Billy's son and successor) were best known within GOP circles for their respective work on prison reform and international relief. A few years into the Bush administration, however, they received mention in the same breath as Jerry Falwell and Pat Robertson. Colson was the most striking case of Bush-era politicization. While remaining a loyal Republican, Colson generally adopted the posture of a wise ex-politico. During the 1976 presidential campaign, he warned evangelicals against uniting behind one presidential candidate, and he offered similar advice as a *Christianity Today* columnist during the 1980s and 1990s. In *Kingdoms in Conflict* and other forums, he stressed the limits of the Christian Right. Colson continued to position himself as a voice of evangelical conscience during the George W. Bush years, even as he frequented the White House. The distance between Republican evangelicals and those evangelicals who specifically identified with Christian Right organizations grew smaller.[19]

Something similar happened regarding evangelicals and Catholics on the right. The Bush team stood to gain from this political dynamic. As a prospective candidate, Bush courted Father Richard John Neuhaus, Catholic-evangelical mediator par excellence. In office, Bush attended the funeral mass of Pope John Paul II. Catholic conservatives, such as Princeton theologian and ethicist Robert George, gained increasing stature in Christian Right circles; James Dobson regularly consulted with George. Intellectually, the Catholic-evangelical relationship was something of a one-way street. Catholic thinkers offered the evangelical right greater scholarly rigor and theological coherence, and the pattern of evangelical public figures gravitating toward the high church tradition continued. Senator Sam Brownback and former Speaker of the House Newt Gingrich entered the fold as "John Paul II Catholics." Evangelical conservative leaders also developed increasing sympathy for Catholic objections to contraception and family planning, both long accepted in Protestant churches. Still, evangelical populism continued to dominate the world of faith-based politicking. For every Brownback or Gingrich, there were more Republicans, such as Minnesota governor Tim Pawlenty, who left the Catholic parish for an evangelical megachurch, or Indiana congressman Mike Pence, who described himself as an evangelical Catholic.[20]

At the start of the 2000s, the handiest label for any president who moved comfortably with conservative Christian politicos was "religious right," or "Christian Right." Presidential piety has been the rule rather than the exception in US history. Nonetheless, the religiosity of the Bush administration struck friends and foes alike as in a category of its own. "I always laugh when people say George W. is saying this or that to appease the religious right," said the president's cousin John Ellis in a line that circulated widely during Bush's reelection campaign. "He *is* the religious right." Conservative columnist George Will averred in 2001 that a member of the "religious right" now occupied the White House before drily observing that the world had not come to an end. Such declarations ignored Christian Right criticism of Bush for appointing openly gay Republicans to administrative posts and anxiety over his compromise policy of permitting federal funding for research on existing stem-cell lines. Yet the evangelical nature of the Bush White House was apparent to anyone afforded a view. Involvement in White House Bible studies, a modest enterprise in previous White Houses, expanded exponentially in an administration in which cabinet meetings began with prayer. Jewish speechwriter David Frum quickly learned to his discomfort that "attendance at Bible study was, if not compulsory, not quite *uncompulsory*, either." To Frum, Bush was unquestionably a product of "the culture of modern Evangelicalism." So were many key players in the White House besides Gerson and Attorney General John Ashcroft. Identifiable evangelicals were by no means a statistical majority in the administration, but in the first term alone they filled such positions as Secretary of Commerce, National Security Advisor, chair of the Council of Economic Advisors, and White House Deputy Chief of Staff. *Washington Post* journalist Hanna Rosin concluded that Beltway "evangelicals are the new Episcopalians—established, connected, respectable." This was a far cry from "poor, uneducated, and easy to command."[21]

The tragic events of September 11, 2001, reinforced Bush's status as "the de facto leader of the evangelical right." Bush effectively replaced figures like Falwell and Robertson. The latter duo, however, caused a stir following a conversation on *The 700 Club* two days after the terrorist attacks. In speculating about why God had permitted the 9/11 attacks to occur, Falwell cited "abortionists," "pagans," "feminists," "gays," "lesbians," and "all the Christ-haters." Franklin Graham and others focused on Islam, which he called "a very evil and wicked religion." While Bush consciously avoided such incendiary language, the evangelicals who lined up to support his War on Terror saw him as a Christian statesman. A national Presidential Prayer Team appeared days after 9/11. In the fall of 2002, as attention turned toward a possible invasion of Iraq, Colson, Bill Bright, and leading Southern Baptist conservative Richard Land wrote a letter supporting the president. Friendly Catholics contributed to the war cry as well. Neuhaus defended the doctrine of preemption on National Public Radio, while Robert George linked the invasion with the just-war tradition. In his 2003 State of the Union address, the president again spoke Gerson's language, paraphrasing a classic evangelical hymn when referring to the "power, wonder-working power" of compassion. On the cusp of a new war and a reelection campaign, though, the context had shifted.[22]

The centripetal pull of President Bush obscured the fact that American evangelicals remained far from monolithic in politics or anything else. On the cusp of the 2004 election, the National Association of Evangelicals (NAE)— which had been tacitly aligned with the Christian Right since the 1980s— released a statement that seemed to portend a new era of evangelical politics. Drafted by David Neff of *Christianity Today* to speak for a group cochaired by Ron Sider and Diane Knippers (representatives of the evangelical left and right, respectively), "For the Health of the Nation" reflected long-standing efforts to move the NAE toward the political center and away from its ties to conservative religious broadcasters. "Evangelical Christians in America face a historic opportunity," the statement declared. "We make up fully one quarter of all voters in the most powerful nation in history. Never before has God given American evangelicals such an awesome opportunity to shape public policy in ways that could contribute to the well-being of the entire world." The statement took predictably conservative positions on social issues, but not on other matters. The "family wage," a reduction of income disparity, "just-war principles," and environmental stewardship all received explicit backing. "For the Health of the Nation" was a remarkably balanced and moderate document—all the more striking because it garnered the signatures of Colson, Land, and Dobson. The last of those leaders had recently resigned the presidency of Focus on the Family, a move that freed him to campaign for GOP candidates and endorse President Bush in 2004. Thus, "For the Health of the Nation" appeared at a time when evangelical right politics never had been more partisan. It was easily overshadowed.[23]

In 2004, the Bush reelection team adopted a base strategy and presumed that evangelicals were the core of the base. The ultimate base issue concerned a matter that was far from the centerpiece of "For the Health of the Nation." Opposition to same-sex marriage—especially following a late 2003 Massachusetts Supreme Judicial Court ruling in favor of gay marriage—promised to galvanize many of the evangelicals whom Rove thought had stayed home in 2000. Christian Right leader Gary Bauer candidly called gay marriage "the new abortion." At the start of the 2004 election year, Bauer and other leaders of the anti-gay-marriage Arlington Group successfully prodded Bush to endorse a federal constitutional amendment outlawing same-sex marriage. Karl Rove encouraged Bush's use of the "narrow cast," appearing in contexts or using language that held special meaning to evangelical voters but that flew right past potential critics. For the most part, though, the base strategy was quite transparent. Ralph Reed headed evangelical outreach, helping pro-Bush ministers to avoid hangups with their tax statuses. David Barton, a wildly influential evangelical amateur historian who also was the longtime vice chair of the Texas GOP, worked for the national party in 2004. The Bush team left few evangelical stones unturned. On one occasion, during the run-up to the convention season, the president held an extemporaneous, private meeting with around fifty Amish residents of Lancaster County, Pennsylvania. Earlier that day, Bush had received an Amish-made quilt reading, "I Love America." The moment captured the extent to which Bush-era politics conflated and subsumed nearly all forms of Christian conservatism. The Amish are biblical pacifists, and their leaders did not encourage voting in national elections, never mind voting for what one Amish leader called a "war president." Yet Bush's appearance in Pennsylvania Dutch country was part of an effort among GOP activists to mobilize the tiny "Amish vote" in that swing state. The minority of Lancaster Amish who did cast their ballots almost unanimously saw Bush as a godly man who defended traditional values. Those values were firmly on display at the 2004 Republican National Convention, which one journalist likened to "a four-day mega-church service." The convention featured performances by contemporary Christian musicians and screenings of a privately produced documentary titled *George W. Bush: Faith in the White House*. Pitched as "an alternative program" to left-wing documentarian Michael Moore's anti-Bush *Fahrenheit 9/11*, the film took up the leading questions of whether Bush's deep faith was sincere and, if so, whether it was a net positive for the American republic. The answers were an unsurprising yes and yes. The documentary cast Bush's reference to Jesus at the 1999 Iowa candidates' debate as an earth-shattering event even as it likened the president's piety in trying times to that of George Washington and Abraham Lincoln.[24]

In November 2004, Ralph Reed's vision of Christian Right politics as mainstream politics, first crafted in the 1990s to steer opposition to Clinton toward a constructive end, stood on the verge of becoming conventional wisdom. To the media, "values voters" ruled the day. A White House official placed a thank-you call to Dobson the morning after the election. Fundamentalist stalwart Bob Jones III, whose university Bush courted during the 2000 primaries, wrote a public letter to the president, using the same scriptural language that Jimmy Carter employed when announcing his campaign back in 1975: "We the people expect your voice to be like the clear and certain sound of a trumpet. Because you seek the Lord daily, we who know the Lord will follow that kind of voice eagerly." Jones reminded Bush that he did not "owe the liberals" anything. "They despise you because they despise your Christ." Many conservative evangelicals cared little for Jones's crass chauvinism, but they shared his enthusiasm for the president. Never had the evangelical right looked more powerful.[25]

The Passion of Evangelical Popular Culture

The same could be said of evangelicalism's reach in popular culture. Many evangelical entrepreneurs, including the founder of the online dating service eHarmony, rode the Bush-era media wave even as they sought to avoid being hemmed in by the president's politics. Neil Clark Warren, the psychologist who founded eHarmony in 2000, had deep evangelical ties. A former dean at Fuller Theological Seminary, he originally described eHarmony as "based on the Christian principles of Focus on the Family author Dr. Neil Clark Warren."

James Dobson's radio show gave the dating service invaluable publicity during its early years. As eHarmony sought to maintain momentum in the mid-2000s, though, Warren dropped all references to Focus on the Family, citing its polarizing politics. The organization maintained a straight-edge reputation, however, as a space for twenty million heterosexuals to find a life partner. Applicants looking for a fling would not find matches. Nor were the service's "29 dimensions of compatibility" applicable to same-sex matches. Lawsuits over the latter policy forced eHarmony to establish a separate website for homosexuals by the end of the decade.[26]

Less controversial but more explicitly evangelical were two of the most pervasive expressions of the 2000s: "What would Jesus do?" and "purpose driven." The question "What would Jesus do?" (WWJD) loomed large during the 2000 campaign season, when Al Gore employed it to accentuate his evangelical credentials. Its rise, or rebirth, as a cultural fad dated from the 1989 whim of Janie Tinkleberg, a youth minister in Holland, Michigan. Tinkleberg thought the slogan would work well on friendship bracelets for the thirty-five teenagers in her youth group. Holland was just down the road from the evangelical publishing center of Grand Rapids, and the born-again marketing machine quickly ran with the catchy slogan. The "WWJD" brand evolved into a multimillion-dollar industry replete with bracelets, books, T-shirts, and sundry other accessories. Evangelical publisher Zondervan and other marketers, both Christian and secular, maneuvered to deny Tinkleberg the royalties from sales—a fitting development, perhaps, since the slogan's originator, Charles Sheldon, never secured a copyright for the century-old novel that begat the very question.[27]

"Purpose driven" was a brand from the start. Megachurch pastor Rick Warren's 2002 devotional book, *The Purpose Driven Life*, followed a familiar path from Christian bookstores to national best-seller lists. By late 2004, it stood as "the fast-selling book of all time, and the best-selling hardback in American history," according to *Publishers Weekly*. A successor to Warren's 1995 *The Purpose Driven Church*, *The Purpose Driven Life* was a self-help book pitched as a spiritual antidote to that very genre. "It's not about you," the first line of the book famously states, even though the dedication page reads, "This book is dedicated to you." Geared to the small-group model of ministry that underlay the growth of Warren's Saddleback Church, *The Purpose Driven Life* laid out a forty-day process of personal commitment and renewal (forty being a number rich in biblical resonance). Warren's sentimental and empowering message hardly distinguished him from fellow celebrity pastors and best-selling authors, such as T. D. Jakes, Max Lucado, and Joel Osteen. In the spirit of Billy Graham, though, the Saddleback pastor captured the imagination of the secular press.[28]

The dramatic story of Ashley Smith took Warren's fame to new heights. Smith was a suburban Atlanta resident in her twenties who had been working through *The Purpose Driven Life*. In March 2005, she was taken hostage by Brian Nichols, an alleged rapist on the run after a dramatic and deadly courtroom escape. At various points during a night of captivity, Smith and Nichols discussed her Christian faith and read a passage from the book. The two achieved a degree of rapport, and the following morning Nichols freed Smith before peacefully surrendering to the authorities. Her use of Warren's book made for a riveting story. In a memoir released later that year by Zondervan (which had also published Warren's book), Smith revealed an additional detail about her desperate night of captivity. Well before discussing her faith with Nichols, she gave him some of the crystal methamphetamine that she stored in her refrigerator. Smith had struggled with substance abuse for years, although she understandably kept those details from journalists and the authorities. This twist, far from undermining her heartwarming tale, only reinforced an already redemptive narrative. After the book appeared, Smith and Warren appeared together on *The Oprah Winfrey Show*. Soon afterward, Starbucks announced that it would begin featuring a quotation from *The Purpose Driven Life* on select coffee cups.[29]

The *Left Behind* end-times thrillers more unambiguously reflected the worldview of conservative evangelicalism, and their reach extended nearly as far as Warren's book. The series of novels first appeared in 1995 but came to resonate with the post-9/11 era. *Left Behind* made a household name of longtime Christian Right and fundamentalist leader Tim LaHaye, who supplied the theological outlines while coauthor Jerry Jenkins handled the plots. The story line follows the exploits and travails of pilot Rayford Steele, his daughter Chloe (a Stanford undergrad), and celebrity journalist Cameron "Buck" William. When all believing Christians, including Mrs. Steele, suddenly disappear—having been raptured to heaven—the protagonists realize that they have been "left behind" to experience up to seven years of tribulation. Like the 1970s thriller *A Thief in the Night*, *Left Behind* substituted a chilling end-times epiphany for the more conventional deathbed conversion. Yet the book's cautionary message quickly yielded to the rising action. Branding themselves the Tribulation Force, Steele and his crew proceed to wage holy counterinsurgency against the demonic Antichrist, one Nicolae Carpathia. The name is Romanian and hence Latinate enough to conform to the usual association of the Antichrist with a revived Roman Empire.

Flight attendant Hattie Durham is a stand-in for the Book of Revelation's Whore of Babylon. In keeping with genre conventions, *Left Behind* also featured the ineluctably named Rabbi Tsion Ben-Judah; like Charles Colson's Hyman Levin, Ben-Judah is a Jewish convert to Christianity who knows the prophetic score. Carpathia moves the United Nations to Babylon, co-opts the beleaguered nation of Israel, and commences the countdown to Armageddon and the Second Coming. The *Left Behind* series updated the end-times clock for the post–Cold War era. In the process, it blended the genres of fundamentalist tract and right-wing jeremiad with an all-American tale of second chances. Wielding what one scholar called "evangelical worldliness" to complement their converts' zeal, the protagonists of *Left Behind* are sophisticated instruments of God's will.[30]

Left Behind really took off after 9/11. The ninth volume in the twelve-part series appeared a few weeks after the terrorist attacks and quickly became the best-selling hardcover of the year. Like *The Purpose Driven Life*, *Left Behind* rendered the shopworn category "crossover" increasingly irrelevant. By 2002, evangelicals comprised only around half of the book's total readership, and LaHaye and Jenkins had each netted around $50 million from the venture. Total sales exceeded sixty-two million copies two years later, by which time the publisher, Tyndale, sponsored a NASCAR driver. Other spinoffs appealed more directly to the books' original audience. Christians concerned about friends and family members likely to be left behind could purchase a postrapture explanatory video (similar to the one Rayford Steele conveniently views).[31]

The evangelical blockbuster for the ages, however, was the movie *The Passion of the Christ*. A deeply Catholic film produced by Hollywood star Mel Gibson, *Passion* evolved into an evangelical spectacle well before its official release on Ash Wednesday 2004. As word surfaced that Gibson was working on a passion film, the actor received unsolicited overtures from an interfaith group of would-be consultants. They were worried about Gibson's brand of anti–Vatican II Catholicism, which was more eccentric than orthodox. After the working screenplay leaked, Gibson faced allegations that his film would perpetuate the charge that Jews were responsible for the death of Jesus. The blatantly anti-Semitic beliefs of Gibson's father lent further credence to these concerns. Gibson responded by unsheathing the sword of the culture wars. With help from an evangelical-friendly marketing firm, he turned *Passion* into a proxy vote on whether Christ had a place in Hollywood. Influential conservative religious leaders and media figures, along with groups of evangelical ministers, saw advance screenings of the film. Evangelicals turned the movie into a box-office success, embracing *Passion* despite its obvious Catholic qualities. For example, the movie focuses far more on Christ's agony than his resurrection, employs Aramaic instead of vernacular English, and relies on extra-biblical revelations to spice up the graphic brutality. Rumors swirled that, upon viewing the film, the aging Pope John Paul II had declared "it is as it was." If *Passion* had a Catholic soul, though, it had an evangelical publicity strategy. Whatever the combustible Gibson's limits as a Christian role model, he found his most loyal defenders among evangelicals. Rick Warren and Bill Hybels promoted the film, while George and Laura Bush spoke warmly of it. More provocatively, NAE president Ted Haggard wondered out loud why Jewish critics would "risk alienating 2 billion Christians over a movie."[32]

Evangelicals interpreted *The Passion of the Christ* through a born-again lens. As one observer argued, they "assessed the realism of the film by its emotional impact," shifting the focus from Christ's suffering to the experience of witnessing it and turning the film into an opportunity for outreach. A small-group devotional book was titled *Experiencing the Passion of Jesus*. The theological meaning of "passion" thus received a distinctively evangelical gloss, amounting to a kind of youth-group pathos. "Christ Is My Passion, & I'm His Passion Too" read a slogan found on T-shirts, coasters, and even infant bibs. While hardly a seeker-friendly flick, *Passion* was equal parts reverence and entertainment. At one stadium-style cinema in Memphis, two employees conducted a Bible quiz competition before a showing of the film.[33]

Hollywood moguls took notice when *The Passion of the Christ* grossed more than $350 million during the Lenten season of 2004. The hunt began for additional "*Passion* dollars." Evangelical-tinted movies like *The Exorcism of Emily Rose* and the film adaptation of C. S. Lewis's *The Chronicles of Narnia: The Lion, the Witch and the Wardrobe* were greenlighted. Disney, long a boycott target of the Southern Baptist Convention, helped to produce the latter, which became one of the twenty-five highest-grossing films in history. The producer of the movie adaptation of *The Da Vinci Code*—a notably unorthodox thriller concerning a conspiracy to conceal knowledge about Jesus' wife and children—even created a website allowing evangelical intellectuals to debunk the book's claims. Evangelical entrepreneurs took advantage of the moment as well. Evangelical pollster George Barna launched a film-previewing service for Christians, while Denver business mogul Philip Anschutz bankrolled the 2006 film *Amazing Grace*, which celebrated evangelical hero William Wilberforce. That same year, NBC purchased the Saturday morning rights to the children's television show *Veggie Tales*, another

example of evangelicalism's modest but enduring foothold in popular entertainment. *Veggie Tales*, argued its creator Phil Vischer, offered a reassuring
"wink" to Christian viewers.[34]

To be sure, evangelicals—particularly those of a Pentecostal persuasion—
remained handy fodder for exposés and satires. A 2002 documentary explored
the complex spiritual and emotional terrain of a "Hell House" run by an
Assemblies of God church in Texas. Christian haunted houses designed to
remind Halloween celebrants of the fate awaiting those who take the wide
path, the increasingly graphic Hell Houses mushroomed in evangelical circles
during the late 1990s and early 2000s. The 2006 documentary *Jesus Camp*
spoke more directly to Bush-era fears, focusing on a children's summer camp
that combined charismatic worship and militant patriotism. A more sophisticated effort was the 2004 movie *Saved!*, a send-up of conservative Christian
education. Set in American Eagle Christian High School, *Saved!* skewered
evangelical paranoia about homosexuality and hypocrisy about premarital
sex. An advance showing of the film to evangelical elites, similar to what
Gibson had done so successfully with *The Passion of the Christ*, backfired when
conservative columnist Cal Thomas walked out of the film and likened its
portrayal of born-again Christians to the minstrel antics of *Amos 'n' Andy*. Yet
the movie's conceit of an unplanned teenage pregnancy (in this case, the outcome of the protagonist's attempt to rid her boyfriend of same-sex attraction)
resembled other mid-2000s films that portrayed the decisions of millennials
to, as the ubiquitous bumper stickers and license plates put it, "Choose Life."
By the end of the decade, twenty-four states permitted specialty plates bearing
that slogan.[35]

The Second Evangelical Scare

"Now we're on during prime time," declared a *Christianity Today* editorial in
July 2005. Thoroughly "mainstreamed," the piece continued, evangelicals
could "no longer complain about a media conspiracy against them." The editors closed with a cautionary allusion to a popular reality television show:
"Now that we're prime-time, we don't want to start acting like American
idols."[36] The warning arrived much too late. By the time of George W. Bush's
reelection campaign, the president himself had joined the cast. The excess of
the mid-2000s precipitated a second evangelical scare, which gave new life
both to the evangelical left and to Democratic Party efforts to reach the
born-again electorate.

The saga of Alabama Supreme Court Chief Justice Roy Moore set the tone for the evangelical right's era of excess. Elected to his post in 2000, the fiery conservative judge immediately proceeded to install a two-and-a-half-ton monument of the Ten Commandments in the Supreme Court building. The self-proclaimed "Ten Commandments judge" was practically begging for a legal challenge. When a federal judge unsurprisingly ordered "Roy's Rock" removed, Moore appealed to a higher law—and to conservative luminaries. A special ethics court removed Moore from office in 2003, but not before Christian Right veterans D. James Kennedy and James Dobson turned him into a martyr of the naked public square. Dobson likened Moore to Rosa Parks, although other evangelical conservatives balked at a judge's brazen defiance of a court order.[37]

The school board of Dover, Pennsylvania, likely had not sought such publicity when it turned the small town into the twenty-first-century version of Dayton, Tennessee. In late 2004, the Dover school board voted by a 6-to-3 margin to require ninth-grade biology students to hear a prepared statement declaring that evolution "is not a fact" but a "theory" containing "gaps." The statement introduced Intelligent Design as "an explanation of the origin of life that differs from Darwin's view" and pointed students toward available copies of the pro-ID "reference book" *Of Pandas and People*. The school board majority tried to open the door to teaching alternatives to evolution without also appearing to sponsor a religious point of view. This amounted to a wholesale endorsement of the "wedge strategy" (theorized by Phillip Johnson and embraced by the Discovery Institute), which saw a "teach the controversy" approach as critical to the eventual defeat of scientific materialism. The slipperiness of the word "theory" assisted the wedge strategy. A scientific theory is an accepted explanatory principle, whereas in popular parlance the same word had come to mean an abstract product of conjecture. Hence, evolution could be cast as "just a theory." Dover became the first national test case for ID. The legal question concerned whether ID really was a stand-in for religion and, thus, whether teaching it in schools violated the Establishment Clause. Indeed, ID was "nothing less than the progeny of creationism," ruled US District Judge John E. Jones III in late 2005. In his scathing and lengthy opinion, Jones called ID "a religious view, a mere re-labeling of creationism, and not a scientific theory." A George W. Bush appointee and a Lutheran, he blasted the Dover school board for attempting to conceal transparently religious pretexts. "The students, parents, and teachers of the Dover Area School District deserved better than to be dragged into this legal maelstrom, with its resulting utter waste of monetary and personal resources."

A month earlier, the Dover school board elections had appeared to anticipate the judge's assessment; every incumbent fell. While ID lost in the courtroom and at the ballot box, it already had gained valuable political allies. Evolution theory had few public defenders within the GOP leadership. Courtesy of Pennsylvania senator Rick Santorum, ID-friendly language appeared in the explanatory notes of the 2001 No Child Left Behind Act. President Bush and numerous high-ranking Republicans were on record embracing "teach the controversy," and even John Kerry, Bush's Democratic opponent in 2004, adopted a similar line.[38]

With conservative Republicans in control of both Congress and the White House, evangelical right elites set their sights on the courts. In the first half of 2005, Terri Schiavo of Florida emerged as a significantly more sympathetic figure than Judge Moore or the Dover school board members. Since 1990, Schiavo had been in a comalike condition (known as a "persistent vegetative state") in which her facial movements could give her the appearance of reacting to external stimuli. Eight years into the condition, Michael Schiavo, Terri's husband and legal guardian, requested the removal of her feeding tubes. Schiavo's parents, Robert and Mary Schindler, opposed the move. The dispute centered on Terri's precondition opinions about life support, as well as her present medical state. A multiyear court battle ensued, and the Schindlers sought out allies in the Christian Right, twice turning to Randall Terry, the antiabortion firebrand. Terry, whose profile had fallen since Operation Rescue's heyday in the late 1980s and early 1990s, was then in the process of converting to Catholicism. The Schiavo case showed how the growing Catholic-evangelical convergence on "life" issues extended well beyond abortion—a trend that Francis Schaeffer and C. Everett Koop's *Whatever Happened to the Human Race?* had anticipated back in 1979. Opposition to euthanasia, traditionally a Catholic concern, galvanized evangelical conservatives as well. The Republican-majority Congress also entered the picture in early 2005 after the Florida judicial process continued to affirm Michael Schiavo's request. GOP Senate Majority Leader Bill Frist, who saw evangelical support as essential to a future presidential bid, deployed his credentials as a transplant surgeon to diagnose Terri Schiavo as "clearly responsive." He relied on video footage of her movements. In March, both houses of Congress, with bipartisan support but GOP impetus, voted to give the federal courts jurisdiction over the matter. President Bush—whose brother, the governor of Florida, had previously intervened on the Schindlers' behalf— interrupted his vacation in Texas, flying back to Washington to sign the legislation at 1:11 a.m. Federal judges ultimately refused to override the state court's opinion. Terri Schiavo's autopsy noted that her brain had shriveled to half its normal size and that she had been blind.[39]

Despite Republican expectations to the contrary, the Schiavo case backfired politically. Americans took end-of-life issues seriously, and many sympathized with both sides of the family dispute. But most did not see the matter as a political issue and thus strongly opposed the intervention of Bush and Congress. The Schiavo controversy intensified conservative hostility toward the judiciary. In 2005 and 2006, evangelical right luminaries, including Dobson and Colson, organized a series of Justice Sunday telecasts, hosted by conservative megachurches, to protest against liberal judicial activism. Frist made a cameo at the first such event, although he soon lost favor by coming out for federal funding of stem-cell research. The Schiavo case inspired social conservatives but confirmed others' suspicions that faith was merely a political tool in the Bush White House.[40]

Insider critiques of WHOFBCI from two of its most influential policy players, John DiIulio and David Kuo, bolstered that line of reasoning. DiIulio's discontent first surfaced in a 2003 *Esquire* article by Ron Suskind, which offered an early window into how the famously secretive Bush White House operated. Having resigned his position after less than a year on the job, DiIulio sent Suskind a long memo, using language he included in earlier letters to the president. The former WHOFBCI head praised Bush as "a godly man and a moral leader," but he blasted the White House's policy-thin "Mayberry Machiavellis" for politicizing WHOFBCI and other domestic programs. DiIulio had never gotten along well with evangelical elites. Pat Robertson fretted that faith-based grants might go to Hare Krishnas, Scientologists, and other groups outside of the Judeo-Christian tradition. DiIulio belittled such concerns. His early departure, which he insisted was in keeping with his original terms for accepting the position, drew cheers from conservative evangelicals. To Reverend Eugene Rivers, though, it was "a signal that the faith-based office will just be a financial watering hole for the right-wing white evangelicals." Then details surfaced about which conservative groups were receiving Compassion Capital Fund grants through cabinet agencies. One recipient was the South Carolina–based Heritage Community Services, a pro-abstinence organization that grew out of an antiabortion pregnancy crisis center. Robertson's relief organization, Operation Blessing, came in for $20 million, while one of Charles Colson's prison programs received $22.5 million and Atlanta's explicitly evangelistic Youth for Christ got $455,000. Critics branded faith-based funding "a spoils system for evangelical ministries." A *New Yorker* cartoon featured a congregational prayer requesting "that we get our hands on some of that government scratch." The remaining progressive allies of Bush's faith-based agenda wore thin. Tony Campolo lamented the budget-draining effects of the Bush tax cuts and the mission-sapping regulations that came with federal funding. Jim Wallis recounted a tense 2003 meeting between White House officials and religious leaders in which a progressive evangelical (most likely Ron Sider) exclaimed, "I voted for President Bush, I supported you all because I liked the language of 'compassionate conservatism.' But I am just a hair's breadth away from concluding the whole thing was a trick, just to focus our attention away from poverty policy and put the whole burden of reducing poverty back on the shoulders of the faith community."[41]

David Kuo's tell-all book advanced a similar point. A protégé of John Ashcroft, Kuo served as the deputy director of WHOFBCI until 2003. In a 2006 memoir and a *60 Minutes* appearance, Kuo reported that White House staffers routinely mocked leading evangelicals. He concluded that most conservatives, Christians included, simply did not care about the compassion agenda, and he even questioned the depth of Bush's own commitment to faith-based action. Kuo traced his involvement in political activism to a 1987 encounter with Charles Colson. Now, he followed earlier insider critics of the Christian Right by calling for a "fast from politics." From the vantage point of Kuo and other spurned supporters, the Bush team had taken an issue that promised to alleviate the culture wars and widen the electoral horizons of the GOP and turned it into a source of bitter partisanship.[42]

While Kuo wondered whether evangelicals truly had a place in the Republican Party, many Bush critics speculated that evangelicals were the true face of the GOP. Patrick Henry College offered evidence toward that end. Headed by Christian Right veteran Michael Farris, the Northern Virginia–based Patrick Henry appeared to exist for the purpose of inserting evangelical conservatives into positions of power. The tiny "Harvard for Homeschoolers," which opened only in 2000, garnered an excessive amount of media attention. It was, though, disproportionately successful in placing interns in the White House. Those in search of "Young Evangelicals in High Places" needed to look no further than the Justice Department, the first-term domain of longtime Christian Right ally John Ashcroft. There, Monica Goodling demonstrated that some Mayberry Machiavellis were evangelicals in good standing. Goodling quickly rose from a Republican National Committee opposition researcher to become, in her early thirties, a senior counsel to Alberto Gonzales, Ashcroft's replacement as Attorney General. Goodling was in charge of ninety-three US attorneys. She played a leading role in the hiring and firing of political appointees and was implicated in the controversial dismissal of several US attorneys in 2006. The following year, by which time Democrats controlled Congress, Goodling admitted to a House committee that she had "crossed the line" in using political criteria for Justice Department hires. She even researched applicants' political donations. The transition from hack to hapless was swift for Goodling, who resigned under pressure. Comedians mocked the sanctimonious name of her undergraduate alma mater, the moderate evangelical Messiah College (home of the "Fighting Christies," proclaimed comedian Bill Maher). Her more politically significant affiliation, though, was with Pat Robertson's Regent School of Law, Ashcroft's employer after he left the Justice Department. The former dean of Regent University, Kay Coles James, served as head of the US Office of Personnel Management. Much higher up in the administration than Goodling or Cole was White House counsel Harriet Miers, Bush's surprising 2005 nomination to the Supreme Court. While Miers was a member of an evangelical church in Texas, she was not a product of evangelical power networks. Still, the administration turned to evangelical leaders to promote her nomination. James Dobson vouched for Miers's piety and pro-life credentials, based largely on Karl Rove's assurances. Other conservatives grew suspicious about her lack of a paper trail, however, and worried that she was simply a Bush crony; they successfully pressured her to withdraw. The aging Dobson's influence gradually flickered.[43]

Ralph Reed's reputation, on the other hand, took a dramatic nosedive following revelations of his collaboration with disgraced GOP lobbyist Jack Abramoff. The two longtime friends worked to close or block casinos on certain Native American reservations. Opposition to legalized gambling was an abiding priority of evangelicals. Limiting its expansion also was of interest to Abramoff's clients, other Native American tribes eager to protect their existing gaming enterprises. Reed's funding came from the latter. He was operating with a Bible in one hand, a stacked deck in the other.[44]

The most dramatic fall of all involved Colorado Springs pastor and NAE president Ted Haggard. By 2006, Haggard was one of the more prominent symbols of Bush-era evangelicalism. An Assemblies of God minister, Haggard built a Colorado Springs megachurch from scratch, growing it into the largest such congregation in that booming evangelical capital. When Haggard assumed the presidency of NAE in 2003, he talked about distancing the organization from the Christian Right. To the casual observer, the move of the NAE headquarters to Colorado Springs (for logistical convenience) only confirmed the connection. So did Haggard's own behavior. He appeared repeatedly in *George W. Bush: Faith in the White House*, the 2004 campaign documentary, praising the president as a "servant leader." He also spoke at a Justice Sunday gathering. Haggard's greatest media exposure came days before the November 2006 midterm elections, when news broke of a Denver-based male prostitute who claimed that the pastor had paid him for sexual services, as well as for methamphetamine. By coincidence, an ebullient, prescandal Haggard was a prominent presence in not one but two mainstream documentaries about evangelical culture that appeared around the time the allegations broke. His hypocrisy thus was on full display. Having confessed his transgressions and submitted himself to the authority of fellow ministers he hitherto had supervised, Haggard received neither cheap grace nor a golden parachute. His severance agreement exiled him (and, by extension, his wife and two sons) from the state of Colorado for a period of eighteen months. During that time, Haggard quickly spent down his savings and was reduced to selling health insurance door to door on commission. His fall intensified a backlash against Bush's "faith-based presidency" that was well under way.[45]

The second evangelical scare surpassed its early 1980s predecessor both in breadth and intensity. Born-again faith was no longer a public novelty. More than ever, though, its political dynamics were under a magnifying glass. The presidency of George W. Bush served as an obvious reference point for evaluating the degree and propriety of evangelical influence on American public life. Journalists came to grips with the fact that evangelicals were "not just another special interest group, like the NRA. This is Bush's base." Even some historians trained to judiciously weigh surface changes against structural continuities saw themselves as living in exceptional times. "Seldom has the wall of separation between church and state seemed so fragile as in the America of George Walker Bush," wrote two academic critics of the Christian Right in 2005. "The religious politics of Ronald Reagan and George Herbert Walker Bush look statesmanlike when compared to the tactics used by the incumbent administration." The events of September 11, 2001, helped to revitalize academic interest in global fundamentalism, although scholars of fundamentalism generally now were more hesitant to include the Christian Right in their narratives. Still, journalist Esther Kaplan cited Israel's Likud Party and India's Bharatiya Janata Party—"in thrall to ultra-Orthodox settlers" and "violent Hindu nationalism," respectively—to argue that "our governing Republican Party is unmistakably in the grips of its own Christian theocratic base." Former New York Times reporter Chris Hedges had observed politicized religion while working abroad in the Middle East and the Balkans. Now he saw similar trends at home. His book title warned of "fascists," but his more specific target was something called "dominionism."[46]

Dominionism was the phantasm of the second evangelical scare—a nightmarish vision of the Christian Right's presumed ultimate goal. Dominionism amounted, in the words of its most influential mid-2000s interpreter, to "the idea that Christians have a God-given right to rule." The name referred to a common translation of Genesis Chapter 1, especially verses 26 and 28, in which God grants mankind "dominion" over the rest of creation. Modern American dominionism had numerous sources. Its boldest forms were the postmillennialist theologies of Rousas John Rushdoony and his estranged brother-in-law, Gary North. They were proponents of Christian Reconstructionism, or theonomy ("God's law"). Rushdoony, North, and their insular but prolific band of sympathizers blended libertarian economics and right-wing constitutionalism with a radicalized version of the Reformed impulse to transform society along Christian lines. Rushdoony, who passed away less than a month after Bush took office, embraced the imposition of Old Testament law on American society, including capital punishment for sodomy. Dominionism was the name critics commonly applied to Reconstructionism's "political theory," although most observers conceded that few dominionists were as extreme as Rushdoony himself. Despite Rushdoony's extremism, even he never advocated political revolution. Still, dominionism's obvious theocratic notes made it a magnet for alarmism. As longtime Christian Right watchers well knew, softer versions of Rushdoony's ideas had filtered into the broader evangelical right. Francis Schaeffer, Randall Terry, and especially Pat Robertson had sympathized with aspects of Reconstructionist theology, while Rushdoony emerged by the 1980s as a leading advocate for homeschooling. These threads of connection confirmed the worst fears of those who were not inclined to believe that the evangelical right might contain competing political visions, never mind confused ones, within its ranks. Even those who acknowledged such differences wondered whether Marvin Olasky's compassionate conservatism or Ralph Reed's emphasis on religious freedom were but stalking horses for a broader agenda of "Christian nationalism." If the GOP was "perhaps the first fundamentally religious party in U.S. history" (as pundit Kevin Phillips argued in a book titled *American Theocracy*), then such questions seemed more pressing with each day.[47]

Many leading voices of the second evangelical scare chafed at faith-based rhetoric and its rosy image of an ecumenical civil society. Religion, ran one long-standing progressive critique, undermined the salience of class politics. "What's the matter with Kansas?" asked Thomas Frank about the conservative-driven culture wars raging in his normally placid home state (which, a century earlier, had been disproportionately socialist). The so-called new atheists dialed the rhetoric up another level. They launched a frontal attack on the deference to faith that ran through the older civil religion and the newer civil society movement. Some of them also criticized the political left for its squishy embrace of pluralism. The new atheists saw religion as a pernicious force in modern life, arguing that moderate believers bore some culpability for the sins of their zealous cousins. Sam Harris, Christopher Hitchens, Richard Dawkins, and other new atheists were not agnostics; they knew that they did not believe in a higher power. In the post-9/11 era, radical Islamism represented the new atheists' best (and mostly commonly cited) case against religion. Harris was particularly exercised about Islam, in contrast to his soft spot for Buddhist practices. Still, his and similar best-selling books did not spare an American society saturated in Christian piety. The new atheists' ultimate target was irrationalism as much as organized religion; this, in their view, was the problem that Islamist terrorists and Christian Right leaders shared. It was also what linked them to the much bloodier twentieth-century sins of atheistic totalitarianism. Thus, Pol Pot was a "quasi-religious" fanatic, while Billy Graham shared with Osama Bin Laden a belief in a heaven. The new atheists did not hesitate to find the shock value in reason.[48]

Other voices offered a less hyperbolic critique of Bush-era political religion. While the new atheists could be humorless to a fault, wit abounded nearby. The most politically influential comedic venue of the era was cable television's *The Daily Show with Jon Stewart*. During the mid-2000s, *The Daily Show* ran a feature called "This Week in God." Cast member Stephen Colbert, the usual host of the sketch, summoned his "God Machine" to produce an interfaith survey of the religious news of the weird. Colbert did not suffer from what satirist Robert Lanham called "Evangophobia." He managed both to make fun of chauvinistic piety—evangelical faith, no more or less than Catholic or Islamic—and to celebrate the comedic material routinely served up by America's religious pluralism. His public square kept its clothes, if not its dignity.[49]

Finally, some secular progressives reversed Thomas Frank's rhetorical question, asking why the left had a problem with so many God-fearing Kansans. Liberals, they argued, needed to come to grips with why they had lost so many of the faithful. Historian Michael Kazin authored a sympathetic biography of William Jennings Bryan, the turn-of-the-century political leader who blended progressive politics and evangelical Protestantism. Bryan was an "anti-Darwinist reformer," an awkward fit eighty years after the Scopes Monkey Trial. In the interest of creating a more viable left, Kazin embraced the progressive evangelical search for a usable past, one that might reveal the reign of the Christian Right to be a finite moment in American evangelical history. This strategy became the most politically salable response to Bush-era evangelical politics.[50]

A new group of thoughtful evangelicals, notably more liberal than their 1990s counterparts, sought to reclaim their brand of Protestant Christianity. While they wanted to change the evangelical status quo, they made their case to largely secular audiences. Their favorable reception belied progressive assumptions that the Bush administration had irreversibly poisoned the well of evangelical politics. Prominent voices, such as theologian Charles Marsh, historian Randall Balmer, and President Jimmy Carter, proudly waved the evangelical flag when attacking the Christian Right and the Bush administration in 2005 and 2006. They helped to steer the energies of the second evangelical scare toward the promotion, or at least tolerance, of alternative forms of religious political engagement. Marsh's January 2006 *New York Times* op-ed, titled "Wayward Christian Soldiers," was the most widely e-mailed *Times* article that month. A telling moment occurred the previous year, when George W. Bush delivered the commencement address at Calvin College, long an intellectual center of evangelicalism. A third of the school's faculty signed an advertisement protesting the Iraq War, while a quarter of the graduating students sported pins reading, "God is not a Republican or a Democrat."[51]

As Bush's popularity began to wane by the start of his second term, he took comfort in his belief (likely inspired by scholar Robert Fogel) that the United States was in the midst of a religious "Third Awakening" rooted in the struggle against global terrorism. The president used the term when addressing a group of conservative journalists in the fall of 2006, a time when Bush perhaps still assumed that he stood to benefit from a national revival.[52] The remainder of his presidency, however, challenged the conventional political wisdom that religion was the Democrats' problem and the Republicans' opportunity. If Jimmy Carter's evangelical critics in the late 1970s saw his born-again presidency as a tragedy, then Bush's small but vocal band of evangelical left critics saw its revival in the 2000s as a farce. Bush, who had campaigned as an agent of evangelical social concern, galvanized an evangelical left that by 2008 was eager to vote the GOP out of the White House. The evangelical left had a second coming, too.

6 HOPE FOR A CHANGE

The decade of evangelical second comings was also one of closures no less ambiguous than Charles Colson's tale of President Shelby Hopkins. A real-life Texan president had changed everything for evangelical politics. Yet by the end of Bush's second term, even past supporters could not agree about whether he was a godly leader or an empty suit. Amid the second evangelical scare, some moderate evangelical leaders moved to distance themselves from the president. It was the evangelical left, though, that changed the conversation, giving Democrats a reason not to write off the born-agains. No Democratic politician better understood these political dynamics than did Illinois senator Barack Obama.

In the summer of 2006, Obama delivered a widely cited speech at a conference sponsored by Call to Renewal, a group associated with Jim Wallis and Sojourners. Deftly manipulating faith-based language, the likely presidential contender made a substantive and strategic argument that Democrats should reach out to believers. Obama argued for a faith-friendly "public square" and endorsed a narrative of American history rooted in the progressive evangelical tradition. He extolled Baptist John Leland (an early advocate of religious liberty), Frederick Douglass, William Jennings Bryan, and Martin Luther King Jr. Yet Obama did not pose as a Democratic version of Michael Gerson. His roots were in Hyde Park, not Wheaton. "Democracy demands that the religiously motivated translate their concerns into universal, rather than religion-specific, values," Obama said. He spoke of his respect for the pro-life position, but he reiterated his own pro-choice stance. Unlike Jimmy Carter in 1976, or George W. Bush in 2000, the Illinois senator was not running as an evangelical. Instead, as Ronald Reagan had done in 1980, Obama was asking an evangelical audience to join a new coalition.[1]

The Reemergence of the Evangelical Left

The unraveling of Bush's faith-based coalition made the vast diversity within the American evangelical world more apparent to outside observers. Journalists perceived an evangelical "crackup" and "identity crisis," highlighting the numerous conservative ministers who distanced themselves from the Christian Right after 2004. Orlando megachurch pastor Joel Hunter fit the narrative well. In 2006, Hunter was named president of the Christian Coalition, an organization still associated with its past leader, Ralph Reed. Hunter was a surprising choice because of his long-standing criticism of what he saw as the narrowness and arrogance of the Christian Right. He announced his intention to steer the organization toward "compassion issues," such as poverty and care for the environment. The Christian Coalition board strongly resisted this proposed move into stereotypically liberal territory. Hunter's presidency was over before it ever started; he never formally assumed office.[2]

European evangelicals offered a model for how American evangelicals might recalibrate their priorities, as the former had neither the hope nor the desire to assume dominion over their overwhelmingly secular societies. A common source of inspiration was John Stott, an evangelical Anglican long cast as a more contemplative version of his American contemporary, Billy Graham. While hardly analogous to Graham in fame or to the pope in influence (despite the claims of some American admirers), Stott offered a comforting vision of conservative Protestantism an ocean removed from the Christian Right's "bozos." Best represented in the United States by InterVarsity Christian Fellowship, a student ministry that had migrated from the Anglosphere in the 1930s and 1940s, Stott-style evangelicalism was theologically conservative and politically moderate.[3]

A complementary perspective came from moderate forces within the National Association of Evangelicals (NAE) who had a new lease on life with the departure of Ted Haggard. Veteran NAE staffer Richard Cizik offered outspoken support for "creation care," a Christian euphemism for environmentalism. Cizik became a media favorite, in no small part because he sparked outrage from the Christian Right's old guard. Jerry Falwell called creation care "Satan's attempt to redirect the church's primary focus." Cizik held onto his position at the NAE until 2008, when he came out in support of civil unions for gay couples.[4]

Rick Warren emerged as the flagship post–Christian Right evangelical, eventually rivaling President Bush himself as the paradigmatic evangelical of the 2000s. By the end of the decade, *The Purpose Driven Life* had sold nearly thirty-five million copies in sixty languages. Warren's Saddleback megachurch had more than 100,000 members (fourth-highest in the nation), with a weekly attendance of around one-fifth that number. His Purpose Driven

Network of pastors likewise exceeded 100,000 members. The twenty-fifth anniversary celebration of Saddleback, in 2005, took place in a Major League Baseball stadium. Despite Warren's seeker-sensitive tactics, such as not advertising Saddleback's Southern Baptist affiliation, his theology remained generically evangelical. His politics were no more exotic. To commemorate 9/11, his congregation distributed yard signs picturing an American flag and, in small print, the words "Saddleback Church." Before the 2004 election, Warren sent an e-mail to the Purpose Driven Network. Without formally endorsing George W. Bush, Warren listed "five issues that are nonnegotiable": abortion, stem-cell research, euthanasia, same-sex marriage, and human cloning. Bush and Kerry, Warren noted, "could not have more opposite views" on those matters. Yet Warren managed to keep his public image largely apolitical. His success, media savvy, and irenic personally allowed him to escape the media hatchets that had befallen many stalwarts on the evangelical right. Communitarian-minded academics saw Saddleback as, in its own way, a bulwark against a fraying civil society.[5]

Warren thus had a stockpile of goodwill following the 2004 election, when he embraced a more conspicuously moderate form of social concern and distanced himself from the Bush administration. The development was more than a little ironic, since Warren was, in many respects, the very model of a compassionate conservative. Prisoners in the state of California who followed Saddleback's addiction recovery program could win an early furlough. Flush with wealth and fame after the publication of *The Purpose Driven Life* in 2002, Warren and his wife, Kay, began to reverse tithe, giving away all but 10 percent of their income. They did not stop there. At Saddleback's twenty-fifth-anniversary celebration, Warren formally unveiled an ambitious plan to promote church involvement to combat the "global giants" of disease, education, economic poverty, and spiritual deprivation. Warren put particular emphasis on global poverty and HIV prevention. Both were issues that Michael Gerson promoted, with some success, in the Bush administration. By the mid-2000s, though, the Dover school board and Terri Schiavo scandals dominated impressions of evangelical politics. Warren appeared to offer a nonpartisan alternative. "How do you get [political] coordinates for a guy who talks about poverty like a liberal Catholic?" gushed John DiIulio. Warren found a receptive audience in Rwandan president Paul Kagame. Although a nonbeliever, Kagame welcomed Warren's capital, social and otherwise. They talked of turning the impoverished, genocide-ravaged country of Rwanda into a "purpose-driven nation." Warren also looked for ways to steer around controversial issues back home, remaining strongly pro-life, but preferring to call himself "whole life." He hung out with rock star Bono, whose status as an evangelical fellow-traveler grew to the point where he spoke at the 2006 National Prayer Breakfast. Warren became something of a rock star himself. "All of a sudden," he told the *Financial Times* with a note of boast-fulness that often came through more in print than in person, "I'm getting invitations to Davos, and to TED and to Harvard and Yale and the UN."[6]

Much more novel than Warren was the emerging church, an energetic, if somewhat amorphous, community of young evangelicals who sought to break away from the modern evangelical establishment. The "emergents" had centers in both North America and Western Europe, but they reacted in particular against US evangelicalism. Their eclectic and innovative worship styles explic-itly repudiated the sentimentalist trappings of contemporary Christian culture. Like mid-twentieth-century neoevangelicals, emergents sought to evangelize the world by way of engaging it. Like the evangelical left of the 1970s, they questioned the shibboleths of their spiritual elders. They took their reaction in new directions, however. As avowed postmodernists, they wanted to deconstruct barriers between church and world. Their open-ended blend of word and deed, faithfulness and worldliness, was captured by the expansive term "missional." The goal was to be open to the work of God in unexpected places. This vision of faithfulness appealed to a broad range of evangelicals, along with a few mainline Protestants, as they came to terms with the fact that "post-Christian" North America, and the West in general, was no longer the epicenter of global Christianity.[7]

A disposition as much as a cause, the emerging church balanced the prophet's moral gravitas with the hipster's inquisitive playfulness. Emergents were enchanted with the language of postmodernism—from technical terms like "deconstruct" to colloquial ones like "framing story" and even the word "postmodern" itself. Postmodernism offered an intellectual space seemingly far removed from the commonsense language of traditional evangelicalism. Brian McLaren, a middle-aged nondenominational pastor in suburban Maryland, was the closest thing to a spokesperson that the emerging scene could tolerate. McLaren had moved across the postwar evangelical spectrum. He grew up in the dispensationalist and separatist Plymouth Brethren tradi-tion, went through a Francis Schaeffer phase, and then embraced a seeker-friendly church ministry that still left him spiritually and intellectually thirsty. Finally, in the mid-1990s, McLaren came to doubt the relevance of the church in a world that was up to other things. He wrestled with those questions in his breakthrough 2001 philosophical dialogue, *A New Kind of Christian*. In a self-reflexive style that "blur[red] the line between fiction and nonfiction,"

McLaren chronicled an alternative to the conventional Christianity he had known. "Doesn't the religious community see that the world is changing? Doesn't it have anything fresh and incisive to say? Isn't it even asking any new questions?" he wondered.[8]

The language of departure was a bit misleading though. The emerging church drew from the very evangelical script against which McLaren and others defined themselves. Emergents generally looked down on seeker-sensitive mega-churches, but proved no less adept at outreach and self-promotion. Their enthusiastic embrace of postmodernism was thoroughly in keeping with evangelical traditions of popularization and reuse—akin to Francis Schaeffer's remixing of Western civilization itself, albeit in an intentionally nondogmatic manner. Like the thoughtful evangelicals of the 1990s, emergents offered an opportunistic interpretation of postmodernity. They saw an opening for a more profound faith that rolled with the very crisis of intellectual authority that Schaeffer had sought to roll back. Postmodern times called for "epistemological humility." Moving away from a "foundationalist" reading of scripture (which amounted to an insistence on its rational transparency), emergents embraced a "generous orthodoxy." The latter part of that formulation sometimes checked their impulses toward social liberalism. In almost every other respect, though, they were political progressives, part of a revived evangelical left.[9]

The evangelical left, of course, had never really gone away. Indeed, by the mid-2000s, many of its veterans occupied prominent positions within the broader evangelical world. Wesley Granberg-Michaelson, a former staffer for Mark Hatfield and an early Sojourners member, served as president of the Reformed Church in America and helped to found Christian Churches Together in the USA, an ecumenical organization designed to be more inclusive than the conservative NAE or the liberal National Council of Churches. Ron Sider was well respected in NAE circles even as he criticized the conservative drift of evangelical politics. At the same time, the evangelical right was a much more powerful force in the mid-2000s than it had been in the early 1970s. When the Chicago Declaration of Evangelical Social Concern was drafted in 1973, the Christian Right was not yet a named entity. "One of my biggest concerns about American Evangelicalism today," wrote Tony Campolo three decades later, "is that, in the minds of many, it has become synonymous with the Religious Right."[10] Challenges aside, Campolo, Sider, and other founding members of the evangelical left had come a long way since the notable but quixotic 1972 Evangelicals for McGovern campaign. Amid the Judge Moore, Dover school board, and Terri Schiavo flaps, they were finally positioned for a return to national relevance.

Jim Wallis led the way. The Washington, DC–based activist long had stood as a handy contrast to Jerry Falwell for journalists. But he did not emerge as a truly national figure until the 1990s. In 1995, when the Christian Coalition was at its zenith, Wallis founded the antipoverty group Call to Renewal with help from Campolo and like-minded Christian activists. Wallis was able to stake out a place on the left end of the civil society consensus, drawing support from high-profile progressive allies such as Garry Wills and Cornel West. Starting in the late 1990s, he occasionally taught at Harvard's Divinity School and John F. Kennedy School of Government. The Sojourners community by then extended well beyond its evangelical base. While Jerry Falwell and others routinely questioned Wallis's born-again bona fides, Wallis proudly kept the label, clarifying that he was "a nineteenth-century evangelical." His new fame began with journalist Ron Suskind's dissection of the "faith-based presidency," published in the *New York Times* just before the 2004 election. Wallis was the hero of the story. He recalled a December 2000 meeting in which the president-elect admitted candidly that he did not understand the daily lives of poor people. "I'm a white Republican guy who doesn't get it. How do I get it?" Bush supposedly asked Wallis. Early in 2002, Wallis and the president encountered each other again in a very different, post-9/11 context. According to Wallis, the president offered no response to his argument that global poverty should be a higher priority than the war on terror.[11]

Wallis then reached out to the Democratic Party, which eventually reciprocated. The process began during the run-up to the 2004 election and intensified with Wallis's 2005 best seller, *God's Politics: Why the Right Gets It Wrong and the Left Doesn't Get It*. Wallis positioned himself as a critic of conservative civil religion and liberal secular chauvinism alike—all while continuing to look askance at partisan politics. His disillusionment with Bush, though, made him more willing to identify with the Democratic Party as a sympathetic critic. In this respect, Wallis's role resembled Richard John Neuhaus's early relationship to the Republican right. "God is always personal, but never private," Wallis wrote in a late 2003 *New York Times* op-ed. "The Democrats are wrong to restrict religion to the private sphere—just as the Republicans are wrong to define it solely in terms of individual moral choices and sexual ethics." During the 2004 convention season, Sojourners released a widely noted public statement declaring, "God is Not a Republican. Or a Democrat." One day before the election, a more pointed ad in *USA Today* directly condemned the Christian Right's "Theology of War" and cited support from prominent evangelicals, as well as Catholic and mainline

Protestant leaders. Democrats were already taking notice, and Wallis testified before the 2004 Democratic Platform Drafting Committee. Greater influence came with the publication of *God's Politics*. In it, Wallis criticized Bush, but he savaged the Democrats for their vapidity on religious matters. Howard Dean, the great liberal presidential hope of 2004, left his Episcopal congregation over a dispute related to a bike path. On the campaign trail, Dean cited the Old Testament Book of Job as his favorite part of the New Testament. Democrats must learn to talk about faith in a respectful manner, Wallis argued. It was especially critical that they find a new way to address abortion, an issue that gave many evangelicals a handy reason to vote conservative. Wallis promoted a politically pragmatic version of the "consistent ethic of life," or "seamless garment," argument, which progressive evangelicals first borrowed in the 1980s from Joseph Cardinal Bernardin and other pro-life but otherwise progressive Catholics. Abortion was one of many pro-life issues. "Someday," Wallis wrote, "a smart Democrat will figure out how both pro-choice and pro-life people could join together in concrete measures to dramatically reduce the abortion rate by focusing on teen pregnancy, adoption reform, and real support for low-income women." On homosexuality, he crafted a position that separated the civil questions from the moral ones. While he "strongly affirmed the critical importance of strengthening marriage and family and of supporting parents in the most difficult and important task in our society," he "also supported gay civil rights and legal protection for same-sex couples." Wallis was not saying that Democratic leaders needed to come to Jesus. But, he contended, they should have something to say to Jesus' followers. Most important, they should not make abortion rights the litmus test for whether one could be a legitimate Democrat. Such arguments resembled the Clinton-style "third way" politics of the previous decade, but they gained new salience when evangelical leaders themselves started making them.[12]

Wallis revealed the newfound relevance of the evangelical left. The national media had spent a quarter of a century fixating on the Christian Right as the most important religious force in American public life. The compensatory coverage of a renewed progressive evangelicalism during the Bush years ensured that the evangelical left effectively functioned as a proxy for the religious left as a whole. The religious left, like its conservative counterparts, was difficult to quantify. A mere 7 percent of Americans identified with something called the "religious left," according to a Pew poll taken in 2006, compared to 11 percent with the "religious right." The left's share grew significantly, though, if it also included the 32 percent of Americans who identified as "liberal or progressive Christians." Sojourners' mailing list numbered around 200,000 people in the mid-2000s; Focus on the Family's surpassed two million. Yet with evangelicals widely understood to make up at least a quarter of the population, Wallis's message had a vast potential constituency. Unlike other veteran faith-based progressives, such as Rabbi Michael Lerner, Wallis did not like the moniker "religious left," and indeed he did not share the social liberalism of Lerner or many mainline Protestant leaders. Wallis and Campolo preferred the term "Red-Letter Christians," a reference to the highlighted words of Jesus in many versions of the gospels. In the eyes of many journalists and politicians, though, Wallis stood as the de facto "leader" of the religious left.[13]

Evangelicalism dominated the discourse of the Bush-era religious left. A variety of Bush critics had every incentive to take back the word "evangelical" from the right. Mel White, a former ghostwriter for Billy Graham and Jerry Falwell who became an anti–Christian Right activist after coming out as gay, generously listed the decidedly liberal Protestant iconoclast William Sloane Coffin as "another of my evangelical heroes." Many mainline Protestant and liberal Catholic critics of Bush seemed defensive by comparison. "I love my country. I love my church...I think I am a patriot," wrote the well-known journalist Ray Suarez, an observant Catholic. Others dwelled on a loss of public influence that Wallis never imagined having held in the first place. "Did it happen when no one was looking?" wrote one liberal Protestant journalist of the Christian Right's power within the GOP. Former senator and ambassador John Danforth, a respected Republican moderate and an ordained Episcopal priest, conceded that some might find it odd that he did not speak out against the Christian Right until the Terri Schiavo controversy. As a pro-life candidate in Missouri, he had benefited from conservative Christian votes. What Danforth objected to by 2005 was the peculiar constellation of issues that the Christian Right had thrust upon his party—not just opposition to abortion, but also to stem-cell research and gay marriage. Mainline Protestant voices tended to focus more on the need for civility. "Deeply religious people," Danforth wrote, "come to different conclusions about how faith should influence public policy." Wallis had a sharper message: "The monologue of the religious right is over."[14]

As Democrats processed Bush's reelection victory, they had good reason to listen to Wallis. That even the most stereotypically liberal Democrats did so was a sign of how shell-shocked the party was in the aftermath of the 2004 elections. Talk of a "God gap" between the two parties led many Democrats to ponder missed opportunities for evangelical outreach. Why had presidential nominee John Kerry turned down an interview request with *Christianity Today*? Why was megachurch pastor Bill Hybels passed over for a speaking slot at the Democratic convention that same year? Why were secular party elites comfortable with the demonstrable religiosity of many African American Democrats, but so wary of white evangelicals? Wallis was a logical target for outreach. House and Senate Democrats, as well as Democratic National Committee chair Howard Dean, sought him out after the 2004 election. A repentant Dean even appeared on Pat Robertson's *The 700 Club*, while John Kerry belatedly established rapport with Rick Warren. House Minority Leader Nancy Pelosi helped to set up a Faith Working Group within her party's caucus and attended the opening service of the increasingly prominent megachurch pastor Joel Osteen's new arena in Houston. Other Democrats rediscovered the middle-road theme of abortion reduction, which Bill Clinton had embraced during the 1992 presidential race. Ohioan Ted Strickland (an ordained Methodist minister) and Michigander Jennifer Granholm (a Catholic) adopted such language during their successful 2006 gubernatorial campaigns. Both politicians hired a new Democratic consulting firm specializing in faith-based outreach. A number of groups and forums emerged to promote or cover religiously informed progressive politics. The specifically partisan FaithfulDemocrats.com appeared in 2006. Before the midterm elections that year, Sojourners and Catholics in Alliance for the Common Good released voter guides to counter the ones produced by the Christian Coalition. Despite Wallis's pretensions to political independence, he had become an adjunct Democrat. He gave the party's weekly radio address on December 2, 2006, as the Democrats prepared to take over Congress. Two years after the peak of the evangelical right, and thirty years after George Gallup announced the Year of the Evangelical, progressive evangelicals never had been more prominent as political actors. Prospective Democratic presidential candidates, especially Barack Obama, took notice.[15]

The Obama Pivot

Postmortems for the Christian Right abounded well before George W. Bush left office with a Gallup approval rating of around 34 percent. In its pioneering poll of 1976, Gallup had calculated the number of born-again Christians as a similar percentage of the American populace. That number had risen slightly by 2011, when George Gallup Jr. passed away. Many other pollsters since had followed the lead of the original evangelical number cruncher. The resulting statistics showed a striking, seemingly countervailing trend: The number of persons without a stated religious affiliation grew sharply in those same decades.

In a landmark 2010 study, two leading social scientists cited a connection between "the rise of the nones" and "the visibility of the Religious Right in the public media." The two trend lines were likely to cross, and the long denouement of the Bush administration pushed evangelical watchers to take stock. "The era of the religious Right is over," announced journalist E. J. Dionne in 2008. To progressive evangelicals, "a seismic shift" was under way, one that would soon reveal just how exceptional a moment the Christian Right's rise and fall had been. Evangelicalism had a center, and it—not the aging lions of the Christian Right—would hold. The new commentary reflected the extent to which evangelicalism had become the public face of Christianity itself. *Newsweek* editor Jon Meacham announced "the end of Christian America," a demographic shift that the hyperevangelical Bush years had done much to conceal.[16]

The rapid ascension of Barack Obama only seemed to bolster these arguments. Obama and his fellow Democrats ultimately benefited from the excesses of the Christian Right and a Republican Party that seemed bound to do its bidding. Still, no Democratic candidate with national ambitions could dream of running in 2008 as an atheist or even as an agnostic. Obama was unusually well positioned to promote a progressive brand of faith-based politics. The prominence of the evangelical left during the Obama campaign altered the terms of evangelical influence on American politics, setting the stage for an overall decline in sway.

Obama was not an evangelical in the sense that most Americans understood the term. The rising politician's religious background was no less variegated than his racial and ethnic identity. His Kansan mother came from a nominally Christian background. She was, in his words, "an agonistic," a seeker appreciative of all faiths. His absentee Kenyan father was raised as a Muslim but became "a confirmed atheist." When, as a young adult, Obama negotiated the burdens and opportunities of his own identity, he took comfort in a black church tradition that to him symbolized the triumph of the Civil Rights Movement. He occasionally visited Harlem's famous Abyssinian Baptist Church while an undergraduate at Columbia University during the early 1980s. Obama became, as he later described himself, "a Christian by choice." While working as a community organizer in Chicago, he started attending Jeremiah Wright's Trinity United Church of Christ. Trinity was a mostly black congregation affiliated with a liberal, largely white denomination. Obama joined the church as a baptized convert. In his best-selling autobiography, *Dreams from My Father*, the discovery of Trinity forms the emotional climax of the section on his adopted city of Chicago. Trinity stood at the fault line of the liberal and black Protestant communities, two core

Democratic constituencies. So did Obama. As a mature politician, he would move gracefully (but not unconsciously) between the measured tone associated with the former and the uplifting cadence associated with the latter.[17]

Obama's national coming out came in 2004, when, as a Senate candidate, he delivered the keynote address at the Democratic National Convention. His personal story was his deepest asset; it was the American Dream, writ progressive. But he spoke as someone who was as comfortable with his religious faith as he was with his political liberalism. "We worship an awesome God in the Blue States," Obama stated in an oft-quoted closing passage, "and we don't like federal agents poking around our libraries in the Red States." He spoke of the "audacity of hope," a phrase he borrowed from a Jeremiah Wright sermon and one that soon became Obama's own trademark. Yet in other ways his liberal vision represented an effort to make hope more reasonable. Religious and secular folks should be able to get along, Obama averred. In an overwhelmingly religious nation, he knew, secularists would have to bear the burden first. "Over the long haul," Obama told a television news network in 2006, "I think we make a mistake when we fail to acknowledge the power of faith in the lives of the American people, and join a serious debate about how to reconcile faith with our modern, pluralistic democracy....Secularists are wrong when they ask believers to leave their religion at the door before entering into the public sphere."[18]

Candidate Obama was not about to concede religious voters to the Republicans. Moreover, faith-based appeals were a way of demonstrating his desire to transcend partisanship. Joshua DuBois, a black Pentecostal pastor, headed religious outreach during the campaign. The Obama campaign titled a late 2007 tour of the important primary state of South Carolina "40 Days of Faith and Family," a narrowcasted riff on the structure of Rick Warren's *The Purpose Driven Life*. Obama's language of hope had religious connotations that resonated with progressive Christians. "Hope" was a favorite word of Brian McLaren.[19]

Obama saw progressive and moderate evangelicals as important symbolic allies. His ties to Jim Wallis dated back to the late 1990s, when Obama was a young, ambitious state senator. The two shared a frustration with the polarized discourse of left and right, remembered Wallis, whom Obama thanked in the acknowledgments of his 2006 campaign book, *The Audacity of Hope*. As that book revealed, Obama had internalized the decades-old narrative of mainline Protestant slippage and evangelical ascent. Obama's speech at the Call to Renewal conference was a crucial moment in his outreach to progressive evangelicals and, through them, to the broader religious left. Wallis called it "perhaps the most important speech on the subject of religion and public life" since John F. Kennedy addressed skeptical Southern Baptist leaders in 1960. Obama echoed themes he would soon highlight in the faith chapter of *The Audacity of Hope*. Tellingly, Obama had asked Rick Warren to review the section. The likely presidential candidate knew well Warren's symbolic significance. Later in 2006, the Illinois senator appeared at Warren's World AIDS Day summit. Also on stage was his Senate colleague, Sam Brownback, a strong political conservative and recent evangelical convert to Catholicism. The two had shared an audience before—at a gathering of the National Association for the Advancement of Colored People—as Brownback noted to the Saddleback crowd. He then turned to Obama and quipped, "Welcome to *my* house." The Kansan offered the awkward line as a good-natured joke, and the crowd responded in kind. Obama played along, as well, while seizing the moment to make a point. "There is one thing I've got to say, Sam: This is my house, too. This is God's house," he retorted, to another round of laughter.[20]

To be sure, the desire for a rapprochement with values voters was not unique to Obama. Heading toward 2008, all three Democratic front-runners (Obama, Hillary Clinton, and former North Carolina senator John Edwards) spoke regularly about their religiosity. In 2007, Sojourners hosted and CNN broadcasted a forum with the Democratic contenders. Edwards, Clinton, and Obama discussed their faith with ease, employing autobiographical flourishes to steer around the divisive issues associated with the culture wars. Obama was the only candidate who made a specific reference to evangelicalism, citing its belief in "second chances" as "an area where I think we can get past the left and right divide." He also took advantage of his ties to Jim Wallis to wish the host a happy birthday.[21]

Moderate evangelicals likewise embraced the spirit of postpartisanship as the Bush years wound down. In April 2008, Obama and Clinton participated in a "Compassion Forum" at Messiah College, the alma mater of Monica Goodling, poster child of the second evangelical scare. Rick Warren hosted a follow-up event in August featuring Obama and his GOP opponent, John McCain. Warren, then at the height of his public influence as a born-again moderate, solicited each nominee with a cell phone call. Saddleback was significantly less friendly territory for Obama than a Call to Renewal gathering. The audience at Warren's congregation consisted largely of church members who had made donations in order to secure a seat. Warren had suggested that he would steer away from cultural issues during the forum, but his questions ultimately leaned more toward gay marriage and abortion than poverty and climate change. Moreover, like most national Republicans, McCain understood how to speak about life issues, and he seized the chance to remind socially conservative evangelicals of why they usually voted for the GOP. McCain's generic profession of Christian faith made him hardly less pious than the beloved Ronald Reagan. Overall, though, the 2008 GOP nominee was not as deft as Reagan, George W. Bush, or even George H. W. Bush in dealing with conservative evangelicals and Catholics. He had sat out the earlier Messiah forum, despite its location in a swing state.[22]

By contrast, Obama had a remarkable ability to attract otherwise right-leaning evangelicals and Catholics who suffered from Bush fatigue. Like Jimmy Carter, he could employ an evangelical tone without supporting specifically evangelical policies. Obama's campaign skills were more comparable to those of Bill Clinton, however. The Illinois senator was as strong a supporter of abortion rights as Clinton or any Democratic nominee since Carter. Three decades into the alliance of the pro-life movement and the Republican Party, however, *Roe v. Wade* remained the law of the land. Obama, some pro-life moderates reasoned, was at least willing to talk with them. The resulting goodwill helped him to survive the worst crisis of his primary campaign, the controversy surrounding revelations of past sermons by Jeremiah Wright in which the reverend embraced conspiracy theories and uttered the incendiary rhetorical lines "Not God *bless* America. God *damn* America." In one of the sermons in question, dating from 1993, Wright actually paraphrased a Tony Campolo speech criticizing Americans for tolerating global hunger. Wright had joined Campolo in supporting Jim Wallis's Call to Renewal back in 1995. The Wright flap was the most reported political news story over the first four months of 2008 and lingered well beyond Obama's narrow primary upset of Hillary Clinton.[23]

The evangelical left backed Obama in a manner not seen since Jesse Jackson in the 1980s or even George McGovern during the 1970s. Journalist and Beliefnet cofounder Steven Waldman, an influential chronicler of the God gap, now touted the emergence of the "Obamagelicals." They included an influential portion of the evangelical center, too—potential swing voters whom the Obama campaign targeted through a series of house parties and events at Christian colleges. Joel Hunter and a more reliably Democratic evangelical leader, Tony Campolo, helped to write abortion-reduction language into the party's platform. While supporting *Roe v. Wade* in no uncertain terms, the plank acknowledged the value of health care and education to "help reduce the number of unintended pregnancies and thereby also reduce the need for abortions." Hunter gave an invocation at the Democratic National Convention in Denver. Jim Wallis rang in the campaign year by heralding a

"Post–Religious Right America." He fantasized about "linking the tradition of Billy Graham with the tradition of Martin Luther King Jr." to create a new "Great Awakening." Wallis was something of a celebrity by 2008, albeit an ambivalent one. He continued to eschew political labels even as he led a proxy campaign for Obama. His message was unstated but obvious: Electing a Democrat to replace Bush was the best way to sink the Christian Right's ship. In April 2008, Sojourners held a 10,000-strong "Justice Revival" at the Vineyard Church of Columbus, Ohio. Other progressive evangelicals were more explicit in their partisan support for Obama and his party. Liberal activist Mara Vanderslice founded the Matthew 25 Network, a political action committee that spent $500,000 on Christian radio advertisements in strategic states. Brian McLaren, a Matthew 25 Network supporter, posted a five-part explanation of his decision to vote for Obama and urged readers to follow his lead.[24]

Evangelical progressives saw 2008 as a critical election, a sign that younger evangelicals were freeing themselves from the yoke of Republican affiliation. Obama's convincing election victory, wrote one enthusiastic theologian, portended "the birth of a new prophetic evangelical politics" to replace the older "evangelical warrior politics." Despite having supported the winning presidential candidate, however, most progressive evangelicals were not eager to turn Sojourners into the Moral Majority. Randall Balmer hoped that evangelicals would "position themselves once again at the margins of society." The election had helped to overturn the reigning evangelical paradigm, freeing evangelicals to go back to being faithful.[25]

As president, Obama made a similar calculation about the limits of evangelical left politics. Support from progressive evangelicals and select moderates had assisted his efforts to look faith-friendly and protected him from attacks by the much larger forces on the evangelical right. In terms of evangelical politics, though, the analogy between 1980 and 2008 was an imperfect one. A significant evangelical shift toward the Democratic Party was not in the offing. A more feasible goal for Obama was to stay on civil terms with the broad swath of evangelical voters. Rick Warren, not Jim Wallis, was of use toward that end. Obama invited Warren to deliver the invocation at his inauguration, a move in keeping with his campaign theme of moving beyond conventional political labels. In the inaugural address, Obama quoted the Apostle Paul on the need "to set aside childish things." Warren likewise linked his presence at the inauguration with the larger cause of promoting "civility in America." Still, the Warren invitation failed to transcend the culture wars. As progressive critics of the invitation noted, he had supported Proposition 8, a successful 2008 initiative to amend California's constitution to ban legal recognition of gay marriages. In his prayer, Warren violated the supposed convention of invoking the Judeo-Christian God, rather than the Christian Jesus. Franklin Graham had crossed this line back in 2001, as had others before him. His father, Billy Graham, sent Warren the Homburg hat that he had worn for past inaugurations, literally passing the cap to one of his many presumed successors. "It's your turn, Rick," the enclosed note read. "It's your hat now."[26]

In office, Obama made a number of moves to engage his allies on the evangelical left and center. He did so, however, in a low-key way that opened him up to criticism from pundits and activists who doubted his religious sincerity and even his Christian faith. Jim Wallis and Joel Hunter were among the five pastors with whom the president regularly consulted. Obama nominated Francis Collins, an outspoken evangelical Christian, to lead the National Institutes of Health. The former head of the Human Genome Project, Collins was on record as calling for "a truce in the escalating war between science and spirit." Obama kept Bush's faith-based office, renaming it the White House Office of Faith-Based and Neighborhood Partnerships. Joshua DuBois served as director, with Mara Vanderslice as a chief aide. Hunter, Wallis, and former Southern Baptist Convention president Frank Page served on the advisory council. As a result of the 2009 stimulus legislation, Obama kept pace with Bush-era funding for faith-based organizations. While campaigning, Obama had pledged to lift Bush's executive order exempting faith-based funding recipients from federal bans on religious discrimination in hiring. Campolo and Wallis opposed the idea and joined conservatives in supporting protections for what they term "co-religionist hiring." At the end of Obama's first term, the exemption remained intact.[27]

The Christian Right was much too institutionally entrenched to disappear, of course—a fact evident even in November 2008. On an obvious level, though, its forces seemed in disarray heading toward the campaign. Two Christian Right patriarchs, Jerry Falwell and D. James Kennedy, had recently passed away, and Bush's popularity was at its nadir. Moreover, no consensus evangelical right candidate existed for 2008. Mike Huckabee, an ordained Southern Baptist minister and a strong social conservative, received surprisingly little support from evangelical elites. Pat Robertson curiously endorsed former New York City mayor Rudy Giuliani, the most socially liberal of the major GOP contenders. In the end, John McCain, arguably the least evangelical-friendly of the candidates, got the nomination. Eager to win, he was not about to reprise his "agents of intolerance" speech of 2000. In selecting the obscure Alaska governor Sarah Palin as his running mate, McCain chose someone whose cultural ties to grassroots evangelicalism equaled and perhaps exceeded those of George W. Bush. Palin was yet another evangelical who operated outside the organizational parameters of the Christian Right. Despite two years of media hype about the evangelical left, evangelical voters themselves clearly remained a reliably Republican bloc in 2008. John McCain received 73 percent of the white evangelical vote, according to the Pew Research Center, with Obama taking 26 percent—a five-point jump from John Kerry's performance in 2004.[28]

The evangelical right did not take the Obama presidency sitting down. James Dobson published a "Letter from 2012 in Obama's America," warning of a future in which same-sex marriage was legal in every state, abortion more accessible than ever, and homeschooling outlawed. Ralph Reed resurfaced as a defender of the religious liberties that the Obama presidency purportedly threatened. "The Obama administration better be careful," Franklin Graham cryptically declared in a 2010 *Newsweek* interview. "Millions of evangelical Christians voted for him in the last election." Graham failed to express much outrage at the persistent and, by 2009 and 2010, growing misbelief that the president was a stealth Muslim. To the contrary, he occasionally perpetuated the rumor. When a backlash against Obama took shape in the form of the Tea Party movement, it was touted for prioritizing economic libertarianism over social conservatism. Still, many prominent Tea Party supporters moved in the orbit of a Christian Right that had grown increasingly ecumenical, if only out of political necessity. Talk-show celebrity Glenn Beck, for example, was a convert to Mormonism. His huge "Restoring Honor" rally of 2010—held on the National Mall on the anniversary of the 1963 civil rights march—resembled a megachurch service. A year earlier, in 2009, the Manhattan Declaration further enshrined the alliance between conservative evangelicals and Catholics on matters of family planning, end-of-life care, and religious liberty. Charles Colson, who passed away in 2012, helped to draft the declaration. In his last public address, Colson attacked the Obama administration's policy of requiring most health insurance plans to fully cover contraception. The policy, Colson charged, was but "the latest manifestation of a growing hostility to Christianity."[29]

It remained to be seen, then, whether the pragmatism of Rick Warren and other prominent evangelicals who belatedly recognized the limits of Bush's faith-based politics represented a substantial departure from the alliance of born-again power brokers with the GOP. The evangelical right no longer monopolized popular impressions of evangelical public engagement. Yet few signs pointed to a wholesale "Great Reversal" that would favor the evangelical left.

BORN AGAIN, AGAIN

By 2012, the Age of Evangelicalism was winding down. It remained unclear, however, whether evangelicalism was waving or drowning in the sea of public influence. Evangelical and Catholic conservatives remained a powerful force in the Republican Party, although they spoke for a shrinking share of the American population. GOP primary candidate Rick Santorum, a Catholic who spliced his speeches with dominionist notes, appealed largely to evangelical voters. He lost to a Mormon opponent, erstwhile moderate Mitt Romney, who followed the lead of previous GOP nominee John McCain by traveling in penitent fashion to speak at Liberty University, "the spiritual heart of the conservative movement." Romney also retraced McCain's path to Billy Graham's North Carolina home for a mid-October visit. Meanwhile, the Billy Graham Evangelistic Association (run by enthusiastic Romney booster Franklin Graham) removed from its website a reference to Mormonism as a cult, stating a desire to avoid "a theological debate about something that has become politicized during this campaign." The elder Graham soon appeared in newspaper advertisements urging Americans to back "candidates who base their decisions on biblical principles," including "the sanctity of life" and "the biblical definition of marriage." Religious liberty was the most prominent faith-based issue of 2012, however. Catholic bishops vigorously attacked the Obama administration over mandatory contraception coverage. Rick Warren scheduled another "civil forum" for the presidential nominees, but he soon canceled it, citing the campaign's lack of civility. In doing so, Warren criticized Obama for not adequately supporting religious freedom. Ralph Reed, who remained a media magnet, headed up a lucrative, if ultimately outgunned, get-out-the-vote operation. While the purported "Mormon moment" and the growing partisanship of Catholic bishops made the Christian Right look more ecumenical than ever, evangelicals clearly retained the rhetorical upper hand. Brief spectacles aside, though, even they rarely made headline news during an election year when Michael Gerson, compassionate conservative par excellence, chided his party for spouting "libertarian nonsense."[1]

President Obama did not advance an evangelical strategy during his successful 2012 campaign. The symbolic cachet of taking God back from the Christian Right had diminished during his four years in office. For that reason alone, Obama did not need to court moderate and progressive evangelicals for his second run. He campaigned as an unabashed social liberal. To be sure, his ministerial advisers described the president as "born again" and noted his spiritual growth while in office.[2] But neither Obama nor Romney could muster a faith story that fit comfortably within an evangelical narrative. On obvious levels, they both spoke to the nation's dynamic religious pluralism, even if they balked at celebrating that fact.

If the 2008 election demonstrated the limits of the evangelical right, then 2012 suggested the waning salience of evangelical politics as a whole. Evangelicalism barely surfaced in the postelection spin cycle. A month before the election, the Pew Forum on Religion and Public Life published statistics indicating that the United States was no longer a majority Protestant nation. As earlier studies had revealed, religiously unaffiliated "nones" composed 20 percent of the population. Commentators continued to characterize the "nones" as a reaction to the earlier prominence of the Christian Right. Around the same time, Sojourners released a survey suggesting that young evangelicals were not the tools of any political party, even if a majority of them still leaned Republican. Four years removed from the jubilant tone of the 2008 campaign, Sojourners was content to celebrate the relative decline of the "culture wars." In 2013, Jim Wallis followed President Obama and most Democratic Party leaders in stating his support for same-sex marriage. He argued that the larger issue was strengthening the institution of marriage itself.[3] Evangelicalism was unlikely to remain the standard or the foil it had been since the 1970s.

Evangelicals and evangelical observers sometimes still acted like it was 1976, however. Born-again Christianity now lacked the explanatory punch it had possessed back then, when old-time faith managed to look like a new force in American politics and culture. Yet so many words about evangelicalism remained the same. Articles reconsidered its usefulness for a new century. Scholars furthered the evangelical left's project of expanding the genealogy of American evangelicalism. The term "new evangelicals" resurfaced as evangelical centrists sought to resist new forms of the old fundamentalism. Essays appeared touting "a comeback of the 'evangelical mind.'" Partnerships and manifestos abounded. Some talked of a "new Christian convergence" on the religious left, while others debated whether the Christian Right still existed. A prestigious magazine profiled the American Family Association, the latest candidate for the most-influential Christian Right group despite the fact that it had been around since 1977. A newly disgruntled ex-GOP insider published a book lamenting the party's captivity to "politicized religious fundamentalism." Liberals complained when lazy journalists conflated "Christian" with evangelical, a move one writer saw as akin to having Hasidic Jews stand in for the entire faith. Christians on the left generally declined to label themselves, period. Through it all, evangelical popular culture kept pulsing, making Christian celebrities appear much more exotic than they actually were. A still-recovering Ted Haggard wound up on the reality television show *Celebrity Wife Swap*, while National Football League quarterback Tim Tebow, a missionary kid and homeschooling product, gained notoriety for his end-zone genuflections. Finally, the search for the next Billy Graham continued ad infinitum.[4]

In 2008, a group of elite evangelicals, largely moderate by inclination, came together to reassert a theological understanding of the label "evangelical." It should be a proper noun, stated "An Evangelical Manifesto," to be capitalized, not dangled as a modifier. The desire to disaggregate "evangelical" from the very culture that had given it resonance was understandable, coming from religious leaders weary of spectacles and wary of stereotypes. Numerous Americans—left, right, and center—no doubt shared their fatigue and frustration. Evangelicalism was bound to lose its elasticity at some point, even if a proper noun would likely not suffice to vanquish the preceding four decades. The desire to make all things new was itself nothing new. Yet it seemed especially poignant to imagine that evangelicalism itself could be born again.

NOTES

INTRODUCTION

1. Alan Wolfe, *The Transformation of American Religion: How We Actually Live Our Faith* (New York: New Press, 2003), 36.
2. James Sturdivant, "Focusing on Faith," *Books Business*, May 2007, 22–25; Terry Mattingly, "Why We're Here," Get Religion blog, http://www.patheos.com/blogs/getreligion/why-were-here/.
3. Steven P. Miller, "Evangelicalism—the End of an Era?" History News Network, May 17, 2009, http://hnn.us/node/82628.
4. I am indebted to Professor Leigh Schmidt and the participants in the 2012–2013 Danforth Center on Religion and Politics Colloquium for suggesting the term "discursive sway" to characterize the influence of evangelicalism in recent American history.
5. Notable recent histories covering post-1970 conservative evangelicalism, the evangelical left, and/or evangelical thought include Darren Dochuk, *From Bible Belt to Sunbelt: Plain-folk Religion, Grassroots Politics, and the Rise of Evangelical Conservatism* (New York: W. W. Norton, 2010); Seth Dowland, "Defending Manhood: Gender, Social Order, and the Rise of the Christian Right in the South, 1965–1995" (Ph.D. dissertation, Duke University, 2007); J. Brooks Flippen, *Jimmy Carter, the Politics of Family, and the Rise of the Religious Right* (Athens: University of Georgia Press, 2010); Brantley Gasaway, "An Alternative Soul of Politics: The Rise of Contemporary Progressive Evangelicalism" (Ph.D. dissertation, University of North Carolina, 2008); Darren Grem, "The Blessings of Business: Corporate America and Conservative Evangelicalism in the Sunbelt Age, 1945–2000" (Ph.D. dissertation, University of Georgia, 2010); Eileen Luhr, *Witnessing Suburbia: Conservatives and Christian Youth Culture* (Berkeley: University of California Press, 2009); Bethany Moreton, *To Serve God and Wal-Mart: The Making of Christian Free Enterprise* (Cambridge, MA: Harvard University Press, 2009); Jeff Sharlet, *The Family: The Secret Fundamentalism at the Heart of American Power* (New York:

HarperCollins, 2008); Axel R. Schäfer, *Countercultural Conservatives: American Evangelicalism from the Postwar Revival to the New Christian Right* (Madison: University of Wisconsin Press, 2011); Randall J. Stephens and Karl W. Giberson, *The Anointed: Evangelical Truth in a Secular Age* (Cambridge, MA: The Belknap Press of Harvard University, 2011); David R. Swartz, *Moral Minority: The Evangelical Left in an Age of Conservatism* (Philadelphia: University of Pennsylvania Press, 2012); John G. Turner, *Bill Bright and Campus Crusade for Christ: The Renewal of Evangelicalism in Postwar America* (Chapel Hill: University of North Carolina Press, 2008); Daniel K. Williams, *God's Own Party: The Making of the Christian Right* (New York: Oxford University Press, 2010); and Molly Worthen, *Apostles of Reason: The Crisis of Authority in American Evangelicalism* (New York: Oxford University Press, 2013).

6. Amy Johnson Frykholm, *Rapture Culture: "Left Behind" in Evangelical America* (New York: Oxford University Press, 2004), 183; Jon Butler, "Jack-in-the-Box Faith: The Religion Problem in Modern American History," *Journal of American History* 90, no. 4 (March 2004): 1357–1378; Stephens and Giberson, *The Anointed*, 10; James Davison Hunter, "The Evangelical Worldview since 1890," 51 (Hunter was summarizing Martin Marty's analysis), in Richard John Neuhaus and Michael Cromartie, eds., *Piety and Politics: Evangelicals and Fundamentalists Confront the World* (Washington, DC: Ethics and Public Policy Center, 1987).

CHAPTER 1

1. Erling Jorstad, *Popular Religion in America: The Evangelical Voice* (Westport, CT: Greenwood, 1993), 27; Kenneth L. Woodward, "Born Again! The Year of the Evangelicals," *Newsweek*, October 25, 1976, 69, 68; "Back to that Oldtime Religion," *Time*, December 26, 1977.

2. Richard Quebedeaux, *The Worldly Evangelicals* (San Francisco: Harper and Row, 1978), xi, 3; William G. McLoughlin, "Is There a Third Force in Christendom?" *Daedalus* 96, no. 1 (Winter 1967): 43–68; "Protestants: The Evangelical Undertow," *Time*, December 20, 1963.

3. "Man and Woman of the Year: The Middle Americans," *Time*, January 5, 1970. On Nixon, see Matthew D. Lassiter, *The Silent Majority: Suburban Politics in the Sunbelt South* (Princeton, NJ: Princeton University Press, 2006), 225–250; Robert Mason, *Richard Nixon and the Quest for a New Majority* (Chapel Hill: University of North Carolina Press, 2004); and Rick Perlstein, *Nixonland: The Rise of a President and the Fracturing of America* (New York: Scribner, 2008). On Nixon's "evangelical strategy," see Daniel K. Williams, *God's Own Party: The Making of the Christian Right* (New York: Oxford University Press, 2010), 89–103.

4. John Herbers, "Thousands Voice Faith in America at Capital Rally," *New York Times*, July 5, 1970; John Herbers, "Graham Defends Patriotic Rally," *New York Times*, July 3, 1970; Lowell D. Streiker and Gerald S. Strober, *Religion and the New Majority:*

Billy Graham, Middle America, and the Politics of the 70s (New York: Association Press, 1972), 74–77; "Rennie Davis Scores Honor America Day," *New York Times*, June 25, 1970.

5. Wendy L. Wall, *Inventing the "American Way": The Politics of Consensus from the New Deal to the Civil Rights Movement* (New York: Oxford University Press, 2008), 5, 9–10, 78; William Inboden, *Religion and American Foreign Policy, 1945–1960: The Soul of Containment* (New York: Cambridge University Press, 2008); Jeff Sharlet, *The Family: The Secret Fundamentalism at the Heart of American Power* (New York: HarperCollins, 2008), 180–204; Angela M. Lahr, *Millennial Dreams and Apocalyptic Nightmares: The Cold War Origins of Political Evangelicalism* (New York: Oxford University Press, 2007), 200; William Martin, *A Prophet with Honor: The Billy Graham Story* (New York: William Morrow, 1991), 143. See also Axel R. Schäfer, "The Cold War State and the Resurgence of Evangelicalism: A Study of the Public Funding of Religion since 1945," *Radical History Review* 99 (Fall 2007): 19–50.

6. Robert N. Bellah, "Civil Religion in America," *Daedalus* 96, no. 1 (Winter 1967): 1–21 (quoted on p. 18); Robert N. Bellah, "Habits of the Heart: Implications for Religion," February 21, 1986, lecture (St. Mark's Catholic Church, Isla Vista, CA), http://robertbellah.com/lectures_5.htm; Robert James Eells, "Mark O. Hatfield and the Search for an Evangelical Politics" (Ph.D. dissertation, University of New Mexico, 1976), 16; "Rennie Davis Scores Honor America Day"; "Graham Defends Patriotic Rally"; "July 4 Group Bars Radicals' Demands," *New York Times*, June 27, 1970.

7. Streiker and Strober, *Religion and the New Majority*, 189; Kevin P. Phillips, *The Emerging Republican Majority* (New Rochelle, NY: Arlington House, 1969); Richard Scammon and Ben J. Wattenberg, *The Real Majority* (New York: Coward-McCann, 1970); Herbers, "Thousands Voice Faith in America"; David R. Swartz, "Left Behind: The Evangelical Left and the Limits of Evangelical Politics, 1965–1988" (Ph.D. dissertation, University of Notre Dame, 2008), 222.

8. J. David Fairbanks, "The Politics of *Christianity Today: 1956–1986*," in Corwin E. Smidt, ed., *Contemporary Evangelical Political Involvement: An Analysis and Assessment* (Lanham, MD: University Press of America, 1989), 35; Steven P. Miller, *Billy Graham and the Rise of the Republican South* (Philadelphia: University of Pennsylvania Press, 2009), 184–194; Robert Eells and Bartell Nyberg, *Lonely Walk: The Life of Senator Mark Hatfield* (Chappaqua, NY: Christian Herald Books, 1979), 59–70, 81–83, 127; Mark O. Hatfield (as told to Diane N. Solomon), *Against the Grain: Reflections of a Rebel Republican* (Ashland, OR: White Cloud, 2001), 165; "Senators Observe a Day of Prayer; Split on 'Humility,'" *New York Times*, May 1, 1974; Darren Dochuk, *From the Bible Belt to the Sunbelt: Plain-Folk Religion, Grassroots Politics, and the Rise of Evangelical Conservatism* (New York: W. W. Norton, 2010), 355; "The New Evangelicals," *Newsweek*, May 6, 1974, 86. The conversation between Billy Graham and Richard Nixon, February 21, 1973, is at

Nixon Presidential Library and Museum, Tape 43, Conversation 161, http://nixon.archives.gov/forresearchers/find/tapes/tape043/043-161.mp3.

9. David John Marley, *Pat Robertson: An American Life* (Lanham, MD: Rowman Littlefield, 2007), 40; John B. Anderson, *Vision and Betrayal in America* (Waco, TX: Word, 1975), 110, 111, 118.

10. Garry Wills, "'Born Again' Politics," *New York Times*, August 1, 1976; Charles Colson, *Born Again* (Old Tappan, NJ: Revell, 1976); "Decisions for Christ," *Newsweek*, October 25, 1976, 75; James C. Hefley and Edward E. Plowman, *Washington: Christians in the Corridors of Power* (Wheaton, IL: Tyndale House, 1975), 37–58; Carol Flake, *Redemptorama: Culture, Politics, and the New Evangelicalism* (New York: Penguin, 1984), 162.

11. Howard Brick, "Optimism of the Mind: Imagining Postindustrial Society in the 1960s and 1970s," *American Quarterly* 44, no. 3 (September 1992): 348–380; Daniel Bell, *The Coming of Post-Industrial Society: A Venture in Social Forecasting* (New York: Basic, 1973); Seymour Martin Lipset, ed., *The Third Century: America as a Post-Industrial Society* (Stanford, CA: Hoover Institution Press, 1979); Alvin Toffler, *Future Shock* (New York: Random House, 1970), 3; Alvin Toffler, ed., *The Futurists* (New York: Random House, 1972); Matthew Connelly, "Future Shock: The End of the World as They Knew It," in Niall Ferguson et al., eds., *The Shock of the Global: The 1970s in Perspective* (Cambridge, MA: Belknap Press of Harvard University Press, 2010), 341–343.

12. Peter L. Berger, *Adventures of an Accidental Sociologist: How to Explain the World without Becoming a Bore* (Amherst, NY: Prometheus, 2011), 72, 135–140; Linda Woodhead, "Introduction" (1–7) and Steve Bruce, "The Curious Case of Unnecessary Recantation: Berger and Secularization" (87–100), both in Linda Woodhead, ed., with Paul Heelas and David Martin, *Peter Berger and the Study of Religion* (London: Routledge, 2001); Alan Petigny, *The Permissive Society: America, 1941–1965* (New York: Cambridge University Press, 2009), 55; Robert T. Handy, *A Christian America: Protestant Hopes and Historical Realities*, 2nd edition (New York: Oxford University Press, 1984), 201; Harvey Cox, *The Secular City: Secularization and Urbanization in Theological Perspective* (New York: Macmillan, 1965); Peter L. Berger, "A Call for Authority in the Christian Community," *Christian Century*, October 27, 1971, 1257–1263 (italics in original); "Secularism in Retreat," *National Interest* 43 (Winter 1996/97); "The Hartford Heresies," *Time*, February 10, 1975.

13. Dean M. Kelley, *Why Conservative Churches Are Growing: A Study in Sociology of Religion* (New York: Harper and Row, 1972), viii, xii, 37; Dean M. Kelley, *Why Conservative Churches Are Growing*, paperback edition (New York: Harper and Row, 1977), viii; Gustav Niebuhr, "Dean Kelley, 70, Advocate for Religious Freedom, Dies," *New York Times*, May 14, 1997; Jeffrey K. Hadden, *The Gathering Storm in the Churches* (Garden City, NY: Doubleday, 1969); Richard John Neuhaus, *Time toward Home: The American Experiment as Revelation* (New York:

Seabury, 1975), 9–21; Pamela D. H. Cochran, *Evangelical Feminism: A History* (New York: New York University Press, 2005), 144–145; David Gates, "Of Profits and Prophesies," *Newsweek*, December 27, 1982.

14. Richard Quebedeaux, *The New Charismatics II: How a Christian Renewal Movement Became Part of the American Religious Mainstream* (San Francisco: Harper and Row, 1983), 237–238; Dochuk, *From the Bible Belt to the Sunbelt*, 281–285; David W. Stowe, *No Sympathy for the Devil: Christian Pop Music and the Transformation of American Evangelicalism* (Chapel Hill: University of North Carolina Press, 2011), 121–123; David Edwin Harrell Jr., *All Things Are Possible: The Healing and Charismatic Revivals in Modern America* (Bloomington: Indiana University Press, 1975), 3.

15. Ronald M. Enroth, Edward E. Ericson Jr., and C. Breckinridge Peters, *The Jesus People: Old-Time Religion in the Age of Aquarius* (Grand Rapids, MI: Eerdmans, 1972), 9; Robert S. Ellwood Jr., *One Way: The Jesus Movement and Its Meaning* (Englewood Cliffs, NJ: Prentice-Hall, 1973), 118–120, 59; Lisa McGirr, *Suburban Warriors: The Origins of the New American Right* (Princeton, NJ: Princeton University Press, 2001), 243–249; Dochuk, *From Bible Belt to Sunbelt*, 313, 311, 282–283; Edward P. Plowman, *The Jesus Movement in America: Accounts of Christian Revolutionaries in Action* (Elgin, IL: David C. Cook, 1971), 109–110; David Wilkerson, with John Sherill and Elizabeth Sherill, *The Cross and the Switchblade* (New York: B. Geis Associates, 1963); *The Cross and the Switchblade* (Worcester, PA: Gateway Films, 1970); Robert Booth Fowler, *A New Engagement: Evangelical Political Thought, 1966–1976* (Grand Rapids, MI: Eerdmans, 1982), 148–150; Larry Eskridge, *God's Forever Family: The Jesus People Movement in America* (New York: Oxford University Press, 2013), 128–132.

16. Two Brothers from Berkeley, *Letters to Street Christians* (Grand Rapids, MI: Zondervan, 1971), 62; Jerry Halliday, *Spaced Out and Gathered In: A Sort of an Autobiography of a Jesus Freak* (Old Tappan, NJ: Fleming H. Revell, 1972), 22–28, 11, 13, 61–99; Ellwood, *One Way*, 55; Heather Hendershot, *Shaking the World for Jesus: Media and Conservative Evangelical Culture* (Chicago: University of Chicago Press, 2004), 21–22; William D. Romanowski, "Roll Over Beethoven, Tell Martin Luther the News: American Evangelicals and Rock Music," *The Journal of American Culture* 15, no. 3 (September 1992): 79; Larry Eskridge, "'One Way': Billy Graham, the Jesus Generation, and the Idea of an Evangelical Youth Culture," *Church History* 67, no. 1 (March 1998): 84–85, 102–103; John G. Turner, *Bill Bright and Campus Crusade for Christ: The Renewal of Evangelicalism in Postwar America* (Chapel Hill: University of North Carolina Press, 2008), 138–146; Stowe, *No Sympathy for the Devil*, 165–166; Eskridge, *God's Forever Family*, 177.

17. Paul Baker, *Why Should the Devil Have All the Good Music? Jesus Music—Where It Began, Where It Is, and Where It Is Going* (Waco, TX: Word, 1979), 47–50, 207, 131–134; Stowe, *No Sympathy for the Devil*, 47, 118; Plowman, *The Jesus Movement in America*, 109; "The New Rebel Cry: Jesus Is Coming!" *Time*, June 21, 1971.

18. Amanda Porterfield, *The Transformation of American Religion: The Story of a Late-Twentieth-Century Awakening* (New York: Oxford University Press, 2001), 114; Larry Christenson, *A Charismatic Approach to Social Action* (Minneapolis: Bethany Fellowship, 1974), 74–75; Stephen A. Kent, *From Slogans to Mantras: Social Protest and Religious Conversion in the Late Vietnam Era* (Syracuse, NY: Syracuse University Press, 2001), 48–49, 35–36, 136–142; Kevin Mattson, *"What the Heck Are You Up to, Mr. President?": Jimmy Carter, America's "Malaise," and the Speech That Should Have Changed the Country* (New York: Bloomsbury, 2009), 36; Sara Davidson, "The Rush for Instant Salvation," *Harper's*, July 1971, 40.

19. Garry Wills, "Measuring Mystical Experience," *Meriden* (CT) *Morning Record*, July 26, 1976.

20. George H. Gallup, *The Gallup Poll: Public Opinion, 1972–1977, Volume Two, 1976–1977* (Wilmington, DE: Scholarly Resources, 1978), 859–862; *Religion in America: The Gallup Opinion Index, 1977–78*, Report No. 145 (Princeton, NJ: American Institute of Public Opinion, 1978), 41–42; D. Michael Lindsay, *Faith in the Halls of Power: How Evangelicals Joined the American Elite* (New York: Oxford University Press, 2007), xi; Woodward, "Born Again!" 68–69; *George Gallup Polls America on Religion* (Carol Stream, IL: *Christianity Today*, 1981), front matter, 2–3, 9; *Religion in America: The Gallup Opinion Index, 1976*, Report No. 130 (Princeton, NJ: American Institute of Public Opinion, 1976), 1–5; "Counting Souls," *Time*, October 4, 1976; Tim LaHaye, *The Battle for the Mind* (Old Tappan, NJ: Fleming H. Revell, 1980), 10; Jerry Falwell, *Listen, America!* (Garden City, NY: Doubleday, 1980), xi; R. Stephen Warner, "Theoretical Barriers to the Understanding of Evangelical Christianity," *Sociological Analysis* 40, no. 1 (1979): 1–9; Timothy Jones et al., "George Gallup Jr.: The Pollster Saint [updated]," *Christianity Today* blog, November 23, 2011, http://blog.christianitytoday.com/ctliveblog/archives/2011/11/the_pollster_sa.html; Kate Zernike, "George Gallup Jr., 81; Expanded Polling Firm," *New York Times*, November 23, 2011. Interestingly enough, Gallup probably was not the first person to describe 1976 as "Year of the Evangelical." *Christianity Today*'s managing editor, David Kucharsky, employed the phrase in July 1976, although the words did not appear in print until later that year. See David Kucharsky, *The Man from Plains: The Mind and Spirit of Jimmy Carter* (San Francisco: Harper and Row, 1976), vii, ix; and David Kucharsky, "The Year of the Evangelical," *Christianity Today*, October 22, 1976, 12–13.

21. "Back to That Oldtime Religion"; Flake, *Redemptorama*, 106–113; Roger Staubach with Sam Blair and Bob St. John, *Staubach: First Down, Lifetime to Go* (Waco, TX: Word, 1974); Roger Staubach with Frank Luska, *Time Enough to Win* (Waco, TX: Word, 1980); John Powell, "Eric Clapton, In the Presence of the Lord," *Christianity Today* (web only), April 2008, http://www.christianitytoday.com/ct/2008/april-web-only/115-32.0.html; *Top Entertainers Are Born Again* (Carol Stream, IL: Creation House, 1977), 30–42.

22. Eldridge Cleaver, *Soul on Fire* (Waco, TX: Word, 1978), 210–212, 224–230, 177, 235–238; T. D. Allman, "The 'Re-birth' of Eldridge Cleaver," *New York Times*, January 16, 1977; John Kifner, "Eldridge Cleaver, Black Panther Who Became a G.O.P. Conservative, Is Dead at 62," *New York Times*, May 2, 1998; Dorothea Marvin Nyberg, "Militant for the Lord," *Christian Herald*, November 1978, 26; Donn Downing, "Ex-Panther Eldridge Cleaver: 'I Just Wish I Could Be Born Again Every Day,'" *People*, October 25, 1976, http://www.people.com/people/archive/article/0,20067024,00.html; Horacio Silva, "Radical Chic," *New York Times*, September 23, 2001.

23. Stowe, *No Sympathy for the Devil*, 220–237; Donald E. Miller, *Reinventing American Protestantism: Christianity in the New Millennium* (Berkeley: University of California Press, 1997), 46–51; *Inside Bob Dylan's Jesus Years: Busy Being Born...Again!* (Oaks, PA: MVD Visual/Highway 61 Entertainment, 2008); Robert Shelton, *No Direction Home: The Life and Music of Bob Dylan* (New York: Beach Tree/William Morrow, 1986), 487–490; Wesley G. Pippert, *An Ethics of News: A Reporter's Search for Truth* (Washington, DC: Georgetown University Press, 1989), 97.

24. "Brother's Presidency Shaped Ruth Stapleton's Life," *Washington Post*, May 6, 1977; Howard Norton and Bob Slosser, *The Miracle of Jimmy Carter* (Plainfield, NJ: Logos International, 1976), 34–36; Martin Schram, *Running for President 1976: The Carter Campaign* (New York: Stein and Day, 1977), 88; Kenneth L. Woodward, "Sister Ruth," *Newsweek*, July 17, 1978; Rusty Unger, "Elected Again," *Village Voice*, November 27, 1978, 22.

25. Larry Flynt (with Kenneth Ross), *An Unseemly Man* (Los Angeles: Dove, 1996), 163–166, 176; Tony Schwartz, "Hustling for the Lord," *Newsweek*, December 5, 1977; Rodney A. Smolla, *Jerry Falwell v. Larry Flynt: The First Amendment on Trial* (New York: St. Martin's Press, 1988), 39; James N. Baker, "Back to Hustling," *Newsweek*, December 18, 1978.

26. Flake, *Redemptorama*, 6; Christopher Lasch, *The Culture of Narcissism: American Life in an Age of Diminishing Expectations* (New York: Warner, 1979), 33; Tom Wolfe, "The 'Me' Decade and the Third Great Awakening," *New York*, August 23, 1976, http://www.nymag.com/news/features/45938/; Garry Wills, "What Religious Revival?" *Psychology Today*, April 1978, 74; Beth Bailey and David Farber, "Introduction," in Bailey and Farber, eds., *America in the 70s* (Lawrence: University Press of Kansas, 2004), 6. On the link between the therapeutic and recent evangelicalism, see Peter Clecak, *America's Quest for the Ideal Self: Dissent and Fulfillment in the 60s and 70s* (New York: Oxford University Press, 1983), 115–156; and Mark Shibley, *Resurgent Evangelicalism in the United States: Mapping Cultural Change since 1970* (Columbia: University of South Carolina Press, 1996), 4–5. Reflecting trends in American society as a whole, the evangelical version of the therapeutic turn began during the postwar years but became especially pronounced in the 1970s. See Randall J. Stephens and Karl W. Giberson, *The*

Anointed: Evangelical Truth in a Secular Age (Cambridge, MA: Belknap Press of Harvard University Press, 2011), 101–102.

27. Amy DeRogatis, "What Would Jesus Do? Sexuality and Salvation in Protestant Evangelical Sex Manuals, 1950s to the Present," *Church History* 74, no. 1 (March 2005): 98; Bruce Larson, *Ask Me to Dance* (Waco, TX: Word, 1972), 93.

28. Dochuk, *From Bible Belt to Sunbelt*, 351; DeRogatis, "What Would Jesus Do?" 106, 111, 112; Tim LaHaye and Beverly LaHaye, *The Act of Marriage: The Beauty of Sexual Love* (Grand Rapids, MI: Zondervan, 1976), 5, 30, 170, 213, 25, 61–65, 6–7; Robert J. Levin and Amy Levin, "Sexual Pleasure: The Surprising Preferences of 100,000 Women," *Redbook*, September 1975, 51–58.

29. Andy Taylor, "Marabel and Charlie Morgan: Being a *Total Woman* May Mean Love under the Dinner Table," *People*, April 7, 1975, http://www.people.com/people/archive/article/0,20065122,00.html; "The New Housewife Blues," *Time*, March 14, 1977; "Back to that Oldtime Religion"; Marabel Morgan, *The Total Woman* (Old Tappan, NJ: Fleming H. Revell, 1973), 180–181.

30. Morgan, *Total Woman*, 93–99, 118; Flake, *Redemptorama*, 67; Helen B. Andelin, *Fascinating Womanhood* (Santa Barbara, CA: Pacific Press, 1965), 115; "Total Fascination," *Time*, March 10, 1975; Fannie Flagg, *Fried Green Tomatoes at the Whistle-Stop Café* (New York: McGraw-Hill, 1988), 42–43; *Fried Green Tomatoes* (Universal City, CA: MCA Universal Home Video, 1992).

31. Morgan, *The Total Woman*, 18, 110; Marabel Morgan, *Total Joy* (Old Tappan, NJ: Fleming H. Revell, 1976), 90–93, 224n14; Fowler, *New Engagement*, 209; Flagg, *Fried Green Tomatoes*, 43; "Marabel Morgan: 'Preferring One Another,'" *Christianity Today*, September 10, 1976, 15.

32. DeRogatis, "What Would Jesus Do?" 128; "Marabel Morgan: 'Preferring One Another,'" 14; Joyce Maynard, "The Liberation of Total Woman," *New York Times Magazine*, September 28, 1975; Claire Safran, "Can the Total Woman 'Magic' Work for You?" *Redbook*, February 1976, 130; "Marabel and Charlie Morgan," *People*, April 7, 1975; Quebedeaux, *Worldly Evangelicals*, 77; David Harrington Watt, *A Transforming Faith: Explorations of Twentieth-Century American Evangelicalism* (New Brunswick, NJ: Rutgers University Press, 1991), 134; David R. Douglass, "*The Total Woman*: Totaled," *Moody Monthly*, September 1975, 102, 107.

33. Maynard, "The Liberation of Total Woman"; "Marabel Morgan: 'Preferring One Another,'" 12–13; Morgan, *Total Woman*, 11; "Marabel and Charlie Morgan"; Watt, *Transforming Faith*, 132; Randall Balmer, *Blessed Assurance: A History of Evangelicalism in America* (Boston: Beacon, 1999), 97; "The New Housewife Blues"; Matthew D. Lassiter, "Inventing Family Values," in Bruce J. Schulman and Julian Zelizer, eds., *Rightward Bound: Making America Conservative in the 1970s* (Cambridge, MA: Harvard University Press, 2008), 13–28.

34. James Dobson, *Dare to Discipline* (Wheaton, IL: Tyndale House, 1970), 13, 20, 26, 14; Ann Hulbert, *Raising America: Experts, Parents, and a Century of Advice*

about Children (New York: Knopf, 2003), 329; Petigny, *The Permissive Society*, 37–41; Dale Buss, *Family Man: The Biography of James Dobson* (Carol Stream, IL: Tyndale, 2005), 45, 72.

35. Edwin McDowell, "Publishers: A Matter of Faith," *New York Times*, April 6, 1980; "Religious Books," *New York Times*, April 6, 1980; Stella Dong, "Faith in Trade Houses," *New York Times*, April 11, 1982; "Paper Back Talk," *New York Times*, October 31, 1976; "Paper Back Talk," *New York Times*, November 7, 1976; Safran, "Can the Total Woman 'Magic' Work for You?" 91.

36. Hal Lindsey (with C. C. Carlson), *The Late Great Planet Earth* (Grand Rapids, MI: Zondervan, 1970), 18; Ray Walters, "Ten Years of Best Sellers," *New York Times*, December 30, 1979; Edward B. Fiske, "There Are Those Who Think It Is Imminent," *New York Times*, October 8, 1972; Melani McAlister, *Epic Encounters: Culture, Media, and U.S. Interests in the Middle East, 1945–2000* (Berkeley: University of California Press, 2001), 165–167.

37. George M. Marsden, *Fundamentalism and American Culture: The Shaping of Twentieth-Century Evangelicalism, 1870–1925* (New York: Oxford University Press, 1980), 48–55; Joel A. Carpenter, *Revive Us Again: The Reawakening of American Fundamentalism* (New York: Oxford University Press, 1997), 247–249; Lindsey, *Late Great Planet Earth*, 137, 43, 59, 82, 94, 98; John F. Walvoord, *Armageddon, Oil, and the Middle East Crisis: What the Bible Says about the Future of the Middle East and the End of Western Civilization* (Grand Rapids, MI: Zondervan, 1974); Caitlin Carenen, *The Fervent Embrace: Liberal Protestants, Evangelicals, and Israel* (New York: New York University Press, 2012), 141–145, 178; Paul Boyer, *When Time Shall Be No More: Prophecy Belief in Modern American Culture* (Cambridge, MA: Harvard University Press, 1992), 252.

38. Lindsey, *Late Great Planet Earth*, 64, 122; Ellwood, *One Way*, 90; McAlister, *Epic Encounters*, 166; Gershom Gorenberg, *The End of Days: Fundamentalism and the Struggle for the Temple Mount* (New York: Oxford University Press, 2002), 121–122; Curt Gentry, *The Last Days of the Late, Great State of California* (New York: G. P. Putnam's Sons, 1968); "The Deluge of Disastermania," *Time*, March 5, 1979; Lasch, *Culture of Narcissism*, 28; Phillip K. Jenkins, *Decade of Nightmares: The End of the Sixties and the Making of Eighties America* (New York: Oxford University Press, 2006), 84–85.

39. *The Late Great Planet Earth* (Robert Amram Films and RCR Productions/American Cinema, copyright 1976); "The Deluge of Disastermania"; Toffler, *Future Shock*; Boyer, *When Time Shall Be No More*, 5; Lindsey, *Late Great Planet Earth*, 95–96, 144, 184; Jenkins, *Decade of Nightmares*, 70–74; Turner, *Bill Bright*, 182; Plowman, *Jesus Movement*, 119–120.

40. Janet Maslin, "Film: A 'Planet' Doomed," *New York Times*, January 18, 1979; Mattson, *"What the Heck Are You Up to, Mr. President?"* 34, 88; *The Late Great Planet Earth* (film); Jeremy Rifkin with Ted Howard, *The Emerging Order: God in*

the *Age of Scarcity* (New York: G. P. Putnam's Sons, 1979), 211, xi; Alvin Toffler, *The Third Wave* (New York: William Morrow, 1980), 382–383, 415.

41. Quebedeaux, *Worldly Evangelicals*, 132; Nathan O. Hatch with Michael S. Hamilton, "Taking the Measure of the Evangelical Resurgence, 1942–1992," in D. G. Hart, ed., *Reckoning with the Past: Historical Essays on American Evangelicalism from the Institute for the Study of American Evangelicals* (Grand Rapids, MI: Baker, 1995), 406; Fowler, *New Engagement*, 2; Jon R. Stone, *On the Boundaries of American Evangelicalism: The Postwar Evangelical Coalition* (New York: St. Martin's Press, 1997); Donald G. Bloesch, *The Evangelical Renaissance* (Grand Rapids, MI: Eerdmans, 1973), 18; Harold Lindsell, *The Battle for the Bible* (Grand Rapids, MI: Zondervan, 1976), 139, 210; Robert K. Johnston, *Evangelicals at an Impasse: Biblical Authority in Practice* (Atlanta: John Knox Press, 1979), 122; Swartz, "Left Behind," 451, 104.

42. "The Top Ten Religious Stories: Evangelical Renaissance Key Event of 1976," *Eternity*, January 1977, 6–7.

43. Wesley Pippert, *Memo for 1976: Some Political Options* (Downers Grove, IL: InterVarsity, 1974), 105.

CHAPTER 2

1. James C. Hefley and Edward E. Plowman, *Washington: Christians in the Corridors of Power* (Wheaton, IL: Tyndale House, 1975), 195.

2. Claude A. Frazier, ed., *Politics and Religion Can Mix!* (Nashville, TN: Broadman Press, 1974), 98, 120, 91–94, 29, 19.

3. George McGovern, "The Politics of Hunger" (53–72); and Barry Goldwater, "The Politics of Morality" (75–95); both in John B. Anderson, ed., *Congress and Conscience* (Philadelphia: J. B. Lippincott, 1970). On Hart, see Garry Wills, *Under God: Religion and American Politics* (New York: Simon Schuster, 1990), 41–50.

4. Barrie Doyle, "Backing Their Man," *Christianity Today*, October 27, 1972, 38–39; "The Evangelical Vote," *Newsweek*, October 30, 1972, 93; Walden Howard to "Dear Friend" [1972], in Augustus Cerillo Jr. and Murray W. Dempster, eds., *Salt and Light: Evangelical Political Thought in Modern America* (Grand Rapids, MI: Baker, 1989), 149–151; recording of George McGovern speech at Wheaton College, October 11, 1972, http://espace.wheaton.edu/lr/a-sc/archives/ McGovern 1972. mp3; Jefferson Cowie, *Stayin' Alive: The 1970s and the Last Days of the Working Class* (New York: New Press, 2010), 120.

5. Lyman Kellstedt, John Green, Corwin Smidt, and James Guth, "Faith Transformed: Religion and American Politics from FDR to George W. Bush," in Mark A. Noll and Luke E. Harlow, eds., *Religion and American Politics: From the Colonial Period to the Present*, 2nd ed. (New York: Oxford University Press, 2007), 273; Wesley Pippert, *Memo for 1976: Some Political Options* (Downers Grove, IL: InterVarsity, 1974), 15.

6. Donald G. Bloesch, *The Evangelical Renaissance* (Grand Rapids, MI: Eerdmans, 1973), 26. The most comprehensive works on the evangelical left are David R. Swartz, *Moral Minority: The Evangelical Left in an Age of Conservatism* (Philadelphia: University of Pennsylvania Press, 2012); and Brantley W. Gasaway, "An Alternative Soul of Politics: The Rise of Contemporary Progressive Evangelicalism" (Ph.D. dissertation, University of North Carolina, 2008).

7. Carl F. H. Henry, *The Uneasy Conscience of Modern Fundamentalism* (Grand Rapids, MI: Eerdmans, 2003 [1947]); Carl F. H. Henry, "Open Letter to President Ford," *Eternity*, January 1976, 23; Perry Bush, "Anabaptism Born Again: Mennonites, New Evangelicals, and the Search for a Useable Past, 1950–1980," *Fides et Historia* 25 (Winter/Spring 1993): 26–47; Donald W. Dayton, *Discovering an Evangelical Heritage* (San Francisco: Harper and Row, 1976); Clark Pinnock, "Election Reflections," *Post-American* (January–February 1973): 1; Richard Quebedeaux, *The Young Evangelicals: Revolution in Orthodoxy* (San Francisco: Harper and Row, 1974); David O. Moberg, *The Great Reversal: Evangelism and Social Concern*, revised edition (Philadelphia: J. B. Lippincott, 1977), 11; Richard V. Pierard, *The Unequal Yoke: Evangelical Christianity and Political Conservatism* (Philadelphia: J. B. Lippincott, 1970).

8. Ronald J. Sider, "Introduction: An Historic Movement for Biblical Social Concern," in Sider, ed., *The Chicago Declaration* (Carol Stream, IL: Creation House, 1974), 24, 3, 34, 12, 19, 31, 41; David R. Swartz, "Left Behind: The Evangelical Left and the Limits of Evangelical Politics, 1965–1988" (Ph.D. dissertation, University of Notre Dame, 2008), 388–389; Harold O. J. Brown, "Restive Evangelicals," *National Review*, February 15, 1974, 192–194. See also "The New Evangelicals," *Newsweek*, May 6, 1974, 86.

9. Robert Booth Fowler, *A New Engagement: Evangelical Political Thought, 1966–1976* (Grand Rapids, MI: Eerdmans, 1982), 155–162; Swartz, "Left Behind," 415–487; Ron Potter, "Thinking for Ourselves," *The Other Side* (July–August 1975): 2–3; Larry Christenson, *A Charismatic Approach to Social Action* (Minneapolis, MN: Bethany Fellowship, 1974); Perry C. Cotham, *Politics, Americanism, and Christianity* (Grand Rapids, MI: Baker, 1976); Daniel R. Grant, *The Christian and Politics* (Nashville, TN: Broadman, 1968); Paul B. Henry, *Politics for Evangelicals* (Valley Forge, PA: Judson Press, 1974); Robert D. Linder and Richard V. Pierard, *Politics: A Case for Christian Action* (Downers Grove, IL: InterVarsity, 1973); Richard J. Mouw, *Political Evangelism* (Grand Rapids, MI: Eerdmans, 1973).

10. Ronald J. Sider, *Rich Christians in an Age of Hunger: A Biblical Study* (Downers Grove, IL: InterVarsity, 1977), 205, 13; Hal Lindsey with C. C. Carlson, *Satan Is Alive and Well on Planet Earth* (Grand Rapids, MI: Zondervan, 1972); "Sojourners," *Post American* (October–November 1975): 3; William Stringfellow, "Babylon," *Post American* (January–February 1973): 8–9; Jim Wallis, *An Agenda for a Biblical People* (New York: Harper and Row, 1976); Quebedeaux, *The Young Evangelicals*, iii;

"Biblical Feminism Probed at Conference," *Eternity* (February 1976): 8–9; Seth Dowland, "'Family Values' and the Formation of a Christian Right Agenda," *Church History* 78, no. 3 (September 2009): 618; Letha Scanzoni and Nancy Hardesty, *All We're Meant to Be: A Biblical Approach to Women's Liberation* (Waco, TX: Word, 1974), 143; Gasaway, "An Alternative Soul of Politics," 173–175; Pamela D. H. Cochran, *Evangelical Feminism: A History* (New York: New York University Press, 2005), 11–76; Richard Quebedeaux, *The Worldly Evangelicals* (San Francisco: Harper and Row, 1978), 128–131.

11. Edward D. Berkowitz, *Something Happened: A Political and Cultural Overview of the Seventies* (New York: Columbia University Press, 2006), 87; Pierard, *The Unequal Yoke*, 10.

12. "The God Network in Washington," *Time*, August 26, 1974; Haynes Johnson, *Sleepwalking through History: America in the Reagan Years* (New York: Norton, 1991 [2003 paperback edition]), 203–205; Edward B. Fiske, "Washington's Men of Influence Join in Prayer Groups," *New York Times*, January 30, 1974; Edward B. Fiske, "Growing Churches, Controversial Strategies for Washington Witness," *Eternity*, August 1976, 6; Harold E. Hughes (with Dick Schneider), *The Man from Ida Grove: A Senator's Personal Story* (Lincoln, VA: Chosen Books, 1979), 296–298, 300, 315–325; Lon Fendall, *Stand Alone or Come Home: Mark Hatfield as an Evangelical and a Progressive* (Newberg, OR: Barclay, 2008), 18; Robert Eells and Bartell Nyberg, *Lonely Walk: The Life of Senator Mark Hatfield* (Chappaqua, NY: Christian Herald Books, 1979), 28–30; "'Watergate or Something Like It Was Inevitable': An Interview with Charles Colson," *Christianity Today*, March 12, 1976, 4–7; Jeff Sharlet, *The Family: The Secret Fundamentalism at the Heart of American Power* (New York: Harper Perennial, 2008), 228; Robert Sherrill, "Elmer Gantry for President," *Playboy*, March 1975, 96–97, 118, 160–170. On the early history of the Fellowship and its founder, Abraham Vereide, see Patrick Daniel Jackson, "Lost: American Evangelicals in the Public Square, 1925–1955" (Ph.D. dissertation, Vanderbilt University, 2012), 109–134.

13. Wesley Pippert, *Faith at the Top* (Elgin, IL: David C. Cook, 1973), 11–27; Mark Bisnow, *Diary of a Dark Horse: The 1980 Anderson Presidential Campaign* (Carbondale: Southern Illinois University Press, 1983), 222; John B. Anderson, *Between Two Worlds: A Congressman's Choice* (Grand Rapids, MI: Zondervan, 1970), 146, 149; "Get Active Politically? Yes," *Christianity Today*, March 26, 1976, 10.

14. Pippert, *Faith at the Top*, 75; Robert James Eells, "Mark O. Hatfield and the Search for an Evangelical Politics" (Ph.D. dissertation, University of New Mexico, 1976), 277; Garry Wills, "'Born Again' Politics," *New York Times*, August 1, 1976; Swartz, "Left Behind," 92; Fendall, *Stand Alone or Come Home*, xiii–xiv, 155–157.

15. David Kucharsky, *The Man from Plains: The Mind and Spirit of Jimmy Carter* (San Francisco: Harper and Row, 1976), 77.

16. James Hefley and Marti Hefley, *The Church That Produced a President* (New York: Wyden, 1977), 248–249; George McGovern, *Grassroots: The Autobiography of George McGovern* (New York: Random House, 1977), 255, 245, 262–263.

17. David R. Swartz, *Moral Minority: The Evangelical Left in an Age of Conservatism* (Philadelphia: University of Pennsylvania Press, 2012), 109; Richard M. Harley, "The Evangelical Vote and the Presidency," *Christian Science Monitor*, June 25, 1980.

18. Gary Scott Smith, *Faith and the Presidency: From George Washington to George W. Bush* (New York: Oxford University Press, 2006), 295; Swartz, "Left Behind," 495; Foy Valentine, "Engagement—the Christian's Agenda," in Sider, *Chicago Declaration*, 57–77.

19. Wesley G. Pippert, *The Spiritual Journey of Jimmy Carter: In His Own Words* (New York: Macmillan, 1978), 36; Kucharsky, *The Man from Plains*, 119–120, 47; Sharlet, *The Family*, 208–210; "The God Network in Washington"; Marjorie Hyer, "Reagan, Carter, Anderson: Three 'Born Again' Christians Who Differ on Meaning," *Washington Post*, July 25, 1980; Fendall, *Stand Alone or Come Home*, 20; Peter G. Bourne, *Jimmy Carter: A Comprehensive Biography from Plains to Postpresidency* (New York: Scribner, 1997), 267; Robert Shogan, *The Double-Edged Sword: How Character Makes and Ruins Presidents, from Washington to Clinton* (Boulder, CO: Westview, 1999), 144–145; William Safire, "The Night of the Center-Right," *New York Times*, February 26, 1976.

20. Edmund Fuller, "The Conversion of Charles Colson," *Wall Street Journal*, March 23, 1976; Kucharsky, *The Man from Plains*, 45–47; Laura Kalman, *Right Star Rising: A New Politics, 1974–1980* (New York: W. W. Norton, 2010), 153; Jimmy Carter, *Why Not the Best?* (Nashville, TN: Broadman, 1975); Pippert, *Spiritual Journey of Jimmy Carter*, 117.

21. Kucharsky, *The Man from Plains*, 1–2; Kenneth A. Briggs, "Carter's Evangelism Putting Religion into Politics for First Time Since '60," *New York Times*, April 11, 1976; William Martin, *With God on Our Side: The Rise of the Religious Right in America* (New York: Broadway, 1996), 150; Kandy Stroud, *How Jimmy Won: The Victory Campaign from Plains to the White House* (New York: William Morrow, 1977), 329; *Presidential Campaign Posters from the Library of Congress* (Philadelphia: Quirk, 2012), 159–160; Howard Norton and Bob Slosser, *The Miracle of Jimmy Carter* (Plainfield, NJ: Logos International, 1976), 10.

22. Shogan, *The Double-Edged Sword*, 145; "Jimmy Carter Explains His Faith," *Eternity*, September 1976, 80–81.

23. Kucharsky, *The Man from Plains*, 129; Peter N. Carroll, *It Seemed Like Nothing Happened: The Tragedy and Promise of America in the 1970s* (New York: Holt, Rinehart and Winston, 1982), 187; Albert J. Menendez, *Religion at the Polls* (Philadelphia: Westminster Press, 1977), 180; "Does a Dedicated Evangelical Belong in the White House?" *Christianity Today*, July 16, 1976, 43.

24. Menendez, *Religion at the Polls*, 102; "I'm Jimmy Carter, and…," *Time*, January 3, 1977; Wills, "'Born Again' Politics"; Paul Henry, "Is God Still a Republican?"

Eternity, November 1976, 29; Randall Balmer, *God in the White House: A History: How Faith Shaped the Presidency from John F. Kennedy to George W. Bush* (New York: HarperOne, 2008), 87; Edward E. Plowman, "The Democrats: God in the Garden?" *Christianity Today*, August 6, 1976, 34; Lloyd Rohler, *George Wallace: Conservative Populist* (Westport, CT: Praeger, 2004), 84; Hendrik Hertzberg, "Jimmy Carter: 1977–1981," in Robert A. Wilson, ed., *Character Above All: Ten Presidents from FDR to George Bush* (New York: Simon Schuster, 1995), 181–182; R. W. Apple Jr., "A Jubilant Party: Minnesotan Cheered as He Scores Ford on Nixon Pardon," *New York Times*, July 16, 1976.

25. James C. Hefley, "A Change of Mind in Plains," *Christianity Today*, December 3, 1976, 50–53; Pippert, *Spiritual Journey of Jimmy Carter*, 28–29. Edwards's firing led a breakaway group to found Maranatha Baptist Church. Returning to Plains in the summer of 1977, Carter attended Sunday School at Plains Baptist and worshipped at Maranatha Baptist. Stroud, *How Jimmy Won*, 421–422.

26. Bruce Nesmith, *The New Republican Coalition: The Reagan Campaigns and White Evangelicals* (New York: Peter Lang, 1994), 63, 70n12; Robert Scheer, "*Playboy* Interview: Jimmy Carter," *Playboy*, November 1976, 63–86; Milton Viorst, "*Playboy* Interview: George McGovern," *Playboy*, August 1971, 55–70, 190–193.

27. Hefley and Hefley, *Church That Produced a President*, 139, 211–212; Pippert, *Spiritual Journey of Jimmy Carter*, 13; Norman Mailer, "The Search for Carter," *New York Times Magazine*, September 26, 1976; Balmer, *God in the White House*, 92; Daniel K. Williams, *God's Own Party: The Making of the Christian Right* (New York: Oxford University Press, 2010), 126–129; Elizabeth Drew, *American Journal: The Events of 1976* (New York: Random House, 1977), 469; Arthur H. Matthews, "Crusade for the White House: Skirmishes in a 'Holy War,'" *Christianity Today*, November 19, 1976, 48–51; Menendez, *Religion at the Polls*, 186; Gerald R. Ford, *A Time to Heal: The Autobiography of Gerald R. Ford* (New York: Harper and Row, 1979), 417; Stroud, *How Jimmy Won*, 381.

28. Nancy Gibbs and Michael Duffy, "The Other Born-Again President," *Time*, January 15, 2007; Ford, *A Time to Heal*, 417; "President Confers with Evangelicals," *Moody Monthly*, November 1976, 14; Henry, "Is God Still a Republican?" 30; "Should Christians Vote for Christians?" *Christianity Today*, June 18, 1976, 20.

29. Jim Newton, "Look at What's Right, Ford Urges Baptists," June 14, 1974, Southern Baptist Historical Library and Archives (SBHLA), Baptist Press Archives, http://media.sbhla.org.s3.amazonaws.com/3803,14-Jun-1974.PDF; "The God Network," *Time*, August 26, 1974; Hefley and Plowman, *Washington: Christians in the Corridors of Power*, 13; Balmer, *God in the White House*, 69–71.

30. Richard V. Pierard, "Reagan and the Evangelicals: The Making of a Love Affair," *Christian Century*, December 21–28, 1983, 1183; Larry Jones and Gerald T. Sheppard, "The Politics of Biblical Eschatology: Ronald Reagan and the Impending Nuclear Armageddon," *TSF Bulletin* (September–October 1984): 16–19; Williams, *God's Own Party*, 124.

31. Kucharsky, *The Man from Plains*, 68; Wills, "'Born Again' Politics"; Edward E. Plowman, "Southern Baptists: Platform for Presidents," *Christianity Today*, July 16, 1976, 48–51; Martin, *With God on Our Side*, 157; Letter, Phil Strickland to Frank Moore, August 31, 1976, SBHLA, Brotherhood Commission Records (660), Box 17, Folder 34, "Carter, Jimmy Correspondence"; Williams, *God's Own Party*, 128–129; "President Confers with Evangelicals," *Moody Monthly*, 8–14; "Interview and Issues," *Christianity Today*, October 8, 1976, 66–68.

32. Albert J. Menendez, *Evangelicals at the Ballot Box* (Amherst, NY: Prometheus, 1996), 137–139; Kellstedt et al., "Faith Transformed," 272–273; Leo P. Ribuffo, *Right Center Left: Essays in American History* (New Brunswick, NJ: Rutgers University Press, 1992), 222; Kalman, *Right Star Rising*, 178.

33. Hefley and Hefley, *The Church That Produced a President*, 4–11; Richard G. Hutcheson Jr., *God in the White House: How Religion Has Changed the Modern Presidency* (New York: Collier, 1989), 136, 99, 2; Martin, *With God on Our Side*, 158–159; Pippert, *Spiritual Journey of Jimmy Carter*, 9, 21–22, 55; Howard Norton, *Rosalynn: A Portrait* (Plainfield, NJ: Logos, 1977), 76–77; "Text of Carter's Video Address," *The Baptist Digest*, June 27, 1977, SBHLA, Jimmy Allen Papers (661), Box 1, Folder 12; Stan Hastey, "Carter Urges MSC Support; Allen Expects $1 Million," May 3, 1978, SBHLA, Baptist Press Archives, http://media.sbhla.org.s3.amazonaws.com/4623,03-May-1978.pdf; Jack U. Harwell, "We Question This White House Meeting," *The Christian Index*, May 25, 1978, SBHLA, Jimmy Allen Papers (661), Box 2, Folder 4, "MSC Correspondence."

34. Kevin Mattson, *"What the Heck Are You Up To, Mr. President?" Jimmy Carter, America's "Malaise," and the Speech That Should Have Changed the Country* (New York: Bloomsbury, 2009), 18, 30, 141–159, 164, 207–217.

35. Carroll, *It Seemed Like Nothing Happened*, ix; Jerry Falwell, *America Can Be Saved! Jerry Falwell Preaches on Revival* (Murfreesboro, TN: Sword of the Lord, 1979); Jerry Falwell, *Listen, America!* (Garden City, NY: Doubleday, 1980).

36. Tim LaHaye, *The Battle for the Mind* (Old Tappan, NJ: Fleming H. Revell, 1979), 185–186; John Charles Cooper, *Religious Pied Pipers: A Critique of Radical Right-Wing Religion* (Valley Forge, PA: Judson, 1981), 48.

37. "The Sins of Billy James," *Time*, February 16, 1976; David Chilton, *Productive Christians in an Age of Guilt Manipulators: A Biblical Response to Ronald J. Sider* (Tyler, TX: Institute for Christian Economics, 1981), 3; Swartz, "Left Behind," 18n35; James C. Burkee, *Power, Politics, and the Missouri Synod: A Conflict That Changed American Christianity* (Minneapolis, MN: Fortress, 2011); Barry Hankins, *Uneasy in Babylon: Southern Baptist Conservatives and American Culture* (Tuscaloosa: University of Alabama Press, 2002). Axel Schäfer similarly argues that an "internal backlash" against the evangelical left helped to fuel the rise of the "New Christian Right." See Schäfer, *Countercultural Conservatives: American Evangelicalism from the Postwar Revival to the New Christian Right* (Madison: University of Wisconsin Press, 2011), 153.

38. Barry Hankins, *Francis Schaeffer and the Shaping of Evangelical America* (Grand Rapids, MI: Eerdmans, 2008), 132; Frank Schaeffer, *Crazy for God: How I Grew Up as One of the Elect, Helped Found the Religious Right, and Lived to Take All (or Almost All) of It Back* (Cambridge, MA: Da Capo, 2008), 211, 253–270; Francis A. Schaeffer, *How Should We Then Live? The Rise and Decline of Western Thought and Culture* (Old Tappan, NJ: Revell, 1976); "Evangelicals Called to Prayer, Action, Change," *Moody Monthly*, April 1976, 8.

39. *Whatever Happened to the Human Race?* (Muskegon, MI: Gospel Films Video, 1979–1980); Williams, *God's Own Party*, 155.

40. Schaeffer and Koop, *Whatever Happened to the Human Race?*; Dowland, "'Family Values,'" 613–615; Williams, *God's Own Party*, 156; LaHaye, *The Battle for the Mind*, 5; Edward G. Dobson, "Goals of Evangelical Political Involvement: A Fundamentalist Perspective," in Corwin E. Smidt, ed., *Contemporary Evangelical Political Involvement: An Analysis and Assessment* (Lanham, MD: University Press of America, 1989), 163; Charles Marsh, *The Beloved Community: How Faith Shapes Social Justice, from the Civil Rights Movement to Today* (New York: Basic, 2005), 142–144, 257n65; Hankins, *Francis Schaeffer*, 204.

41. On the turn to gender and family issues, see Marjorie J. Spruill, "Gender and America's Right Turn," in Bruce J. Schulman and Julian Zelizer, eds., *Rightward Bound: Making America Conservative in the 1970s* (Cambridge, MA: Harvard University Press, 2008), 71–89; Dowland, "'Family Values,'" 610–612; Gasaway, "An Alternative Soul of Politics," 173; Randall Balmer, *The Making of Evangelicalism: From Revivalism to Politics and Beyond* (Waco, TX: Baylor University Press, 2010), 59–67; Joseph Crespino, "Civil Rights and the Religious Right," 90–105; Schulman and Zelizer, *Rightward Bound*; Martin, *With God on Our Side*, 172; Williams, *With God on Our Side*, 163–164; Scheer, "*Playboy* Interview," 84; Drew, *American Journal*, 414.

42. Southern Baptist Convention (SBC), "Resolution on Abortion," June 1971, http://www.sbc.net/resolutions/amResolution.asp?ID=13 (accessed October 7, 2010); Steven P. Miller, *Billy Graham and the Rise of the Republican South* (Philadelphia: University of Pennsylvania Press, 2009), 288n21; Williams, *God's Own Party*, 117; Foy Valentine to Adrian Rogers, November 21, 1977, and Rodgers to Valentine, November 28, 1977; both in SBHLA, Christian Life Commission Resource Files (138–2), Box 58, Folder 4, "Abortion: Correspondence 1977–1987."

43. R. F. R. Gardner, *Abortion: The Personal Dilemma: A Christian Gynaecologist Examines the Medical, Social and Spiritual Issues* (Grand Rapids, MI: Eerdmans, 1972); Albert Q. Maisel, "The Growing Battle over Abortion Reform," *Reader's Digest*, June 1969, clipping in SBHLA, 138–2, Box 8, Folder 1; Nancy Hardesty, "Should Anyone Who Wants an Abortion Have One?" *Eternity*, June 1967, 32–34; Tim Miller and Tonda Rush, "God and the GOP in Kansas City," *Christianity Today*, September 10, 1976, 60; Pippert, *Faith at the Top*, 23.

44. Harold O. J. Brown, "Legal Aspects of the Right to Life," in Richard L. Ganz, ed., *Thou Shall Not Kill: The Christian Case against Abortion* (New Rochelle, NY: Arlington House, 1978), 111–125; Harold O. J. Brown, "The American Way of Death," *Moody Monthly*, December 1976, 32; SBC, "Resolution on Abortion," June 1976, http://www.sbc.net/resolutions/amResolution.asp?ID=15; SBC, "Resolution on Abortion," June 1980, http://www.sbc.net/resolutions/amResolution.asp?ID=19; Williams, *God's Own Party*, 119; John B. Anderson (on behalf of National Abortion Rights Action League) to "Friend," undated [1980], SBHLA, Christian Life Commission Resource Files (138–2) Box 79, Folder 4; George F. Will, "John Anderson Draws Criticism," *Lawrence* (Kan.) *Journal-World*, March 6, 1980, 4.

45. Martin, *With God on Our Side*, 173; Dochuk, *From Bible Belt to Sunbelt*, 345–347; Balmer, *God in the White House*, 115; Stuart Rothenberg and Frank Newport, *The Evangelical Voter: Religion and Politics in America* (Washington, DC: Free Congress Research and Educational Foundation, 1984), 4.

46. Mark O. Hatfield, "The Christian's True Call," and John Conlan, "You Can Help Guide America," both in *Moody Monthly*, October 1976, 46–47; John G. Turner, *Bill Bright and Campus Crusade for Christ: The Renewal of Evangelicalism in Postwar America* (Chapel Hill: University of North Carolina Press, 2008), 110, 161–164; Jim Wallis and Wes Michaelson, "The Plan to Save America: A Disclosure of an Alarming Political Initiative by the Evangelical Far Right," *Sojourners*, April 1976, 4–12; Irene Conlan, *Women, We Can Do It!* (Glendale, CA: Regal, 1976), 117–118; "Growing Churches, Controversial Strategies for Washington Witness," 6; Kenneth L. Woodward, "Politics from the Pulpit," *Newsweek*, September 6, 1976, 49–50; Dochuk, *From Bible Belt to Sunbelt*, 360–361; LaHaye, *The Battle for the Mind*, 217–218.

47. Rus Walton, *One Nation under God* (Washington, DC: Third Century, 1975), 110; Wallis and Michaelson, "The Plan to Save America," 6; Turner, *Bill Bright and Campus Crusade for Christ,* 165–168; Woodward, "Politics from the Pulpit," 49; Matthews, "Crusade for the White House," 51; Martin, *With God on Our Side*, 212.

48. Ken Kelley, "*Playboy* Interview: Anita Bryant," *Playboy*, May 1978, 74, 250; David John Marley, *Pat Robertson: An American Life* (Lanham, MD: Rowman Littlefield, 2007), 42–46; Pippert, *Spiritual Journey of Jimmy Carter*, 42; Andrew R. Flint and Joy Porter, "Jimmy Carter: The Re-emergence of Faith-based Politics and the Abortion Rights Issue," *Presidential Studies Quarterly* 35, no. 1 (March 2005): 41; Martin, *With God on Our Side*, 151; Duane Murray Oldfield, *The Right and the Righteous: The Christian Right Confronts the Republican Party* (Lanham, MD: Rowman Littlefield, 1996), 87, 248n1.

49. Williams, *God's Own Party*, 164–179, 182–184; Leo P. Ribuffo, "Family Policy Past as Prologue: Jimmy Carter, the White House Conference on Families, and the Mobilization of the New Christian Right," *Review of Policy*

Research 23, no. 2 (March 2006): 311–337; David Chagall, *The New Kingmakers* (New York: Harcourt Brace Jovanovich, 1981), 280; Dochuk, *From Bible Belt to Sunbelt*, 388.

50. Flint and Porter, "Jimmy Carter," 35, 42–45; David W. Stowe, *No Sympathy for the Devil: Christian Pop Music and the Transformation of American Evangelicalism* (Chapel Hill: University of North Carolina Press, 2011), 191–193; Hutcheson, *God in the White House*, 158–159; Robert L. Maddox, *Preacher at the White House* (Nashville, TN: Broadman, 1984), 139–143, 161–165.

51. David Harrington Watt, *A Transforming Faith: Explorations of Twentieth-Century American Evangelicalism* (New Brunswick, NJ: Rutgers University Press, 1991), 50; "50 Faces for America's Future," *Time*, August 6, 1979; Mary Murphy, "The Next Billy Graham," *Esquire*, October 10, 1978, 26–32; "Preachers in Politics," *US News and World Report*, September 24, 1979, 38.

52. Jerry Strober and Ruth Tomczak, *Jerry Falwell: Aflame for God* (Nashville, TN: Thomas Nelson, 1979), 174; Michael Cromartie, "Fixing the World: From Nonplayers to Radicals to New Right Conservatives: The Saga of Evangelicals and Social Action," *Christianity Today*, April 27, 1992, 25; Marjorie Hyer, "Three 'Born Again' Christians Who Differ on Meaning," *Washington Post*, July 25, 1980.

CHAPTER 3

1. Maxwell Glen, "The Electronic Ministers Listen to the Gospel According to the Candidates," *National Journal*, December 22, 1979, in *The New Right: Readings and Commentary*, Vol. 2 (Oakland, CA: The Data Center, 1981), 252–255; Martin Marty, "Sizing-up the Armies of the Moral Majority," *Miami Herald*, December 21, 1980, in *New Right*, Vol. 3, 385–387; Jeffrey K. Hadden and Charles E. Swann, *Prime Time Preachers: The Rising Power of Televangelism* (Reading, MA: Addison-Wesley, 1981); J. Brooks Flippen, *Jimmy Carter, the Politics of Family, and the Rise of the Religious Right* (Athens: University of Georgia Press, 2011), 1–14; Ruth Ravenel, "The Thee Decade: How the Press Tripped Over One of 1980's Biggest Stories," *Washington Journalism Review*, December 1980, in *New Right*, Vol. 4, 468–471; Daniel K. Williams, *God's Own Party: The Making of the Christian Right* (New York: Oxford University Press, 2010), 182.

2. "Preachers in Politics," *US News and World Report*, September 24, 1979, 40; Flippen, *Jimmy Carter*, 265; Michael Sean Winters, *God's Right Hand: How Jerry Falwell Made God a Republican and Baptized the American Right* (New York: HarperCollins, 2012), 128–129; Kathy Sawyer and Robert G. Kaiser, "Evangelicals Flock to GOP Standard Feeling They Have Friend in Reagan," *Washington Post*, July 15, 1980; Hadden and Swann, *Prime Time Preachers*, 130, 152; Williams, *God's Own Party*, 190–191; David Domke and Kevin Coe, *The God Strategy: How Religion Became a Political Weapon in America*, 2nd edition (New York: Oxford University Press, 2010), 3–4; Steven P. Miller, *Billy Graham and the Rise of the*

Republican South (Philadelphia: University of Pennsylvania Press, 2009), 209; William Martin, *With God on Our Side: The Rise of the Religious Right in America* (New York: Broadway, 1996), 214–218; "A Tide of Born-Again Politics," *Newsweek*, September 15, 1980, in *New Right*, Vol. 3, 294–296.

3. Kenneth L. Woodward, "The Evangels and the Jews," *Newsweek*, November 10, 1980; Frances FitzGerald, *Cities on a Hill: A Journey through Contemporary American Cultures*, revised edition (New York: Simon Schuster, 1986), 121, 186.

4. Williams, *God's Own Party*, 178; Kenneth A. Briggs, "Christians on Right and Left Take Up Ballot and Cudgel," *New York Times*, September 21, 1980; Robert Booth Fowler, *A New Engagement: Evangelical Political Thought, 1966–1976* (Grand Rapids, MI: Eerdmans, 1982), 245; Leo P. Ribuffo, *Right Center Left: Essays in American History* (New Brunswick, NJ: Rutgers University Press, 1991), 246; Doug Wead and Bill Wead, *Reagan in Pursuit of the Presidency—1980* (Plainfield, NJ: Haven Books, 1980), 21–27; Edward Walsh, "Carter Turns to Ridicule, Sarcasm in War of Words with Reagan," *Washington Post*, October 22, 1980; Hadden and Swann, *Prime Time Preachers*, 150.

5. Hadden and Swann, *Prime Time Preachers*, 6, 162, 126; Louis Harris, "Polls Show Moral Majority Power Real," *Oakland Tribune*, November 11, 1980, in *New Right*, Vol. 3, 395; "Religious Right Goes for Bigger Game," *US News and World Report*, November 17, 1980; Frances FitzGerald, "The Triumphs of the New Right," *New York Review of Books*, November 19, 1981; Tina Rosenberg, "How the Media Made the Moral Majority," *Washington Monthly*, May 1982, 28; "New Right Tops Religion News," *Christian Century*, December 31, 1980, 1283; Seymour Martin Lipset and Earl Raab, "The Election and the Evangelicals," *Commentary*, March 1981, 25–31; David Chagall, *The New Kingmakers* (New York: Harcourt Brace Jovanovich, 1981), 251, 233; Albert J. Menendez, *Evangelicals at the Ballot Box* (New York: Prometheus, 1996), 142.

6. William Martin, "The Birth of a Media Myth," *The Atlantic*, June 1981, 7, 11; Hadden and Swann, *Prime Time Preachers*, 54; Bill Peterson and Barry Sussman, "Moral Majority Is Growing in Recognition, but Remains Unknown to Half the Public," *Washington Post*, June 13, 1981; Anson Shupe and William A. Stacey, *Born Again Politics and the Moral Majority: What Social Surveys Really Show* (New York: Edwin Mellon, 1982), 30, 45; Rosenberg, "Moral Majority," 28, 34.

7. Willard P. Rose, "Did Moral Majority Win Politics' Soul?" *Miami Herald*, November 23, 1980, in *New Right*, Vol. 3, 390–394; Megan Rosenfeld, "The New Moral America and the War of the Religicos: Born Again Political Forces Not Singing the Same Hymn," *Washington Post*, August 24, 1980; Marguerite Michaels, "Billy Graham: America Is Not God's Only Kingdom," *Parade*, February 1, 1981, in *New Right*, Vol. 4, 597–599. A search of LexisNexis database articles from 1980 through 1984 revealed 48 results for the search term "religious new right," compared with 221 results for the term "christian right" and 34 results for "pro-family

movement" (June 8, 2011, search of LexisNexis Academic ["All News (English)"] database).

8. Domke and Coe, *God Strategy*, 31, 48, 61.

9. Martin, *With God on Our Side*, 222–225; Flippen, *Jimmy Carter*, 325; Curt Suplee, "The Power and the Glory in the New Senate: A Growing Congregation of Born Again Believers," *Washington Post*, December 20, 1981; Sidney Blumenthal, "The Righteous Empire: A Short History of the End of History, and Maybe Even of the G.O.P.," *The New Republic*, October 22, 1984, 18; Allan J. Lichtman, *White Protestant Nation: The Rise of the American Conservative Movement* (New York: Grove, 2008), 375–376; Williams, *God's Own Party*, 203, 210; Haynes Johnson, *Sleepwalking through History: America in the Reagan Years* (New York: W. W. Norton, 1991 [2003 paperback edition]), 211–212.

10. James L. Guth, "The Politics of the Christian Right," in John C. Green et al., *Religion and the Culture Wars: Dispatches from the Front* (Lanham, MD: Rowman Littlefield, 1996), 26; Lichtman, *White Protestant Nation*, 357–360; "An Interview with the Lone Ranger of American Fundamentalism," *Christianity Today*, September 4, 1981, 26; Williams, *God's Own Party*, 195–196.

11. Blumenthal, "Righteous Empire," 20; Williams, *God's Own Party*, 197, 204–205; Bradford Martin, *The Other Eighties: A Secret History of America in the Age of Reagan* (New York: Hill and Wang, 2011), 3–24.

12. Kenneth D. Wald, *Religion and Politics in the United States* (New York: St. Martin's, 1987), 194; Ronald Reagan, *In God I Trust* (Carol Stream, IL: Tyndale House, 1984); Blumenthal, "Righteous Empire," 24, 18; Gary Scott Smith, *Faith and the Presidency: From George Washington to George W. Bush* (New York: Oxford University Press, 2006), 337; John Herbers, "Religious Leaders Tell of Worry on Armageddon View Ascribed to Reagan," *New York Times*, October 21, 1984; Grace Halsell, *Prophecy and Politics: Militant Evangelists on the Road to Nuclear War* (Westport, CT: Lawrence Hill, 1986), 10; "Text of the Second Reagan-Mondale Debate," *Washington Post*, October 22, 1984.

13. Carl F. H. Henry, "Response," in Michael Cromartie, ed., *No Longer Exiles: The Religious New Right in American Politics* (Washington, DC: Ethics and Policy Center, 1993), 83; James Davison Hunter, *Culture Wars: The Struggle to Define America* (New York: Basic, 1991), 276, 386n9; "Mondale's Whipping Boy," *Time*, October 22, 1984; E. J. Dionne Jr., *Why Americans Hate Politics* (New York: Simon Schuster, 1991), 211.

14. Erling Jorstad, *The New Christian Right, 1981–1988: Prospects for the Post-Reagan Decade* (Lewiston, NY: Edwin Mellon, 1987), 157; Ronald Reagan, "Religion and Politics Are Necessarily Related," *Church and State*, October 1984, 9–11; "Text of the First Reagan-Mondale Debate" (Parts 1 and 2), *Washington Post*, October 8, 1984; Chuck Conconi column, *Washington Post*, October 11, 1984; John Schmalzbauer, *People of Faith: Religious Conviction in American Journalism and*

Higher Education (Ithaca, NY: Cornell University Press, 2003), 64–65; Williams, *God's Own Party*, 206.

15. Winters, *God's Right Hand*, 243, 215; FitzGerald, *Cities on a Hill*, 195; Flo Conway and Jim Siegelman, *Holy Terror: The Fundamentalist War on America's Freedoms in Religion, Politics and Our Private Lives* (Garden City, NJ: Doubleday, 1982), 68, 74; Joseph F. Sullivan, "Falwell Warns Jersey Liberals at Capitol Rally," *New York Times*, November 11, 1980; Richard G. Hutcheson Jr., *God in the White House: How Religion Has Changed the Modern Presidency* (New York: Collier, 1989), 69; Flippen, *Jimmy Carter*, 292–293; Warren Brown, "Falwell Denies 'Moral Majority' Seeks to Dictate Nation's Moral Philosophy," *Washington Post*, October 13, 1980, in *New Right*, Vol. 3, 397; Robert Scheer, "The Prophet of 'Worldly Methods,'" *Los Angeles Times*, March 4, 1981, in *New Right*, Vol. 1, 121–128; "*Penthouse* Interview: Reverend Jerry Falwell," *Penthouse*, March 1981, 154, 152; Ed Bruske, "Falwell Loses Courtroom Round to *Penthouse*," *Washington Post*, February 3, 1981, in *New Right*, Vol. 1, 141; Gabriel Fackre, *The Religious Right and the Christian Faith* (Grand Rapids, MI: Eerdmans, 1982), 111n10; Rodney A. Smolla, *Jerry Falwell v. Larry Flynt: The First Amendment on Trial* (New York: St. Martin's, 1988), 313.

16. Francis A. Schaeffer, *A Christian Manifesto* (Westchester, IL: Crossway, 1981), 77–78, 90, 73, 75, 93; Barry Hankins, *Francis Schaeffer and the Shaping of Evangelical America* (Grand Rapids, MI: Eerdmans, 2008), 193–200; Franky Schaeffer, *Bad News for Modern Man: An Agenda for Christian Activism* (Westchester, IL: Crossway, 1984), 93.

17. Faye Ginsburg, "Rescuing the Nation: Operation Rescue and the Rise of Anti-Abortion Militance," in Rickie Solinger, ed., *Abortion Wars: A Half Century of Struggle, 1950–2000* (Berkeley: University of California Press, 1998), 227–250; Kristin Luker, *Abortion and the Politics of Motherhood* (Berkeley: University of California Press, 1984), 196; Larry Martz, "The New Pro-Life Offensive," *Newsweek*, September 12, 1988; David John Marley, "Riding in the Back of the Bus: The Christian Right's Adoption of Civil Rights Rhetoric," in Leigh Raiford and Renee C. Ramono, eds., *The Civil Rights Movement in American Memory* (Athens: University of Georgia Press, 2006), 355–358; Garry Wills, "Evangels of Abortion," *New York Review of Books*, June 15, 1989; Sara Diamond, *Not by Politics Alone: The Enduring Influence of the Christian Right* (New York: Guilford, 1998), 136–137.

18. "If the Moral Majority Has Its Way, You'd Better Start Praying," *New York Times*, November 23, 1980; Dolores A. Barclay, "Moral Majority Decries 'Fear Tactics'" *Miami Herald*, March 28, 1981, in *New Right*, Vol. 3, 364; Moral Majority advertisement, *New York Times*, March 23, 1981.

19. Robert D. McFadden, "Head of Yale Calls Moral Majority 'Peddlers of Coercion' on 'Values,'" *New York Times*, September 1, 1981; "Text of Giamatti Letter to Yale Freshman," *New York Times*, September 6, 1981; Winters, *God's Right Hand*, 221–222; "Moral Majority Terms Attack by Yale President a 'Diatribe,'" *New York Times*,

September 2, 1981; Anthony Lewis, "God and Jonah at Yale," *New York Times*, September 10, 1980; Samuel G. Freedman, "Mr. Falwell Meets an Outspoken Antagonist, Yale's Giamatti," *New York Times*, November 12, 1982.

20. James Luther Adams, "The Fundamentalist Far Right Rides Again: Congress Attacks 'Secular Humanism,'" *The Humanist*, September/October 1976, 8–9; Judy MacLean, "Crusaders Boost Right," *In These Times*, December 13, 1976, in *New Right*, Vol. 4, 522–523; "Who's Who among the Evangelicals and the Right Wing (A Partial Listing)," *Press On!*, Fall 1980, in *New Right*, Vol. 1, 35–38.

21. Rosenberg, "How the Media Made the Moral Majority," 26–27; Jerry Falwell, ed., *The Fundamentalist Phenomenon: The Resurgence of Conservative Christianity* (Garden City, NY: Doubleday, 1981); David T. Courtwright, *No Right Turn: Conservative Politics in a Liberal America* (Cambridge, MA: Harvard University Press, 2010), 117; Daniel C. Maguire, *The New Subversives: Anti-Americanism of the Religious Right* (New York: Continuum, 1982); Perry Deane Young, *God's Bullies: Native Reflections on Preachers and Politics* (New York: Holt, Rinehart and Winston, 1982); Conway and Siegelman, *Holy Terror*, 10; Flo Conway and Jim Siegelman, *Snapping: America's Epidemic of Sudden Personality Change* (Philadelphia: Lippincott, 1978); *Footloose* (Los Angeles: Paramount, 1984); *Dirty Dancing* (Stamford, CT: Vestron, 1987).

22. Conway and Siegelman, *Holy Terror*, 13; Isaac Asimov, "The Blind Who Would Lead," *Maclean's* 94, no. 5 (February 2, 1981), 6; Maguire, *The New Subversives*, 21; Mary Murphy, "The Next Billy Graham," *Esquire*, October 10, 1978, 30; Hadden and Swann, *Prime Time Preachers*, 149; Moral Majority advertisement, *New York Times*, March 23, 1981; George McGovern, "The New Right and the Old Paranoia," *Playboy*, January 1981, in *New Right*, Vol. 4, 555; Margaret Atwood, *The Handmaid's Tale* (Boston: Houghton Mifflin, 1986); "Preachers in Politics," 41; Leo P. Ribuffo, "Liberals and That Old-Time Religion," *The Nation*, November 29, 1980, 572; Andrew M. Greeley, "Moral Majority Is Liberals' Fiction," *Detroit Free Press*, March 22, 1981.

23. Norman Lear, "America Is Strangling on Its Obsession with the Bottom Line," in Herbert F. Vetter, ed., *Speak Out against the New Right* (Boston: Beacon, 1982), 12; "*Penthouse* Interview," 59; Conway and Siegelman, *Holy Terror*, 3; John L. Kater Jr., *Christians on the Right: The Moral Majority in Perspective* (New York: Seabury, 1982), xi. See also James Davison Hunter, "The Liberal Reaction," in Robert C. Liebman and Robert Wuthnow, eds., *The New Christian Right: Mobilization and Legitimization* (New York: Albine, 1983), 149–163.

24. "Preachers in Politics: Decisive Force in '80?" *US News and World Report*, September 15, 1980, 26; "Religious Right Goes for Bigger Game," *US News and World Report*, November 17, 1980, in *New Right*, Vol. 3, 289; Mike Sager, "McGovern Back on Campus, Runs into Moral Majority," *Washington Post*, March 4, 1981, in *New Right*, Vol. 4, 553; Albert R. Hunt, "Ex-Sen. McGovern Forms

Organization to Fight New Right," *Wall Street Journal*, February 3, 1981, in *New Right*, Vol. 4, 554; Rosenberg, "How the Media Made the Moral Majority," 28.

25. Sarah Barringer Gordon, *The Spirit of the Law: Religious Voices and the Constitution in Modern America* (Cambridge, MA: Belknap, 2010), 69–95; Hadden and Swann, *Prime Time Preachers*, 146; William A. Donahue, *The Politics of the American Civil Liberties Union* (New Brunswick, NJ: Transaction, 1985); Samuel Walker, *In Defense of American Liberties: A History of the ACLU* (New York: Oxford University Press, 1990), 341–342, 369.

26. Robert M. Collins, *Transforming America: Politics and Culture during the Reagan Years* (New York: Columbia University Press, 2007), 177; Louise Sweeney, "Norman Lear's PAW Takes a Swipe at the New Right," *Christian Science Monitor*, July 23, 1981; Ben Stein, "The War to Clean Up TV: Norman Lear vs. the Moral Majority," *Saturday Review*, February 1981, 23–27; Chagall, *The New Kingmakers*, 274; Norman Cousins, "The Threat of Intolerance," *Saturday Review*, January 1981, 8.

27. Margaret Hornblower, "Anderson: Steady and Self-Confident," *Washington Post*, October 23, 1980; "Anderson's Church and Its Beliefs," *New York Times*, June 9, 1980; Chagall, *The New Kingmakers*, 233; Dan Hall, "Anderson Raps Christian Right," Associated Press, October 8, 1980; "Preachers in Politics," 25; Blumenthal, "Righteous Empire," 24; Johnson, *Sleepwalking through History*, 203–205; David Bollier, *Liberty and Justice for Some: Defending a Free Society from the Radical Right's Holy War on Democracy* (Washington, DC: People for the American Way, 1982), vii, 10–13; Sweeney, "Norman Lear's PAW"; Hadden and Swann, *Prime Time Preachers*, 146; Erling Jorstad, *The Politics of Moralism: The New Christian Right in American Life* (Minneapolis, MN: Augsburg, 1981), 99; Robert L. Maddox, *Separation of Church and State: Guarantor of Religious Freedom* (New York: Crossroad, 1987); "A Move against the 'New Right'" *Oakland Tribune*, October 22, 1980, in *New Right*, Vol. 4, 579; Willard P. Rose, "Did Moral Majority Win Politics' Soul?" *Miami Herald*, November 23, 1980, in *New Right*, Vol. 3, 393.

28. Kirk Victor, "Feeling Its Way," *National Journal*, December 7, 1996, 2641–2645; Hadden and Swann, *Prime Time Preachers*, 148; David Remnick, "TV Ads Give the Moral Majority PAWs; PAW's Ad Campaign," *Washington Post*, June 25, 1981; Bollier, *Liberty and Justice for Some*, 3, 46, 63, 68, 229, 112; Jorstad, *The New Christian Right*, 267; Lear, "America Is Strangling," 6.

29. Jeffrey K. Hadden and Anson D. Shupe, *Televangelism: Power and Politics on God's Frontier* (New York: Holt, 1988), 194.

30. Martin, *The Other Eighties*, 150–151; Maryann Barasko, *Governing NOW: Grassroots Activism in the National Organization for Women* (Ithaca, NY: Cornell University Press, 2004), 90–120 (quote on p. 90); Courtwright, *No Right Turn*, 193.

31. "Excerpts from Jackson to Convention Delegates for Unity in Party," *New York Times*, July 18, 1984; Garry Wills, *Under God: Religion and American Politics* (New York: Simon Schuster, 1990), 234; Jorstad, *New Christian Right*, 135;

David R. Swartz, "Left Behind: The Evangelical Left and the Limits of Evangelical Politics, 1965–1988" (Ph.D. dissertation, University of Notre Dame, 2008), 608–609; Colman McCarthy, "Jackson's Reversal on Abortion," *Washington Post*, May 21, 1988.

32. Walter Mondale, "Religion Is a Private Matter," *Church and State*, October 1984, 12–15.
33. Robert D. Putnam and David E. Campbell, *American Grace: How Religion Divides and Unites Us* (New York: Simon Schuster, 2010), 120; Victor, "Feeling Its Way," 2645.
34. James T. Richardson, Joel Best, and David G. Bromley, "Satanism as a Social Problem" (3–17), and Bromley, "Satanism: The New Cult Scare" (49–72), both in Richardson, Best, and Bromley, eds., *The Satanism Scare* (New York: Aldine de Gruyter, 1991); Philip Jenkins and Daniel Maier-Katkin, "Satanism: Myth and Reality in a Contemporary Moral Panic," *Crime, Law and Social Change* 17 (1992): 53–75; Bill Ellis, *Raising the Devil: Satanism, New Religions, and the Media* (Lexington: University Press of Kentucky, 2000), 7–14, 177, 104–117. Two valuable introductions to the satanic panic are Philip Jenkins, *Moral Panic: Changing Conceptions of the Child Molester in Modern America* (New Haven, CT: Yale University Press, 1998), chapter 8; and W. Scott Poole, *Satan in America: The Devil We Know* (Lanham, MD: Rowman Littlefield, 2009), chapter 6.
35. Jenkins, *Moral Panic*, 172.
36. Jenkins and Maier-Katkin, "Satanism"; Jenkins, *Moral Panic*, 164–188; Hal Lindsey with C. C. Carlson, *Satan Is Alive and Well on Planet Earth* (Grand Rapids, MI: Zondervan, 1972); Ellis, *Raising the Devil*, 185, 177; Jon Trott and Mike Hertenstein, "Selling Satan: The Tragic History of Mike Warnke," *Cornerstone Magazine* 21, no. 98 (1992) (copy in possession of author); *Selling Satan: The Tragic History of Mike Warnke* (Chicago: Cornerstone Press, 1993); Mike Warnke with Dave Balsiger and Les Jones, *The Satan Seller* (Plainfield, NJ: Logos, 1972); "The Devil Worshippers," *20/20* episode (May 16, 1985); *Hell's Bells: The Dangers of Rock "N" Roll* (Reel to Reel Ministries, 1989); Jon Pareles, "For Slayer, the Mania Is the Message," *New York Times*, September 3, 1988; "Devil Worship: Exploring Satan's Underground," Geraldo Rivera NBC special (October 25, 1988); Peter J. Boyer, "Program on Satan Worship Spurs Controversy at NBC," *New York Times*, October 26, 1988; Jerry Johnston, *The Edge of Evil: The Rise of Satanism in North America* (Dallas, TX: Word, 1989), v, xi.
37. Lawrence Wright, *Remembering Satan* (New York: Knopf, 1994), 80, 179, 146 (quote on p. 195).
38. Mara Leveritt, *Devil's Knot: The True Story of the West Memphis Three* (New York: Atria, 2002); Campbell Robertson, "Rare Deal Frees 3 in '93 Arkansas Child Killings," *New York Times*, August 20, 2011; *Paradise Lost: The Child Murders at Robin Hood Hills* (New York: Home Box Office, 1996); *Paradise Lost 2: Revelations* (New York: Home Box Office, 1999).

39. John A. Saliba, *Christian Reponses to the New Age Movement: A Critical Assessment* (London: Geoffrey Chapman, 1999), 39–88; James R. Lewis, "Works of Darkness: Occult Fascination in the Novels of Frank E. Peretti," in James R. Lewis, ed., *Magical Religion and Modern Witchcraft* (Albany: State University of New York Press, 1996), 339–350; Frank E. Peretti, *This Present Darkness* (Wheaton, IL: Crossway, 1986).

40. Hadden and Swann, *Prime Time Preachers*, 32; "Heaven Can Wait," *Newsweek*, June 8, 1987, 62; Charles E. Shepard, *Forgiven: The Rise and Fall of Jim Bakker and the PFL Ministry* (New York: Atlantic Monthly Press, 1989), 418, 231, 135, 344–347; Thomas C. O'Quinn and Russell W. Belk, "Heaven on Earth: Consumption at Heritage Village, USA," *Journal of Consumer Research* 16, no. 2 (September 1999): 227–238; Frances FitzGerald, "Reflections: Jim and Tammy," *New Yorker*, April 23, 1990, 3, 80; Wills, "Evangels of Abortion"; Wills, *Under God*, 80. To be sure, the Bakkers' denomination, the Assemblies of God, had long been a pillar of the NAE. See Axel R. Schäfer, *Countercultural Conservatives: American Evangelicalism from the Postwar Revival to the New Christian Right* (Madison: University of Wisconsin Press, 2011), 56.

41. Shepard, *Forgiven*, 468–471, 492–494, xv, 298, 306–307, 543, 547–548; "God and Money," *Newsweek*, April 6, 1987, 16–22; "Heaven Can Wait," 58–65 (quote on p. 58); FitzGerald, "Reflections: Jim and Tammy," 46, 79; Susan Friend Harding, *Book of Jerry Falwell: Fundamentalist Language and Politics* (Princeton, NJ: Princeton University Press, 2000), 263.

42. Harding, *Book of Jerry Falwell*, 252; "God and Money," 16, 17; "Heaven Can Wait," 58, 66; Shepard, *Forgiven*, 550, 548, 553; Adam Bernstein, "Televangelist Tammy Faye Bakker Messner," *Washington Post*, July 22, 2007; Hank Stuever, "From Down Here, She Looks Like an Angel Now," *Washington Post*, July 23, 2007.

43. "Fatal Addiction: Ted Bundy's Final Interview," January 23, 1989, www.pureintimacy.org/f/fatal-addiction-ted-bundys-final-interview/; Diamond, *Not by Politics Alone*, 32–33; Ted Guest, "The Drive to Make America Porn-free," *US News and World Report*, February 6, 1989, 26–27; Pamela Ellis-Simons, "The Rising Voice of a Family Crusader," *US News and World Report*, February 6, 1989, 27; Al Goldstein, "Ted Bundy's Last Lie," *New York Times*, February 18, 1989; Mary Ellen Klas, "Bundy's Tale Draws Skeptics," *Palm Beach Post*, January 31, 1989; Lichtman, *White Protestant Nation*, 401; "Bundy Interview to Air," *The Oregonian*, March 4, 1989; "Churches Use Bundy's Video to Warn Pupils," *Toronto Star*, October 19, 1989.

44. Blumenthal, "The Righteous Empire," 20; Preston Shires, *Hippies of the Religious Right* (Waco, TX: Baylor University Press, 2007), 177.

45. David John Marley, *Pat Robertson: An American Life* (Lanham, MD: Rowman Littlefield, 2007), 35; David Edwin Harrell Jr., *Pat Robertson: A Life and Legacy* (Grand Rapids, MI: Eerdmans, 2010), 105; Martin, *With God on Our Side*, 268.

46. Martin, *With God on Our Side*, 280–282; Wills, *Under God*, 171–172; Justin Watson, *The Christian Coalition: Dreams of Restoration, Demands for Recognition*

(New York: St. Martin's, 1997), 40; Cory SerVaas and Maynard Good Stoddard, "CBN's Pat Robertson: White House Next?" *Saturday Evening Post*, March 1985, 50–56, 106–109; Jorstad, *New Christian Right*, 230, 240, 246; Winters, *God's Right Hand*, 298; Schäfer, *Countercultural Conservatives*, 141.

47. Martin, *With God on Our Side*, 262, 311–317; Miller, *Billy Graham and the Rise of the Republican South*, 212; Wills, *Under God*, 80, 152–164, 60–61; Jerry Falwell, *Strength for the Journey: An Autobiography* (New York: Simon Schuster, 1987), dust jacket back cover; George H. W. Bush, *All the Best, George Bush: My Life in Letters and Other Writings* (New York: Scribner, 1999), 319–320; David S. Broder and Bob Woodward, *The Man Who Would Be President: Dan Quayle* (New York: Simon Schuster, 1992), 187; Williams, *God's Own Party*, 221; Courtwright, *No Right Turn*, 202–203.

48. Robert Booth Fowler, "The Failure of the Religious Right," in Cromartie, *No Longer Exiles*, 57; Steve Bruce, *The Rise and Fall of the New Christian Right* (London: Clarendon, 1990), 162.

CHAPTER 4

1. Richard John Neuhaus, *The Naked Public Square: Religion and Democracy in America*, revised edition (Grand Rapids, MI: Eerdmans, 1986), 37.

2. Os Guinness, "Introduction," in James Davison Hunter and Os Guinness, eds., *Articles of Faith, Articles of Peace: The Religious Liberty Clauses and the American Public Philosophy* (Washington, DC: Brookings Institution, 1990), 2; Os Guinness, *The American Hour: A Time of Reckoning and the Once and Future Role of Faith* (New York: Free Press, 1993), 388, 445.

3. Neuhaus, *Naked Public Square*, quoted 37, 260, 93, 156; Richard John Neuhaus, *American Babylon: Notes of a Christian Exile* (New York: Basic, 2009), 39.

4. Richard John Neuhaus, *Time Toward Home: The American Experiment as Revelation* (New York: Seabury, 1975), 214, 210–211; Neuhaus, *Naked Public Square*, 78, 26–27; Allan J. Lichtman, *White Protestant Nation: The Rise of the American Conservative Movement* (New York: Grove Press, 2008), 284.

5. Neuhaus, *Naked Public Square*, 238–239; Neuhaus, *Time Toward Home*, 214, 210–211; Daniel T. Rodgers, *Age of Fracture* (Cambridge, MA: Harvard University Press, 2011), 83; Peter L. Berger and Richard John Neuhaus, *To Empower People: The Role of Mediating Structures in Public Policy* (Washington, DC: American Enterprise Institute for Public Policy Research, 1977), 26–33; "Peter Berger and Richard John Neuhaus Respond," in Michael Novak, ed., *To Empower People: From State to Civil Society* (Washington, DC: AEI, 1996), 145–154; Sunil Khilnani, "The Development of Civil Society," in Sudipta Kaviraj and Khilnani, eds., *Civil Society: History and Possibilities* (Cambridge, UK: Cambridge University Press, 2001), 11–32; Don Eberly, *The Rise of Global Civil Society: Building Communities and Nations from the Bottom Up* (New York:

Encounter, 2008), 42; Olivier Zunz, *Philanthropy in America: A History* (Princeton, NJ: Princeton University Press, 2012), 232–263; J. Brooks Flippen, *Jimmy Carter, the Politics of Family, and the Rise of the Religious Right* (Athens: University of Georgia Press, 2011), 80; "A Tide of Born-Again Politics," *Newsweek*, September 15, 1980, in *The New Right: Readings and Commentary*, Vol. 3 (Oakland, CA: Data Center, 1981), 294, 296.

6. Charles Colson (with Ellen Santilli Vaughn), *Kingdoms in Conflict* (New York: William Morrow/Zondervan, 1987), 373; "The 25 Most Influential Evangelicals in America," *Time*, February 7, 2005; Neuhaus, "Can Atheists Be Good Citizens?" in Neuhaus and George Weigel, eds., *Being Christian Today: An American Conversation* (Washington, DC: Ethics and Public Policy Center, 1992), 295–308; Jacob Heilbrunn, "Neocon v. Theocon," *The New Republic*, December 30, 1996, 20–24.

7. Harvey Cox, "Putting God Back in Politics," *New York Times Book Review*, August 26, 1984; Michael Scully, "Finding a Place for Religion in Public Life," *Wall Street Journal*, July 30, 1984; Robert N. Bellah et al., *Habits of the Heart: Individualism and Commitment in American Life* (Berkeley: University of California Press, 1985), 235, 221; Robert N. Bellah, "Habits of the Heart: Implications for Religion," February 21, 1986 lecture (St. Mark's Catholic Church, Isla Vista, CA), http://www.robertbellah.com/lectures_5.htm; Kenneth A. Briggs, "Protest against Moral Majority Emerges at a Baptist Conference," *New York Times*, March 26, 1981. See also Bellah, "Introduction," in Mary Douglas and Steven Tipton, eds., *Religion and America: Spiritual Life in a Secular Age* (Boston: Beacon, 1983), ix–xiii. On communitarianism, see Rodgers, *Age of Fracture*, 191–198.

8. Stephen L. Carter, *The Culture of Disbelief: How American Law and Politics Trivialize Religious Devotion* (New York: Basic, 1993), 4, 51, 211, 266; Stephen L. Carter, *God's Name in Vain: The Wrongs and Rights of Religion in Politics* (New York: Basic, 2000), quote on 115; Anne C. Loveland, "Later Stages of the Recovery of American Religious History," in Harry Stout and D. G. Hart, *New Directions in American Religious History* (New York: Oxford University Press, 1997), 492–493; John Schmalzbauer, *People of Faith: Religious Conviction in American Journalism and Higher Education* (Ithaca, NY: Cornell University Press, 2003), 64–68.

9. Neuhaus, *Naked Public Square*, 177; Isaac Kramnick and R. Laurence Moore, *The Godless Constitution: The Case against Religious Correctness* (New York: W. W. Norton, 1996), 13, 172; R. Marie Griffith and Melani McAlister, "Introduction: Is the Public Square Still Naked?" *American Quarterly* 59, no. 3 (September 2007): 527–563.

10. Todd Gitlin and Ruth Rosen, "Give the 60's Generation a Break," *New York Times*, November 14, 1987; Steven V. Roberts and Dorian R. Friedman, "The Culture Wars of 1990," *U.S. News*, June 25, 1990; Richard John Neuhaus, "Notes on the Culture Wars," *First Things*, January 1991; James Davison Hunter, *Culture Wars: The Struggle to Define America* (New York: Basic, 1991), quote on 42–43.

11. James Gilbert, "Cultural Skirmishes," *Reviews in American History* 21, no. 2 (June 1993): 346–351; Hunter, *Culture Wars*, 47, 132, 48; Andrew M. Greeley, "With God on Their Sides," November 24, 1991, *New York Times Book Review*; William McLoughlin, "New and Strange Bedfellows," *Washington Post*, December 29, 1991; Robert Wuthnow, *The Restructuring of American Religion: Society and Faith since World War II* (Princeton, NJ: Princeton University Press, 1988); Robert Wuthnow, "Divided We Fall: America's Two Civil Religions," *Christian Century*, April 20, 1988, 395–399.

12. N. J. Demerath III and Younghe Yang, "What American Culture War? A View from the Trenches as Opposed to the Command Posts and the Press Corps," in Rhys H. Williams, ed., *Cultural Wars in American Politics: Critical Reviews of a Popular Myth* (New York: Aldine de Gruyter, 1997), 17–38 (quote on 17); William Martin, *With God on Our Side: The Rise of the Religious Right in America* (New York: Broadway, 1996), 117–143; *Romer v. Evans*, 517 US 620, http://caselaw. lp.findlaw.com/cgi-bin/getcase.pl?court=US&vol=000&invol=U10179; Christian Smith, with Michael Emerson, Sally Gallagher, Paul Kennedy, and David Sikkink, "The Myth of Culture Wars: The Case of American Protestantism," in Williams, *Cultural Wars in American Politics*, 175–195; Alan Wolfe, *One Nation, After All: What Middle-Class Americans Really Think About: God, Country, Family, Racism, Welfare, Immigration, Homosexuality, Work, the Right, the Left, and Each Other* (New York: Viking, 1998), 276; James Davison Hunter and Alan Wolfe, *Is There a Culture War? A Dialogue on Values and American Public Life* (Washington, DC: Pew Research Center and Brookings Institution Press, 2006).

13. James Davison Hunter, *Before the Shooting Begins: Searching for Democracy in America's Culture War* (New York: Free Press, 1994), viii; "Is There a Culture War?" Pew Forum on Religion and Public Life transcript, May 23, 2006, http://pewforum.org/Politics-and-Elections/Is-There-A-Culture-War.aspx; James Davison Hunter, *Evangelicalism: The Coming Generation* (Chicago: University of Chicago Press, 1987); James Davison Hunter, *American Evangelicalism: Conservative Religion and the Quandary of Modernity* (New Brunswick, NJ: Rutgers University Press, 1983); James Davison Hunter, "The New Class and the Young Evangelicals," *Review of Religious Research* 22, no. 2 (December 1980): 155–169; James Davison Hunter, "Flap Will Not Doom Evangelicalism," *Los Angeles Times*, March 27, 1987.

14. James Davison Hunter, "Religious Freedom and the Challenge of Modern Pluralism," 54–73 (quote on 71), in Hunter and Guinness, *Articles of Faith, Articles of Peace*; James Davison Hunter, " 'America's Fourth Faith': A Sociological Perspective on Secular Humanism," *This World* 19 (Fall 1987): 101–110; Hunter, *Culture Wars*, 57–58; *Smith v. Board of School Commissioners*, 655 F. Supp. 939 (US Dist. 1987); Robert Daniel Rubin, "Establish No Religion: Faith, Law, and Public Education in Mobile, Alabama, 1981–1987" (Ph.D. dissertation, Indiana University, 2009).

15. Charles W. Colson, "The Common Cultural Task: The Culture War from a Protestant Perspective," in Charles Colson and Richard John Neuhaus, eds., *Evangelicals and Catholics Together: Toward a Common Mission* (Dallas, TX: Word, 1995), 1–44; Neuhaus, *American Babylon*, 32, 53; David T. Courtwright, *No Right Turn: Conservative Politics in a Liberal America* (Cambridge, MA: Harvard University Press, 2010), 212; R. W. Apple Jr., "G.O.P. Is Flirting with the Dangers of Negativism," *New York Times*, August 19, 1992; Nancy J. Davis and Robert V. Robinson, "Are the Rumors of War Exaggerated? Religious Orthodoxy and Moral Progressivism in America," *American Journal of Sociology* 102, no. 3 (November 1996): 784; Hunter, "Reflections on the Culture Wars Hypothesis," in James L. Nolan Jr., ed., *The American Culture Wars: Current Contests and Future Prospects* (Charlottesville: University of Virginia Press, 1996), 253; John Gallagher and Chris Bull, *Perfect Enemies: The Religious Right, the Gay Movement, and the Politics of the 1990s* (New York: Crown, 1996), xiv.

16. Robert Wuthnow, *The Struggle for America's Soul: Evangelicals, Liberals, and Secularism* (Grand Rapids, MI: Eerdmans, 1989), 169.

17. Joe Conason, "A Political Story—Chapter and Verse," *Columbia Journalism Review* 32, no. 2 (July–August 1993).

18. Jeffrey K. Hadden and Anson Shupe, "Introduction," xii; and Shupe and Hadden, "Is There Such a Thing as Global Fundamentalism?," in Hadden and Shupe, *Secularization and Fundamentalism Reconsidered* (New York: Paragon House, 1989), 109–122; Martin E. Marty, "Fundamentalism Reborn: Faith and Fanaticism," *Saturday Review*, May 1980, 37–42.

19. Martin E. Marty, "Too Bad We're So Relevant: The Fundamentalism Project Projected," *Bulletin of the American Academy of Arts and Sciences* 49, no. 6 (March 1996): 22–38; Susan Friend Harding, *The Book of Jerry Falwell: Fundamentalist Language and Politics* (Princeton, NJ: Princeton University Press, 2000), 268; Martin E. Marty, "Fundamentalism as a Social Phenomenon," *Bulletin of the American Academy of Arts and Sciences* 42, no. 2 (November 1988): 15–29; Martin E. Marty and R. Scott Appleby, *The Glory and the Power: The Fundamentalist Challenge to the Modern World* (Boston: Beacon, 1992); *The Glory and the Power: Fundamentalisms Observed.* Part I, *Fighting Back* (Washington, DC: WTAE/PBS, 1992); and the following titles, all edited by Martin E. Marty and R. Scott Appleby: *Fundamentalisms Observed* (Chicago: University of Chicago Press, 1991); *Fundamentalisms and Society: Reclaiming the Sciences, the Family, and Education* (Chicago: University of Chicago Press, 1993); *Fundamentalisms and the State: Remaking Politics, Economies, and Militance* (Chicago: University of Chicago Press, 1993); *Accounting for Fundamentalisms: The Dynamic Character of Movements* (Chicago: University of Chicago Press, 1994); and *Fundamentalisms Comprehended* (Chicago: University of Chicago Press, 1995). See also Gabriel A. Almond, R. Scott Appleby, and Emmanuel Sivan, *Strong Religion: The Rise of*

Fundamentalisms around the World (Chicago: University of Chicago Press, 2002).

20. Gilles Kepel, *The Revenge of God: The Resurgence of Islam, Christianity and Judaism in the Modern World*, trans. Alan Braley (University Park: Pennsylvania State University Press, 1994), 2; Samuel P. Huntington, *The Clash of Civilizations and the Remaking of World Order* (New York: Simon Schuster, 1996), 95–101. See also Karen Armstrong, *The Battle for God* (New York: Knopf, 2000); Lawrence Kaplan, ed., *Fundamentalism in Comparative Perspective* (Amherst: University of Massachusetts Press, 1992); and David Zeidan, *The Resurgence of Religion: A Comparative Study of Selected Themes in Christian and Islamic Fundamentalist Discourses* (Leiden: Brill, 2003).

21. Barry Hankins, *Francis Schaeffer and the Shaping of Evangelical America* (Grand Rapids, MI: Eerdmans, 2008), x–xi, 77–79, 209–225; Kenneth L. Woodward, "Guru of Fundamentalism," *Newsweek*, November 1, 1982; George M. Marsden, *The Outrageous Idea of Christian Scholarship* (New York: Oxford University Press, 1997), 38–39; Ronald L. Numbers, *The Creationists: From Scientific Creationism to Intelligent Design*, expanded edition (Cambridge, MA: Harvard University Press, 2006), 278–279; Mark A. Noll, Nathan O. Hatch, and George M. Marsden, *The Search for Christian America* (Westchester, IL: Crossway, 1983); Mark A. Noll, Nathan O. Hatch, and George M. Marsden, *The Search for Christian America*, expanded edition (Colorado Springs, CO: Helmers and Howard, 1989), quote on 156; D. G. Hart, *From Billy Graham to Sarah Palin: Evangelicals and the Betrayal of American Conservatism* (Grand Rapids, MI: Eerdmans, 2011), 80.

22. Randall Balmer, *Mine Eyes Have Seen the Glory: A Journey into the Evangelical Subculture in America* (New York: Oxford University Press, 1989); Schmalzbauer, *People of Faith*, 156; Paul Boyer, *When Time Shall Be No More: Prophecy Belief in Modern American Culture* (Cambridge, MA: Harvard University Press, 1992), 447; Numbers, *The Creationists*, 13–14. See also Maxie B. Burch, *The Evangelical Historians: The Historiography of George Marsden, Nathan Hatch, and Mark Noll* (Lanham, MD: University Press of America, 1996).

23. Mark A. Noll, *The Scandal of the Evangelical Mind* (Grand Rapids, MI: Eerdmans, 1994), 3, 11–12, 109, 126, 218; Alan Wolfe, "The Opening of the Evangelical Mind," *Atlantic Monthly*, October 2000; Stephen J. Nichols, *Jesus Made in America: A Cultural History from the Puritans to "The Passion of Christ"* (Downers Grove, IL: Intervarsity Press, 2008), 163. See, for example, Os Guinness, *Fit Bodies Fat Minds: Why Evangelicals Don't Think and What to Do about It* (Grand Rapids, MI: Baker, 1994).

24. Noll, *Scandal of the Evangelical Mind*, 255; Wolfe, "The Opening of the Evangelical Mind"; John Schmalzbauer and Kathleen A. Mahoney, "American Scholars Return to Studying Religion," *Contexts* (Winter 2008): 21; Martin Morse Wooster, *The Great Philanthropists and the Problem of "Donor Intent,"* 3rd edition (Washington, DC: Capital Research Center, 2007), 57–77; D. Michael Lindsay, *Faith in the*

Halls of Power: How Evangelicals Joined the American Elite (New York: Oxford University Press, 2007), 81–85, 97–99.

25. Joel A. Carpenter, "Grantmaking in Religion at the Pew Charitable Trusts: A Survey of Its Past, Present, and a Proposal for Its Future," March 1990 (copy in possession of author), quotes on 19, 24, 32; Lindsay, *Faith in the Halls of Power*, 81–85, 97–99; John Schmalzbauer and Kathleen A. Mahoney, "Religion and Knowledge in the Post-Secular Academy," Social Science Research Council Working Papers (2009), 19, http://blogs.ssrc.org/tif/wp-content/uploads/2009/09/post-secular-academy.pdf; Andrea Sterk, ed., *Religion, Scholarship, and Higher Education: Essays from the Lilly Seminar on Religion and Higher Education* (Notre Dame, IN: University of Notre Dame Press, 2002); Janet L. Kroll and Rebecca A. Cornejo, "Onward, Christian Soldiers," *Trust*, Winter/Spring 2003, 27–29; Marsden, *The Outrageous Idea of Christian Scholarship*, 115; Hunter, *Culture Wars*, xii; Robert Wuthnow, *Growing Up Religious: Christians and Jews and Their Journeys of Faith* (Boston: Beacon, 1999), xiii; Schmalzbauer, *People of Faith*, 198, xvi.

26. Burch, *Evangelical Historians*, 96; James C. Turner, "Something to Be Reckoned With: The Evangelical Mind Awakens," *Commonweal*, January 15, 1999, 11; "Evangelicals and Catholics Together: The Christian Mission in the Third Millennium," in Colson and Neuhaus, *Evangelicals and Catholics Together*, xxiv, xxxii–xxxiii; Colson and Neuhaus, *Your Word Is Truth: A Project of Evangelicals and Catholics Together* (Grand Rapids, MI: Eerdmans, 2002); William M. Shea, *The Lion and the Lamb: Evangelicals and Catholics in America* (New York: Oxford University Press, 2004), 5; Wolfe, "The Opening of the Evangelical Mind."

27. George M. Marsden, *Fundamentalism and American Culture: The Shaping of Twentieth-Century Evangelicalism, 1870–1925* (New York: Oxford University Press, 1980); Nathan O. Hatch, *The Democratization of American Christianity* (New Haven, CT: Yale University Press, 1989), quote on 210, 218; Leonard I. Sweet, "Wise as Serpents, Innocent as Doves: The New Evangelical Historiography," *Journal of the American Academy of Religion* 56, no. 3 (Autumn 1988): 397–416, quote on 397; Harry S. Stout and Robert M. Taylor Jr., "Studies of Religion in American Society: The State of the Art," in Stout and Hart, *New Directions in American Religious History*, 19; Schmalzbauer, *People of Faith*, 153–157.

28. George M. Marsden, *The Soul of the American University: From Protestant Establishment to Established Nonbelief* (New York: Oxford University Press, 1994), xi, quote on 7; George M. Marsden and Bradley J. Longfield, eds., *The Secularization of the Academy* (New York: Oxford University Press, 1992); Marsden, *The Outrageous Idea of Christian Scholarship*, quote in front matter; Mark A. Noll, "Traditional Christianity and the Possibility of Historical Knowledge," in Bruce Kuklick and D. G. Hart, eds., *Religious Advocacy and American History* (Grand Rapids, MI: Eerdmans, 1997), 28–53.

29. Stanley Hauerwas, *Against the Nations: War and Survival in a Liberal Society* (Minneapolis, MN: Winston, 1985); Stanley Hauerwas and William H. Willimon,

Resident Aliens: Life in the Christian Colony (Nashville, TN: Abington, 1989); Stanley Hauerwas, *Hannah's Child: A Theologian's Memoir* (Grand Rapids, MI: Eerdmans, 2010), 116–119; Jean Bethke Elshtain, "Christian Contrarian," *Time*, September 17, 2001; James Davison Hunter, *To Change the World: The Irony, Tragedy, and Possibility of Christianity in the Late Modern World* (New York: Oxford University Press, 2010), 152, 165.

30. Peter Steinfels, "Universities Biased against Religion, Scholar Says," *New York Times*, November 26, 1993; Schmalzbauer, *People of Faith*, 96–98.

31. Heather Hendershot, *Shaking the World for Jesus: Media and Conservative Evangelical Culture* (Chicago: University of Chicago Press, 2004), 10.

32. David Scott, "Notes from the Alternative Nation," *National Review*, June 17, 1996, 49–51; Hendershot, *Shaking the World for Jesus*, 21; Dale D. Buss, "Mass Marketing the Good News," *Christianity Today*, January 8, 1996, 57–60.

33. Hendershot, *Shaking the World for Jesus*, 57, 52; Eileen Luhr, *Witnessing Suburbia: Conservatives and Christian Youth Culture* (Berkeley: University of California Press, 2009), 126; Kenneth L. Woodward, "The New Christian Minstrels," *Newsweek*, August 19, 1985; Nichols, *Jesus Made in America*, 135; Sara Diamond, *Not by Politics Alone: The Enduring Influence of the Christian Right* (New York: Guilford, 1998), 49; Michael S. Hamilton, "The Triumph of the Praise Songs," *Christianity Today*, July 12, 1999.

34. Scott Thumma and Dave Travis, *Beyond Megachurch Myths: What We Can Learn from America's Largest Churches* (San Francisco: Jossey-Bass, 2007), xviii; Gustav Niebuhr, "Where Religion Gets a Big Dose of Shopping-Mall Culture," *New York Times*, April 16, 1995; Kimon Howland Sargeant, *Seeker Churches: Promoting Traditional Religion in a Nontraditional Way* (New Brunswick, NJ: Rutgers University Press, 2000), 2; Anne C. Loveland and Otis B. Wheeler, *From Meetinghouse to Megachurch: A Material and Cultural History* (Columbia: University of Missouri Press, 2003), 115, 127, 131–132; George Marsden, *Reforming Fundamentalism: Fuller Seminary and the New Evangelicalism* (Grand Rapids, MI: Eerdmans, 1987), 238.

35. Stephen Prothero, *American Jesus: How the Son of God Became a National Icon* (New York: Farrar, Straus Giroux, 2003), 154; Larry Eskridge, *God's Forever Family: The Jesus People Movement in America* (New York: Oxford University Press, 2013), 275–276; Sargeant, *Seeker Churches*, 19, 10, 15, 30; Gustav Niebuhr, "The Minister as Marketer: Learning from Business," *New York Times*, April 18, 1995; Robert D. Putnam and David E. Campbell, *American Grace: How Religion Divides and Unites Us* (New York: Simon Schuster, 2010), 113.

36. Gustav Niebuhr, "Megachurches Strive to Be All Things to All Parishioners," *Wall Street Journal*, May 13, 1991; Patricia Leigh Brown, "Megachurches as Minitowns," *New York Times*, May 9, 2002; James B. Twitchell, *Branded Nation: The Marketing of Megachurch, College, Inc., and Museumworld* (New York: Simon Schuster, 2004), 97; Peter F. Drucker, "Management's New Paradigms," *Forbes*, October 5, 1998;

Niebuhr, "The Minister as Marketer"; Shayne Lee and Phillip Luke Sinitiere, *Holy Mavericks: Evangelical Innovators and the Spiritual Marketplace* (New York: New York University Press, 2009), 142; Charles Trueheart, "Welcome to the Next Church," *Atlantic Monthly*, August 1996. See, for example, Robert D. Putnam, *Bowling Alone: The Collapse and Revival of American Community* (New York: Simon Schuster, 2000).

37. Jeff Sharlet, *The Family: The Secret Fundamentalism at the Heart of American Power* (New York: HarperPerennial, 2008), 294; Joshua Hammer, "Good-bye to Dubai," *New York Review of Books*, August 19, 2010; Peter Waldman, "Shifting Sands: With Its Oil Dwindling, Tiny Dubai Is Finding a Future as Cargo Hub," *Wall Street Journal*, July 26, 1994; "Colorado Springs: The Conservative Voice," *The Economist*, May 5, 1994; Marc Cooper, "God and Man in Colorado Springs," *The Nation*, January 2, 1995, 9–12; Darren Dochuk, *From Bible Belt to Sunbelt: Plain-Folk Religion, Grassroots Politics, and the Rise of Evangelical Conservatism* (New York: W. W. Norton, 2010), 406; Daniel K. Williams, *God's Own Party: The Making of the Christian Right* (New York: Oxford University Press, 2010), 236; Hendershot, *Shaking the World for Jesus*, 146.

38. Randall Balmer, *Mine Eyes Have Seen the Glory: A Journey into the Evangelical Subculture in America*, 4th edition (New York: Oxford University Press, 2006 [1989]), 310–321; e-mail communication from Liz Bilbo, Branson, Missouri, November 29, 2011; Jerry Rodnitzky, "Back to Branson: Normalcy and Nostalgia in the Ozarks," *Southern Cultures* 8, no. 2 (Summer 2002): 97–105; Aaron K. Ketchell, "Hillbilly Heaven: Branson Tourism and the Hillbilly of the Missouri Ozarks," 121, in Anthony J. Stanonis, ed., *Dixie Emporium: Tourism, Foodways, and Consumer Culture in the American South* (Athens: University of George Press, 2008); Rick Brunson, "Behind the Boom in Branson," *Charisma*, July 1993, 46–50; Aaron K. Ketchell, *Holy Hills of the Ozarks: Religion and Tourism in Branson, Missouri* (Baltimore: Johns Hopkins University Press, 2007), xiii–xiv, 117–118; Bethany Moreton, *To Serve God and Wal-Mart: The Making of Christian Free Enterprise* (Cambridge, MA: Harvard University Press, 2009), 9–10, 36; Julia Lesage, "Christian Media," in Linda Kintz and Julia Lesage, eds., *Media, Culture, and the Religious Right* (Minneapolis: University of Minnesota Press, 1998), 27.

39. Matthew C. Moen, "From Revolution to Evolution: The Changing Nature of the Christian Right," *Sociology of Religion* 55, no. 3 (Autumn 1994): 345–357.

40. Michael Sean Winters, *God's Right Hand: How Jerry Falwell Made God a Republican and Baptized the American Right* (New York: HarperCollins, 2012), 273–274; Larry Flynt, "My Friend, Jerry Falwell," *Los Angeles Times*, May 20, 2007, http://www.latimes.com/news/opinion/commentary/la-op-flynt20may20,0,2751741.story; *The People vs. Larry Flynt* (Los Angeles: Columbia, 1996); David Edwin Harrell Jr., *Pat Robertson: A Life and Legacy* (Grand Rapids, MI: Eerdmans, 2010), 125–131.

41. Williams, *God's Own Party*, 228; Martin, *With God on Our Side*, 318, 401 (note).

42. Kramnick and Moore, *The Godless Constitution*, 154–161; Ralph Reed, *Active Faith: How Christians Are Changing the Soul of American Politics* (New York: Free Press, 1996), 109–110, 8, 25, 68, 117–118, 200, 265; Diamond, *Not by Politics Alone*, 110, 151; Harrell, *Pat Robertson*, 143.

43. Reed, *Active Faith*, 133, 165; Michael Weisskopf, "Energized by Pulpit or Passion, the Public Is Calling; 'Gospel Grapevine' Displays Strength in Controversy over Military Gay Ban," *Washington Post*, February 1, 1993; James Davison Hunter and Carl Bowman, *The State of Disunion: 1996 Survey of American Political Culture* (Ivy, VA: In Media Res Educational Foundation, 1996), 53; Joann Byrd, "'Blind Spots,'" *Washington Post*, February 7, 1993; "A Dose of Demographic Reality," *Washington Post*, February 6, 1993; Gustav Niebuhr, "Broadcasters Urged to Wage 'Cultural War,'" *Washington Post*, February 20, 1993.

44. Justin Watson, *The Christian Coalition: Dreams of Restoration, Demands for Recognition* (New York: St. Martin's, 1997), 3, 52; Ralph Reed, *Politically Incorrect: The Emerging Faith Factor in American Politics* (Dallas, TX: Word, 1994), 41, 15–16.

45. Watson, *The Christian Coalition*, 57; Williams, *God's Own Party*, 230; Lichtman, *White Protestant Nation*, 398.

46. Ann Southworth, *Lawyers of the Right: Professionalizing the Conservative Coalition* (Chicago: University of Chicago Press, 2008), 25–26, 34, 31, 36.

47. Reed, *Active Faith*, 184–185, 201; Harrell, *Pat Robertson*, 138, 153; Williams, *God's Own Party*, 232–233; Thomas Edsall, "Religious Right Ready to Press GOP on Its Own Social 'Contract,'" *Washington Post*, May 14, 1995; Laurie Goodstein, "Gingrich Vows to Pursue Christian Coalition Agenda," *Washington Post*, May 18, 1995; Andrew Preston, *Sword of the Spirit, Shield of Faith: Religion in American War and Diplomacy* (New York: Knopf, 2012), 608; David Murray Oldfield, *The Right and the Righteous: The Christian Right Confronts the Republican Party* (Lanham, MD: Rowman Littlefield, 1996), 2.

48. Randall A. Terry, "Selling Out the Law of Heaven," *Washington Post*, September 18, 1994; Harrell, *Pat Robertson*, 147; Williams, *God's Own Party*, 239–240, 242.

49. Bill McCartney with Dave Diles, *From Ashes to Glory*, revised edition (Nashville, TN: Thomas Nelson, 1995); Bryan W. Brickner, *The Promise Keepers: Politics and Promises* (Lanham, MD: Lexington, 1999), 42–45; Donald E. Miller, *Reinventing American Protestantism: Christianity in the New Millennium* (Berkeley: University of California Press, 1997), 46–51; Patrick Allitt, *Religion in America since 1945: A History* (New York: Columbia University Press, 2003), 242–243; Michael E. Eidenmuller, "Promise Keepers and the Rhetoric of Recruitment: The Context, the Persona, and the Spectacle," in Dane S. Claussen, ed., *The Promise Keepers: Essays on Masculinity and Christianity* (Jefferson, NC: McFarland and Company, 2000), 92–93.

50. Gerald F. Seib, "Capital Journal: A Man's March: Behaving Right, or Going Right," *Wall Street Journal*, September 10, 1997; Susan Faludi, *Backlash: The Undeclared*

War against American Women (New York: Crown, 1991); Don Terry, "Black March Stirs Passion and Protests," *New York Times*, October 8, 2005; Moreton, *To Serve God and Wal-Mart*, 112–113; Michael J. Chrasta, "The Religious Roots of the Promise Keepers," in Claussen, *The Promise Keepers*, 25; Michael O. Emerson and Christian Smith, *Divided by Faith: Evangelical Religion and the Problem of Race in America* (New York: Oxford University Press, 2000), 52–68; Joe Conason, Alfred Ross, and Lee Cokorinos, "The Promise Keepers Are Coming: The Third Wave of the Religious Right," *The Nation*, October 7, 1996, 15; Brickner, *The Promise Keepers*, 34.

51. Patricia Ireland, "A Look at…Promise Keepers; Beware of 'Feel-Good Male Supremacy,'" *Washington Post*, September 7, 1997; Brickner, *The Promise Keepers*, 107; and the following chapters, all in Claussen, *The Promise Keepers*: Seib, "A Man's March"; Colleen E. Kelley, "Silencing the Voice of God: Rhetorical Responses to the Promise Keepers" (231–232); Ken Waters, "Who Are These Guys? The Promise Keepers' Media Relations Strategy for 'Stand in the Gap'" (259, 255); L. Dean Allen II, "They Just Don't Get It! Promise Keepers' Response to Media Coverage" (269); and Dane S. Claussen, "'So, Far, News Coverage of Promise Keepers Has Been More Like Advertising': The Strange Case of Christian Men and the Print Mass Media" (284).

52. David R. Swartz, "Left Behind: The Evangelical Left and the Limits of Evangelical Politics, 1965–1988" (Ph.D. dissertation, University of Notre Dame, 2008), 589–591.

53. Jerome P. Baggett, *Habitat for Humanity: Building Private Homes, Building Public Religion* (Philadelphia: Temple University Press, 2001), 40–65, 249–250, ix, x; Chris Goodrich, *Faith Is a Verb: On the Homefront with Habitat for Humanity in the Campaign to Rebuild America (and the World)* (Brookfield, CT: Gimlet Eye, 2005), 126–131, back cover.

54. William Aiken, "Habitats of the Heart: Have Nails, Will Hammer," *Commonweal*, January 25, 1991, 38–39; R. Allen Hays, "Habitat for Humanity: Building Social Capital through Faith Based Service," *Journal of Urban Affairs* 24, no. 3 (2002): 258; Jason Hackworth, "Normalizing 'Solutions' to 'Government Failure': Media Representations of Habitat for Humanity," *Environment and Planning A* 41 (2009): 2686–2705; Baggett, *Habitat for Humanity*, 251; Alan Cooperman, "Harassment Claims Roil Habitat for Humanity; As Founder's Supporters Rally, New Allegations Emerge," *Washington Post*, March 9, 2005; Michael G. Maudlin, "God's Contractor: How Habitat for Humanity's Millard Fuller Persuaded Corporate America to Do Kingdom Work," *Christianity Today*, June 14, 1999, 45.

55. Courtwright, *No Right Turn*, 222; David Domke and Kevin Coe, *The God Strategy: How Religion Became a Political Weapon in America*, 2nd edition (New York: Oxford University Press, 2010), 71–72; David L. Holmes, *The Faiths of the Founding Fathers* (New York: Oxford University Press, 2006), 181; Lindsay, *Faith*

in the Halls of Power, 52, 16, 23–24; Jim Wallis, *Who Speaks for God? An Alternative to the Religious Right—A New Politics of Compassion, Community, and Civility* (New York: Delacorte, 1996); Randall Balmer, *God in the White House: A History: How Faith Shaped the Presidency from John F. Kennedy to George W. Bush* (New York: HarperOne, 2008), 139; Hunter and Bowman, *State of Disunion*, 51, 59; Harrell, *Pat Robertson*, 137; Williams, *God's Own Party*, 243.

56. Sean Wilentz, *The Age of Reagan: A History, 1974–2008* (New York: HarperCollins, 2008), 392–393; Louise Branson, "A Pursuer Who Would Not Quit," *Maclean's*, September 21, 1998; David Kuo, *Tempting Faith: An Inside Story of Political Seduction* (New York: Free Press, 2006), 73; Courtwright, *No Right Turn*, 246.

57. Holmes, *The Faiths of the Founding Fathers*, 202n34; Tony Campolo, "Errant Evangelical? A Presidential Counselor in the Line of Fire," in E. J. Dionne Jr. and John J. DiIulio Jr., *What's God Got to Do with the American Experiment?* (Washington, DC: Brookings Institution Press, 2000), 106; Edward P. Wimberly, "African-American Pastoral Theology as Public Theology: The Crisis of Private and Public in the White House" (90–98), "Declaration concerning Religion, Ethics, and the Crisis in the Clinton Presidency" (1–3), and "Transcript of President Clinton's Speech at the Religious Leaders' Prayer Breakfast, September 11, 1998" (185–187), all in Gabriel Fackre, ed., *Judgment Day at the White House: A Critical Declaration Exploring Moral Issues and the Political Use and Abuse of Religion* (Grand Rapids, MI: Eerdmans, 1999); J. Philip Wogaman, *From the Eye of the Storm: A Pastor to the President Speaks Out* (Louisville, KY: Westminster John Knox Press, 1998), 74, 55; Balmer, *God in the White House*, 140–141.

58. Watson, *The Christian Coalition*, 84.

CHAPTER 5

1. Charles Colson (with Ellen Santilli Vaughn), *Kingdoms in Conflict* (Grand Rapids, MI: Zondervan, 1987), 9–40 (quotes on 12, 16, 17, 18, 35).

2. Colson, *Kingdoms in Conflict*, 40, 221.

3. Cal Thomas and Ed Dobson, *Blinded by Might: Can the Religious Right Save America?* (Grand Rapids, MI: Zondervan, 1999); Paul M. Weyrich, "An Open Letter to Conservatives," in Gregory L. Schneider, ed., *Conservatism in America since 1930* (New York: New York University Press, 2003), 428–431.

4. Charles Colson with Ellen Santilli Vaughn, *God and Government: An Insider's View on the Boundaries between Faith and Politics* (Grand Rapids, MI: Zondervan, 2007), 9–44.

5. Guy Lawson, "George W.'s Personal Jesus," *GQ*, February 2005, http://www.gq.com/news-politics/newsmakers/200501/george-bush-jesus-adviser-beliefs; George W. Bush, *Decision Points* (New York: Crown, 2010), 30–34.

6. George W. Bush, *A Charge to Keep* (New York: William Morrow, 1999), 136; Jacob Weisberg, *The Bush Tragedy* (New York: Random House, 2008), 82.

7. Howard Fineman, "Bush and God," *Newsweek*, March 10, 2003; Bush, *Decision Points*, 60–61; Daniel K. Williams, *God's Own Party: The Making of the Christian Right* (New York: Oxford University Press, 2010), 247; Fred Barnes, "The Gospel according to George W. Bush," *Weekly Standard*, March 22, 1999.

8. E. J. Dionne Jr., ed., *Community Works: The Revival of Civil Society in America* (Washington, DC: Brookings Institution Press, 1998); Olivier Zunz, *Philanthropy in America: A History* (Princeton, NJ: Princeton University Press, 2012), 255–259; Allen D. Hertzke, *Freeing God's Children: The Unlikely Alliance for Global Human Rights* (Lanham, MD: Rowman Littlefield, 2004), 183–236; David Grann, "Where W. Got Compassion," *New York Times Magazine*, September 12, 1999; Myron Magnet, *The Dream and the Nightmare: The Sixties' Legacy to the Underclass* (New York: William Morrow, 1993); Marvin Olasky, *The Tragedy of American Compassion* (Washington, DC: Regnery, 1992), 221; Joe Klein, "In God They Trust," *The New Yorker*, June 16, 1997, 40–48; Jim Wallis, *Who Speaks for God? An Alternative to the Religious Right—A New Politics of Compassion, Community, and Civility* (New York: Delacorte, 1996), ix.

9. Amy E. Black, Douglas L. Koopman, and David K. Ryden, *Of Little Faith: The Politics of George W. Bush's Faith-based Initiatives* (Washington, DC: Georgetown University Press, 2004), 51–54, 57–60, 37.

10. Black et al., *Of Little Faith*, 22–24; E. J. Dionne Jr., "In Search of George W.," *Washington Post Magazine*, September 19, 1999, reprinted in Richard A. Clucas, ed., *Readings and Cases in State and Local Politics* (Boston: Houghton Mifflin, 2006), 222–225.

11. Black et al., *Of Little Faith*, 12, 46–48; Harry S. Dent, *The Prodigal South Returns to Power* (New York: John Wiley, 1978), 299; Allan J. Lichtman, *White Protestant Nation: The Rise of the American Conservative Movement* (New York: Grove, 2008), 434; Weisberg, *Bush Tragedy*, 92–93; Marvin Olasky, *Compassionate Conservatism: What It Is, What It Does, and How It Can Transform America* (New York: Free Press, 2000), 9–11; Steven Teles, "Compassionate Conservatism, Domestic Policy, and the Politics of Ideational Change," in Joel D. Aberbach and Gillian Peele, eds., *Crisis of Conservatism? The Republican Party, the Conservative Movement and American Politics after Bush* (New York: Oxford University Press, 2011), 180; David Kuo, *Tempting Faith: An Inside Story of Political Seduction* (New York: Free Press, 2006), 83; Jim Wallis, *God's Politics: Why the Right Gets It Wrong and the Left Doesn't Get It* (San Francisco: HarperCollins, 2005), 11–12; D. Michael Lindsay, *Faith in the Halls of Power: How Evangelicals Joined the American Elite* (New York: Oxford University Press, 2007), 68; Tony Campolo, *Speaking My Mind* (Nashville, TN: Thomas Nelson, 2004), 130–131; Jeff Sharlet, *The Family: The Secret Fundamentalism at the Heart of American Power* (New York: Harper-Perennial, 2008), 276.

12. James Davison Hunter, *To Change the World: The Irony, Tragedy, and Possibility of Christianity in the Late Modern World* (New York: Oxford University Press, 2010),

72–74; Jeff Sharlet, *C Street: The Fundamentalist Threat to American Democracy* (New York: Little, Brown, 2010), 273–280.

13. Kuo, *Tempting Faith*, 56; Jeffrey Goldberg, "Letter from Washington: The Believer," *New Yorker*, February 13, 2006; uncorrected transcript of "Q&A with Michael Gerson," CSPAN, January 7, 2007, http://www.q-and-a.org/Transcript/? ProgramID=1109; Ross Douthat, "The Future of the GOP," *Slate*, November 26, 2007; Michael J. Gerson, *Heroic Conservatism: Why Republicans Need to Embrace America's Ideals (And Why They Deserve to Fail If They Don't)* (New York: HarperCollins, 2007), 27–29, 35–36.

14. Ronald L. Numbers, *The Creationists: From Scientific Creationism to Intelligent Design*, expanded edition (Cambridge, MA: Harvard University Press, 2006), 373–398; Chris Mooney, *The Republican War on Science* (New York: Basic, 2005), 164.

15. Dionne, "In Search of George W.," 221; George W. Bush, "The Duty of Hope," July 22, 1999, http://blog.chron.com/txpotomac/2010/07/today-in-texas-history-gw-bush-delivers-first-presidential-campaign-speech/; Ralph Reed, "Mr. Right: The Conservative Case for George W.," *National Review*, July 12, 1999; Williams, *God's Own Party*, 246–249; "Bob Jones University Ends Ban on Interracial Dating," March 30, 2010, http://articles.cnn.com/2000-03-04/us/bob.jones_1_racist-school-ends-ban-bushs-visit?_s=PM:US; Timothy S. Goeglein, *The Man in the Middle: An Inside Account of Faith and Politics in the George W. Bush Era* (Nashville, TN: B&H Publishing, 2011), 28.

16. Williams, *God's Own Party*, 250; Black et al., *Of Little Faith*, 75–76; Randall Balmer, *God in the White House: A History: How Faith Shaped the Presidency from John F. Kennedy to George W. Bush* (New York: HarperOne, 2008), 146; Wallis, *Who Speaks for God?* 32, back cover; E. J. Dionne, "Foreword," in Hugh Heclo and Wildred M. McClay, *Religion Returns to the Public Square: Faith and Policy in America* (Washington, DC: Woodrow Wilson Center Press, 2003), xv.

17. Richard L. Berke, "Aide Says Bush Will Do More to Marshal Religious Base," *New York Times*, December 12, 2001; Wallis, *God's Politics*, 11–12; Amy Sullivan, *The Party Faithful: How and Why Democrats Are Closing the God Gap* (New York: Simon Schuster, 2008), 95; transcript of George W. Bush's first inaugural address, January 20, 2001, http://www.pbs.org/newshour/inauguration/speech.html.

18. Black et al., *Of Little Faith*, 190, 186, 306–306; Kuo, *Tempting Faith*, 136; Ron Suskind, "Why Are These Men Laughing?" *Esquire*, January 2003, http://ronsuskind.com/articles/000032.html; President George W. Bush, "Rallying the Armies of Compassion," January 2001, http://archives.hud.gov/reports/rally.pdf.

19. Goeglein, *Man in the Middle*, xii; Randall J. Stephens and Karl W. Giberson, *The Anointed: Evangelical Truth in a Secular Age* (Cambridge, MA: Harvard University Press, 2011), 79; Hertzke, *Freeing God's Children*, 35; Bob Cleath, untitled news blurb reprinted in *Moody Monthly*, September 1976, 21; Charles Colson, "From a

Moral Majority to a Persecuted Minority," *Christianity Today*, May 14, 1990, 80; Charles Colson (with Anne Moore), "Evangelical Drift," *Christianity Today*, April 2004, 112.

20. Damon Linker, *The Theocons: Secular America under Siege* (New York: Doubleday, 2006), 113; Goeglein, *Man in the Middle*, 170; David D. Kirkpatrick, "The Right Hand of the Fathers," *New York Times Magazine*, December 20, 2009; Jon A. Shields, *The Democratic Virtues of the Christian Right* (Princeton, NJ: Princeton University Press, 2009), 66; Laurie Goodstein, "Gingrich Represents New Political Era for Roman Catholics," *New York Times*, December 17, 2011; Nia J. Stanley, "What Is Sam Brownback's Religion?" *Politics Daily*, October 27, 2010, http://www.politicsdaily.com/2010/10/27/what-is-sam-brownbacks-religion/; Mark Oppenheimer, "Many Evangelicals See Something to Admire in Candidates' Broods," *New York Times*, January 21, 2012; Martin Kaste, "Tim Pawlenty: The Young Republican Comes of Age," National Public Radio, April 25, 2011, http://www.npr.org/2011/04/25/135409599/tim-pawlenty-the-young-reaganite-comes-of-age; Hanna Rosin, *God's Harvard: A Christian College on a Mission to Save America* (Orlando, FL: Harcourt, 2007), 65.

21. Peter Schweitzer and Rochelle Schweitzer, *The Bushes: Portrait of a Dynasty* (New York: Doubleday, 2004), 465; George F. Will, "Bush's Conservatism," *Washington Post*, April 29, 2001; Esther Kaplan, *With God on Their Side: George W. Bush and the Christian Right* (New York: New Press, 2005), 148–151; Goeglein, *Man in the Middle*, 51–58; David Frum, *The Right Man: The Surprise Presidency of George W. Bush* (New York: Random House, 2003), 4, 17; Lindsay, *Faith in the Halls of Power*, 26, 69; D. Jason Berggren and Nicol C. Rae, "Jimmy Carter and George W. Bush: Faith, Foreign Policy, and an Evangelical Presidential Style," *Presidential Studies Quarterly* 36, no. 4 (December 2006): 614.

22. Williams, *God's Own Party*, 254; Jon Meacham, *American Gospel: God, the Founding Fathers, and the Making of a Nation* (New York: Random House, 2006), 234–235; "Franklin Graham Conducts Services at Pentagon," CNN.com, April 18, 2003, http://www.cnn.com/2003/ALLPOLITICS/04/18/graham.pentagon/; Gary Scott Smith, *Faith and the Presidency: From George Washington to George W. Bush* (New York: Oxford University Press, 2006), 371; Bill Broadway, "Evangelicals' Voices Speak Softly about Iraq," *Washington Post*, January 25, 2003; Linker, *Theocons*, 130; Kirkpatrick, "Right Hand of the Fathers."

23. Axel R. Schäfer, *Countercultural Conservatives: American Evangelicalism from the Postwar Revival to the New Christian Right* (Madison: University of Wisconsin Press, 2011), 136–145; "For the Health of the Nation: An Evangelical Call to Civic Responsibility," in Ronald J. Sider and Diane Knippers, eds., *Toward an Evangelical Public Policy: Political Strategies for the Health of the Nation* (Grand Rapids, MI: Baker, 2005), 363–375; David P. Gushee, *The Future of Faith in American Politics: The Public Witness of the Evangelical Center* (Waco, TX: Baylor University Press, 2008), 101; Peter Goodwin Heltzel, *Jesus and Justice: Evangelicals,*

Race, and American Politics (New Haven, CT: Yale University Press, 2009), 139, 145; Ronald J. Sider, *The Scandal of Evangelical Politics: Why Are Christians Missing the Chance to Really Change the World?* (Grand Rapids, MI: Baker, 2008), 207; Dan Gilgoff, *The Jesus Machine: How James Dobson, Focus on the Family, and Evangelical America Are Winning the Culture War* (New York: St. Martin's, 2007), 2, 11–15.

24. David Domke and Kevin Coe, *The God Strategy: How Religion Became a Political Weapon in America*, updated edition (New York: Oxford University Press, 2010), 117; Williams, *God's Own Party*, 256–260; Kaplan, *With God on Their Side*, 76; David D. Kirkpatrick, "The Evangelical Crackup," *New York Times Magazine*, October 28, 2007; Kevin M. Kruse, "Compassionate Conservatism: Religion in the Age of George W. Bush," in Julian E. Zelizer, ed., *The Presidency of George W. Bush: A First Historical Assessment* (Princeton, NJ: Princeton University Press, 2010), 244; Erik Eckholm, "History Buff Sets a Course for the Right," *New York Times*, May 5, 2011; Donald B. Kraybill and Kyle C. Kopko, "Bush Fever: Amish and Old Order Mennonites in the 2004 Presidential Election," *Mennonite Quarterly Review* 81 (April 2007): 165–205; Jack Brubaker, "Bush Quietly Meets with Amish Here," *Lancaster* (Penn.) *New Era*, July 16, 2004; Sullivan, *Party Faithful*, 137; *George W. Bush: Faith in the White House* (New York: GoodTimes Entertainment, 2004).

25. Sullivan, *Party Faithful*, 179; Kirkpatrick, "Evangelical Crackup"; Richard T. Hughes, *Christian America and the Kingdom of God* (Champaign: University of Illinois Press, 2009), 159–160.

26. Janet Kornblum, "eHarmony: Heart and Soul," *USA Today*, May 19, 2005; Jarrod Dicker, "Religious CEOs: eHarmony Founder, Neil Clark Warren," Minyanville blog, May 19, 2010; Lisa Miller, "An Algorithm for Mr. Right," *Newsweek*, May 5, 2008.

27. David Gibson, "'WWJD' Survives Politics, Parodies, Marketing Fads," *Contra Costa Times*, October 14, 2000; Damien Cave, "What Would Jesus Do—about Copyright?" *Salon*, October 25, 2000, http://www.salon.com/2000/10/25/wwjd/; Alfred Gingold, "Onward, Christian Clothiers," *Slate*, July 11, 1998.

28. Rick Warren, *The Purpose Driven Life: What on Earth Am I Here For?* (Grand Rapids, MI: Zondervan, 2002), 19, 17, 5; Rick Warren, *The Purpose Driven Church: Growth without Compromising Your Message and Mission* (Grand Rapids, MI: Zondervan, 1995); Jeffrey L. Sheler, *Prophet of Purpose: The Life of Rick Warren* (New York: Doubleday, 2009), 182; Malcolm Gladwell, "The Cellular Church," *The New Yorker*, September 12, 2005; David Van Biema, "Spirit Raiser," *Time*, September 17, 2001; Todd M. Brenneman, *Homespun Gospel: The Triumph of Sentimentality in Contemporary American Evangelicalism* (New York: Oxford University Press, 2014).

29. Ashley Smith with Stacy Mattingly, *Unlikely Angel: The Untold Story of the Atlanta Hostage Hero* (Grand Rapids, MI: Zondervan, 2005); transcript of

The Oprah Winfrey Show, September 28, 2005, http://www.saddlebackfamily. com/home/images/OprahTranscriptAshleyRW.pdf; Cathy Lynn Grossman, "Starbucks Stirs Things Up with a God Quote on Cups," *USA Today,* October 19, 2005.

30. Tim LaHaye and Jerry B. Jenkins, *Left Behind* (Carol Stream, IL: Tyndale House, 1995); Sherryll Mleynek, "The Rhetoric of the 'Jewish Problem' in the *Left Behind* Novel," *Literature and Theology* 19, no. 4 (November 2005): 367–383; Melanie McAlister, "Prophecy, Politics, and the Popular: The *Left Behind* Series and Christian Fundamentalism's New World Order," *South Atlantic Quarterly* 102, no. 4 (Fall 2003): 777.

31. Nancy Gibbs et al., "Apocalypse Now," *Time,* July 1, 2002; John Cloud et al., "Meet the Prophet," *Time,* July 1, 2002; David Gates, "The Pop Prophets," *Newsweek*, May 24, 2004; Amy Johnson Frykholm, *Rapture Culture: "Left Behind" in Evangelical America* (New York: Oxford University Press, 2004), 25; Heather Hendershot, *Shaking the World for Jesus: Media and Conservative Evangelical Culture* (Chicago: University of Chicago Press, 2004), 196–197.

32. Mark Silk, "Almost a Culture War: The Making of *The Passion* Controversy" (23–34); J. Shawn Landres and Michael Berenbaum, "Introduction" (1–17); Leslie E. Smith, "Living *in* the World, but Not *of* the World: Understanding Evangelical Support for *The Passion of the Christ*" (52–53); all in J. Shawn Landres and Michael Berenbaum, eds., *After "The Passion" Is Gone: American Religious Consequences* (Walnut Creek, CA: AltaMira, 2004); Peter Boyer, "The Jesus War," *The New Yorker*, September 15, 2003; Monique El-Faizy, *God and Country: How Evangelicals Have Become America's New Mainstream* (New York: Bloomsbury, 2006), 159; James Y. Trammell, "Who Does God Want Me to Invite to See *The Passion of the Christ*? Marketing Movies to Evangelicals," *Journal of Media and Religion* 9, no. 1 (2010): 25; Frank Rich, "The Good News about Mel Gibson," *New York Times* "Week in Review," July 18, 2010, 9.

33. Smith, "Living *in* the World, But Not *of* the World," 51, 53; Stephen R. Haynes, "A March of Passion; or, How I Came to Terms with a Film I Wasn't Supposed to Like," in Landres and Berenbaum, *After "The Passion" Is Gone*, 193–195; Trammell, "Who Does God Want Me to Invite?" 19–29; Lee Strobel and Garry Poole, *Experiencing the Passion of Jesus: A Discussion Guide on History's Most Important Event* (Grand Rapids, MI: Zondervan, 2004).

34. Berenbaum and Landres, Introduction, in *After "The Passion" Is* Gone, 4; Hanna Rosin, "Can Jesus Save Hollywood?" *Atlantic Monthly*, December 2005, 161–162; Lindsay, *Faith in the Halls of Power*, 122, 132, 135, 152; El-Faizy, *God and Country*, 155, 164, 169–170.

35. *Hell House* (Brooklyn, NY: Plexifilm, 2002); Jason C. Bivins, *Religion of Fear: The Politics of Horror in Conservative Evangelicalism* (New York: Oxford University Press, 2008), 129–168; *Jesus Camp* (Los Angeles: Magnolia Home Entertainment, 2006); *Saved!* (Beverly Hills, CA: MGM Home Entertainment, 2004); Lindsay,

Faith in the Halls of Power, 119; Laura Bruno, "Abortion Foes Push for License Plates," *USA Today*, October 13, 2009.

36. "We're Prime Time, Baby!," *Christianity Today*, July 2005, 23.

37. Frederick V. Slocum, "With God on Our Side: Moral and Religious Issues, Southern Culture, and Republican Realignment in the South," in Glenn Feldman, ed., *Painting Dixie Red: When, Where, Why, and How the South Became Republican* (Gainesville: University Press of Florida, 2011), 57–58; Gilgoff, *Jesus Machine*, 1–5.

38. *Tammy Kitzmiller et al. v. Dover Area School District*, US District Court Case No. 04cv2688, December 20, 2005, http://ncse.com/webfm_send/73; Jodi Wilgoren, "Politicized Scholars Put Evolution on the Defensive," *New York Times*, August 21, 2005; Numbers, *The Creationists*, 391–394, 389, 397; Michelle Goldberg, *Kingdom Coming: The Rise of Christian Nationalism* (New York: W. W. Norton, 2006), 201–202.

39. "Schiavo Timeline, Part 1," http://www.miami.edu/index.php/ethics/projects/schiavo/schiavo_timeline/; "Schiavo Timeline, Part 2," http://www.miami.edu/index.php/ethics/projects/schiavo/schiavo_timlinee2/; E. J. Dionne Jr., *Souled Out: Reclaiming Faith and Politics after the Religious Right* (Princeton, NJ: Princeton University Press, 2008), 117–123; Larry Fish, "Schiavo's Parents Recruit Activist in Plea for Daughter," *Philadelphia Inquirer*, February 16, 2005; Jacqueline L. Salmon, "Randall Terry Wants to Lead Rebirth of Antiabortion Fight," *Washington Post*, July 15, 2009; Sheryl Gay Stolberg, "Frist Is Treading a Perilous Path Leading to 2008," *New York Times*, April 3, 2006; William Saletan, "Blind Man's Love," *Slate*, June 17, 2005.

40. Kruse, "Compassionate Conservatism," 247; "The Terri Schiavo Case," PR Newswire, April 15, 2005; Domke and Coe, *God Strategy*, 135; Goldberg, *Kingdom Coming*, 169–170.

41. Suskind, "Why Are These Men Laughing?"; John J. DiIulio Jr., "Afterword: Why Judging George W. Bush Is Never as Easy as It Seems," in Robert Maranto et al., eds., *Judging Bush* (Stanford, CA: Stanford University Press, 2009), 294–310; Kruse, "Compassionate Conservatism," 234–236; John J. DiIulio Jr., *Godly Republic: A Centrist Blueprint for America's Faith-Based Future* (Berkeley: University of California Press, 2007), 135; Frum, *The Right Man*, 103; Frank Lambert, *Religion in American Politics: A Short History* (Princeton, NJ: Princeton University Press, 2008), 205–207; Isaac Kramnick and R. Laurence Moore, *The Godless Constitution: A Moral Defense of the Secular State* (New York: W. W. Norton, 2005), 193; Goldberg, *Kingdom Coming*, 107; Dave Donaldson and Stanley Carlson-Thies, *A Revolution of Compassion: Faith-Based Groups as Full Partners in Fighting America's Social Problems* (Grand Rapids, MI: Baker, 2003), 138; Campolo, *Speaking My Mind*, 132–133; Wallis, *God's Politics*, 250–251.

42. Kuo, *Tempting Faith*, 69–73, 11–14; "A Loss of Faith," *60 Minutes* story transcript, October 15, 2006, http://www.cbsnews.com/stories/2006/10/14/60minutes/main2089778.shtml.

43. Rosin, *God's Harvard*, 13, 47; "The New Establishment: How Evangelicals Became Part of Washington's Fabric," *Washington Post*, May 25, 2007; Alan Cooperman, "Bush Loyalist Rose Quickly at Justice," *Washington Post*, March 30, 2007; Dan Eggen and Paul Kane, "Goodling Says She 'Crossed the Line,'" *Washington Post*, May 24, 2007; Dahlia Lithwick, "Justices Holy Hires," *Washington Post*, April 8, 2007; Richard T. Hughes, "Why the Media Bungled Monica Goodling's Background," *Philadelphia Inquirer*, May 6, 2007, http://www.messiah.edu/offices/publications/the_bridge/summer07/hughes/hughes2.html; El-Faizy, *God and Country*, 205; Williams, *God's Own Party*, 265–267.

44. David D. Kirkpatrick and Philip Shenon, "Ralph Reed's Zeal for Lobbying Is Shaking His Political Faithful," *New York Times*, April 18, 2005.

45. Heltzel, *Jesus and Justice*, 145–148; Sharlet, *The Family*, 293–297; *George W. Bush: Faith in the White House*; *Friends of God: The Evangelical Movement in America* (Princeton, NJ: Films Media Group, 2007); *Jesus Camp*; *The Trials of Ted Haggard* (New York: Home Box Office, 2009). For uses of "faith-based presidency," see Ron Suskind, "Without a Doubt," *New York Times Magazine*, October 17, 2004; and Nancy Gibbs, "The Faith Factor," *Time*, June 21, 2004.

46. Esther Kaplan, *With God on Their Side: George W. Bush and the Christian Right* (New York: New Press, 2005), 3, 277; Kramnick and Moore, *The Godless Constitution*, 178; Gabriel A. Almond, R. Scott Appleby, and Emmanuel Sivan, *Strong Religion: The Rise of Fundamentalisms around the World* (Chicago: University of Chicago Press, 2003); Santosh C. Saha, *Religious Fundamentalism in the Contemporary World: Critical Social and Political Issues* (Lanham, MD: Lexington, 2004); Chris Hedges, *American Fascists: The Christian Right and the War on America* (New York: Free Press, 2006), 9–10.

47. Molly Worthen, "The Chalcedon Problem: Rousas John Rushdoony and the Origins of Christian Reconstructionism," *Church History* 77, no. 2 (June 2008): 399–437; Goldberg, *Kingdom Coming*, 13, 37–40; Sharlet, *The Family*, 44, 347–351; Garry Wills, *Under God: Religion and American Politics* (New York: Simon Schuster, 1990), 174–175; Sara Diamond, *Roads to Dominion: Right-Wing Movement and Political Power in the United States* (New York: Guilford, 1995), 246–249; Kevin Phillips, *American Theocracy: The Perils and Politics of Radical Religion, Oil, and Borrowed Money in the 21st Century* (New York: Penguin, 2006), xxviii.

48. Thomas Frank, *What's the Matter with Kansas? How Conservatives Won the Heart of America* (New York: Metropolitan, 2004); Ronald Aronson, "Faith No More?" *Bookforum*, October/November 2005, 16–19; "The New Atheists," *The Nation*, June 25, 2007, 11–14; Sam Harris, *The End of Faith: Religion, Terror, and the Future of Reason* (New York: W. W. Norton, 2004); Sam Harris, *Letters to a Christian Nation* (New York: Knopf, 2006), 40–41; Sam Harris, "Response to Controversy: Version 2.3," April 7, 2013, http://www.samharris.org/site/full_text/response-to-controversy2; Christopher Hitchens, *God Is Not Great: How*

Religion Poisons Everything (New York: Twelve, 2007), 32; Richard Dawkins, *The God Delusion* (Boston: Houghton Mifflin, 2006).

49. *The Daily Show with Jon Stewart*, clips, September 16, 2004, http://www .thedailyshow.com/watch/thu-september-16-2004/this-week-in-god–falwell-law, and December 16, 2004, http://www.thedailyshow.com/watch/thu-december-16-2004/this-week-in-god–holiday-edition; Robert Lanham, *The Sinner's Guide to the Evangelical Right* (New York: New American Library, 2006), xix.

50. Michael Kazin, *A Godly Hero: The Life of William Jennings Bryan* (New York: Knopf, 2006); Michael Kazin, "A Difficult Marriage: American Protestants and American Politics," *Dissent*, Winter 2006.

51. Charles Marsh, "Wayward Christian Soldiers," *New York Times*, January 20, 2006; Charles Marsh, *Wayward Christian Soldiers: Freeing the Gospel from Political Captivity* (New York: Oxford University Press, 2007), 178; Randall Balmer, *Thy Kingdom Come: How the Religious Right Distorts the Faith and Threatens America: An Evangelical's Lament* (New York: Basic, 2007); Jimmy Carter, *Our Endangered Values: America's Moral Crisis* (New York: Simon Schuster, 2005); Lanham, *Sinner's Guide*, 190.

52. Peter Baker, "Bush Tells Group He Sees a 'Third Awakening,'" *Washington Post*, September 13, 2006. See Robert William Fogel, *The Fourth Great Awakening and the Future of Egalitarianism* (Chicago: University of Chicago Press, 2000).

CHAPTER 6

1. "Obama's Historic 'Call to Renewal' Speech," delivered June 26, 2008 (posted November 2, 2008), http://blog.beliefnet.com/stevenwaldman/2008/11/obamas-historic-call-to-renewa.html.

2. David D. Kirkpatrick, "The Evangelical Crackup," *New York Times Magazine*, October 28, 2007; Lisa Miller, "An Evangelical Identity Crisis," *Newsweek*, November 13, 2006; Francis FitzGerald, "The New Evangelicals," *The New Yorker*, June 30, 2008; Joel Hunter, *A New Kind of Conservative* (Ventura, CA: Regal, 2008), 20–21.

3. Charles Marsh, *Wayward Christian Soldiers: Freeing the Gospel from Political Captivity* (New York: Oxford University Press, 2007), 23–26, 56–57; Alister Chapman, *Godly Ambition: John Stott and the Evangelical Movement* (New York: Oxford University Press, 2012); David Brooks, "Who Is John Stott?," *New York Times*, November 30, 2004; "InterVarsity's History," http://www.intervarsity.org/ about/our/history (accessed March 6, 2013).

4. Peter Goodwin Heltzel, *Jesus and Justice: Evangelicals, Race, and American Politics* (New Haven, CT: Yale University Press, 2009), 153–158; *Fresh Air* (National Public Radio) episode transcript, December 2, 2008, http://www.npr.org/tem-plates/story/story.php?storyId=97690760; David P. Gushee, *The Future of Faith in American Politics: The Public Witness of the Evangelical Center* (Waco, TX: Baylor University Press, 2008), xii.

5. Robert D. Putnam and David E. Campbell, *American Grace: How Religion Divides and Unites Us* (New York: Simon Schuster, 2010), 59, 54–55; Jeffrey L. Sheler, *Prophet of Purpose: The Life of Rick Warren* (New York: Doubleday, 2009), 1, 258; Robert D. Putnam and Lewis M. Feldstein, *Better Together: Restoring the American Community* (New York: Simon Schuster, 2003), 119–141.

6. Pew Forum transcript, "The Future of Evangelicals: A Conversation with Pastor Rick Warren," November 13, 2009, http://www.pewforum.org/Christian/Evangelical-Protestant-Churches/The-Future-of-Evangelicals-A-Conversation-with-Pastor-Rick-Warren.aspx; John Leland, "Offering Ministry, and Early Release, to Prisoners," *New York Times*, June 10, 2004; Sheler, *Prophet of Purpose*, 8–9; Kevin M. Kruse, "Compassionate Conservatism: Religion in the Age of George W. Bush," in Julian E. Zelizer, ed., *The Presidency of George W. Bush: A First Historical Assessment* (Princeton, NJ: Princeton University Press, 2010), 240–242; Miller, "An Evangelical Identity Crisis"; Timothy C. Morgan, "Purpose Driven in Rwanda," *Christianity Today*, October 2005; Monique El-Faizy, *God and Country: How Evangelicals Have Become America's New Mainstream* (New York: Bloomsbury, 2006), 15; Rob Blackhurst, "Mass Appeal," *Financial Times*, August 13, 2011.

7. Shayne Lee and Phillip Luke Sinitiere, *Holy Mavericks: Evangelical Innovators and the Spiritual Marketplace* (New York: New York University Press, 2009), 77–105; Eddie Gibbs and Ryan K. Bolger, *Emerging Churches: Creating Christian Community in Postmodern Churches* (Grand Rapids, MI: Baker Academic, 2005); Andy Crouch, "Emergent Mystique," *Christianity Today*, November 2004, 36–41; Darrell L. Guder, ed., *Missional Church: A Vision for the Sending of the Church in North America* (Grand Rapids, MI: Eerdmans, 1998).

8. Brian McLaren, foreword to John D. Caputo, *What Would Jesus Deconstruct? The Good News of Postmodernism for the Church* (Grand Rapids, MI: Baker Academic, 2007), 9–12; Brian McLaren, *Everything Must Change: Jesus, Global Crises, and a Revolution of Hope* (Nashville, TN: Thomas Nelson, 2007), 5–6; Brian McLaren, *A New Kind of Christian: A Tale of Two Friends on a Spiritual Journey* (San Francisco: Jossey-Bass, 2001), xiv; Gibbs and Bolger, *Emerging Churches*, 283–285.

9. Brian McLaren, *A Generous Orthodoxy* (Grand Rapids, MI: Zondervan, 2004); Brian McLaren, foreword to Richard T. Hughes, *Christian America and the Kingdom of God* (Urbana: University of Illinois Press), xi–xiii; John Blake, "Faith and Values: Voice of 'Sage' Inspires, Unsettles," *Atlanta Journal-Constitution*, January 27, 2007; Carl Raschke, *The Next Reformation: Why Evangelicals Must Embrace Postmodernity* (Grand Rapids, MI: Baker, 2004), 20–24; Lloyd Chia, "Emerging Faith Boundaries: Bridge-Building, Inclusion, and the Emerging Church Movement in America" (Ph.D. dissertation, University of Missouri-Columbia, 2010), 94.

10. Dan Wakefield, *The Hijacking of Jesus: How the Religious Right Distorts Christianity and Promotes Violence and Hate* (New York: Nation, 2006), 192–193; Ronald J.

Sider, *The Scandal of Evangelical Politics: Why Are Christians Missing the Chance to Really Change the World?* (Grand Rapids, MI: Baker, 2008); Tony Campolo, *Letters to a Young Evangelical* (New York: Basic, 2006), 3.

11. D. Michael Lindsay, *Faith in the Halls of Power: How Evangelicals Joined the American Elite* (New York: Oxford University Press, 2007), 28; Jim Wallis, *The Soul of Politics: Beyond "Religious Right" and "Secular Left"* (San Diego, CA: Harcourt Brace, 1994), ix–xi; e-mail exchange with Duane Shank, Senior Policy Adviser for Sojourners, January 26, 2012; David R. Swartz, "Left Behind: The Evangelical Left and the Limits of Evangelical Politics, 1965–1988" (Ph.D. dissertation, University of Notre Dame, 2008), 578–579; Frank Lambert, *Religion in American Politics: A Short History* (Princeton, NJ: Princeton University Press, 2008), 233; Jim Wallis, *God's Politics: Why the Right Gets It Wrong and the Left Doesn't Get It* (San Francisco, CA: HarperCollins, 2005), 67; Ron Suskind, "Without a Doubt," *New York Times Magazine*, October 17, 2004.

12. Jim Wallis, "Putting God Back in Politics," *New York Times*, December 28, 2003; *New York Times* advertisement, August 30, 2004; Sojourners advertisement in *USA Today* (2004), http://www.yuricareport.com/Religion/confessing_christ. pdf (see also http://www.reformedreflections.ca/series/q-a-sojourners.html); Wallis, *God's Politics*, xx, xiv–xxvi, 59, 57, 11, 297–306; Swartz, "Left Behind," 582–583; Thomas G. Fuechtmann, ed., *Consistent Ethic of Life* (Kansas City, MO: Sheed and Ward, 1988).

13. Lambert, *Religion in American Politics*, 222; Lindsay, *Faith in the Halls of Power*, 28; Michael Lerner, *The Left Hand of God: Taking Back Our Country from the Religious Right* (San Francisco: HarperCollins, 2006); Wallis, *God's Politics*, 4–5; Campolo, *Letters to a Young Evangelical*, 7; David D. Kirkpatrick, "Democrats Turn to Leaders of Religious Left," *New York Times*, January 17, 2005.

14. James Davison Hunter made a similar point about the outsize role of the evangelical left. James Davison Hunter, *To Change the World: The Irony, Tragedy, and Possibility of Christianity in the Late Modern World* (New York: Oxford University Press, 2010), 137; Mel White, *Religion Gone Bad: The Hidden Dangers of the Christian Right* (New York: Penguin, 2006), 21; Ray Suarez, *The Holy Vote: The Politics of Faith in America* (New York: HarperCollins, 2006), 1; Wakefield, *Hijacking of Jesus*, 14; John Danforth, *Faith and Politics: How the "Moral Values" Debate Divides America and How to Move Forward Together* (New York: Viking, 2006), 78–79, quote on 10; "In the Name of Politics," *New York Times*, March 30, 2005; Gushee, *Future of Faith*, 57.

15. Amy Sullivan, *The Party Faithful: How and Why Democrats Are Closing the God Gap* (New York: Simon Schuster, 2008), 4, 134, 185, 91–92, 157, 172; Daniel K. Williams, *God's Own Party: The Making of the Christian Right* (New York: Oxford University Press, 2010), 261; Kirkpatrick, "Democrats Turn to Leaders of Religious Left"; David Domke and Kevin Coe, *The God Strategy: How Religion Became a Political Weapon in America*, updated edition (New York: Oxford University Press,

2010), 117, 7; Hunter, *To Change the World*, 148; Lambert, *Religion in American Politics*, 239; Lisa Sharon Harper, *Evangelical Does Not Equal Republican…or Democrat* (New York: New Press, 2008), 11.

16. Lydia Saad, "Bush Presidency Closes with 34 Percent Approval, 61 Percent Disapproval," Gallup Poll News Service, January 14, 2009; Lindsay, *Faith in the Halls of Power*, xi, 255–245n3; Kate Zernike, "George Gallup Jr., 81; Expanded Polling Firm," *New York Times*, November 23, 2011; Putnam and Campbell, *American Grace*, 127; E. J. Dionne Jr., *Souled Out: Reclaiming Faith and Politics after the Religious Right* (Princeton, NJ: Princeton University Press, 2008), 4; Harper, *Evangelical Does Not Equal Republican*, 1; Gushee, *The Future of Faith*; Hunter, *To Change the World*, 111; Jon Meacham, "The End of Christian America," *Newsweek*, April 13, 2009; Michael Spencer, "The Coming Evangelical Collapse," *Christian Science Monitor*, March 10, 2009.

17. Lisa Miller and Richard Wolffe, "Finding His Faith," *Newsweek*, July 21, 2008; Darlene Superville, "Obama 'Christian by Choice': President Responds to Questioner," *Huffington Post*, September 28, 2010, http://www.huffingtonpost.com/2010/09/28/obama-christian-by-choice_n_742124.html; David Remnick, *The Bridge: The Life and Rise of Barack Obama* (New York: Knopf, 2010), 169–177, 244–245; Barack Obama, *Dreams from My Father: A Story of Race and Inheritance* (New York: Crown, 2004), 291–295.

18. "Text of Obama's Address at Convention," Associated Press Online, July 27, 2004; Remnick, *The Bridge*, 170; Lambert, *Religion in American Politics*, 238–239.

19. Laurie Goodstein, "Without a Pastor, Obama Turns to a Circle of Five," *New York Times*, March 15, 2009; Lee and Sinitiere, *Holy Mavericks*, 132; McLaren, *Everything Must Change*.

20. Goodstein, "Without a Pastor"; Barack Obama, *The Audacity of Hope: Thoughts on Reclaiming the American Dream* (New York: Crown, 2006), 364, 195–226; Jim Wallis, *The Great Awakening: Reviving Faith and Politics in a Post–Religious Right America* (New York: HarperCollins, 2008), 45; Sheler, *Prophet of Purpose*, 264; Tim Grieve, "Left Turn at Saddleback Church," *Salon*, December 2, 2006, http://www.salon.com/2006/12/02/obama_155/.

21. Nancy Gibbs and Michael Duffy, "Leveling the Praying Field," *Time*, July 23, 2007; "Special Edition: Sojourners Presidential Forum," transcript of *The Situation Room*, CNN, June 4, 2007.

22. John M. Broder, "At Forum on Faith, Democrats Wrangle over Words and Beliefs," *New York Times*, April 14, 2008; Lauren Collins, "Purpose-driven Hype," *The New Yorker*, August 11, 2008; Amy Sullivan, "What Obama Needs to Know before Meeting Rick Warren Again," *The New Republic* online, July 18, 2012, http://www.tnr.com/blog/plank/105148/what-obama-needs-know-meeting-rick-warren-again.

23. Peter J. Boyer, "Party Faithful," *The New Yorker*, September 8, 2008; Remnick, *The Bridge*, 468–472, 517–533; Jim Wallis, *Who Speaks for God? An Alternative to the*

Religious Right—A New Politics of Compassion, Community, and Civility (New York: Delacorte, 1996), 215; Tiffany Ruby Patterson, "Barack Obama and the Politics of Anger," in Liette Gidlow, *Obama, Clinton, Palin: Making History in Election 2008* (Urbana: University of Illinois Press, 2011), 29.

24. Ronald Eric Matthews Jr. and Michele Gilbert, *Obamagelicals: How the Right Turned Left* (Newcastle upon Tyne, UK: Cambridge Scholars, 2010), 5; Laurie Goodstein, "Obama Made Gains among Younger Evangelical Voters, Data Show," *New York Times*, November 7, 2008; Marcia Pally, *The New Evangelicals: Expanding the Vision of the Common Good* (Grand Rapids, MI: Eerdmans, 2011), 112; 2008 Democratic Party Platform, August 25, 2008, http://www.presidency.ucsb.edu/ws/index.php?pid=78283#axzz1gcPgUvfD; Goodstein, "Without a Pastor"; Wallis, *The Great Awakening*, 308; Jason Gedeik, "10,000 Participate in Sojourners' First Justice Revival, Committing Spiritual, Social and Political Will to End Poverty in Columbus, Ohio," Sojourners press release, April 30, 2008, http://sojo.net/press/10000-participate-sojourners%E2%80%99-first-justice-revival-committing-spiritual-social-and-political-; Brian McLaren, "Why I'm Voting for Obama…and I Hope You Will Too: Reason 5," October 27, 2008, http://brianmclaren.net/archives/blog/why-im-voting-for-barak-obama-and-i-hope-you-will-too-reason-5.html.

25. Robin Rogers and Peter Goodwin Heltzel, "The New Evangelical Politics," *Society* 45, no. 5 (September 2008): 412–414; Heltzel, *Jesus and Justice*, 4, 5; Randall Balmer, *The Making of Evangelicalism: From Revivalism to Politics and Beyond* (Waco, TX: Baylor University Press, 2010), 82.

26. Transcript of President Barack Obama's inaugural address, *Washington Post*, January 21, 2009; "Statement by Dr. Rick Warren, Pastor of Saddleback Church Regarding the Invitation from President-elect Obama to Deliver the Inaugural Invocation," PR Newswire, December 18, 2008; Pew Forum, "The Future of Evangelicals: A Conversation with Pastor Rick Warren," November 13, 2009, http://www.pewforum.org/Christian/Evangelical-Protestant-Churches/The-Future-of-Evangelicals-A-Conversation-with-Pastor-Rick-Warren.aspx; Sheler, *Prophet of Purpose*, 268–269, 277; James L. Guth, "Obama, Religious Politics, and the Culture Wars," in Steven E. Schier, ed., *Transforming America: Barack Obama in the White House* (Lanham, MD: Rowman Littlefield, 2011), 85; "Rick Warren's Inaugural Invocation," *Christianity Today* Politics blog, January 20, 2009, http://blog.christianitytoday.com/ctpolitics/2009/01/rick_warrens_in.html; "Franklin Graham's Inauguration Prayer," January 20, 2001, http://www.beliefnet.com/Faiths/Christianity/2002/08/Franklin-Grahams-Inauguration-Prayer.aspx.

27. Francis S. Collins, *The Language of God: A Scientist Presents Evidence for Belief* (New York: Free Press, 2006), 233; Randall J. Stephens and Karl W. Giberson, *The Anointed: Evangelical Truth in a Secular Age* (Cambridge, MA: Harvard University Press, 2011), 51; Goodstein, "Without a Pastor"; Mara Vanderslice biography, Global Faith Forum, http://www.globalfaithforum.org/speakers/mara-vander-

slice; Guth, "Obama, Religious Politics, and the Culture Wars," 87–89; Sarah Posner, "Obama's Faith-Based Failure," *Salon*, May 4, 2012, http://mobile.salon. com/2012/05/04/obamas_faith_based_failure/singleton/; Pally, *The New Evangelicals*, 211.

28. FitzGerald, "The New Evangelicals"; Williams, *God's Own Party*, 246, 275, 341n88.

29. Hunter, *To Change the World*, 116; Pally, *The New Evangelicals*, 65; Jon Meacham and Lisa Miller interview with Franklin Graham, "'Muhammad Only Leads to the Grave,'" *Newsweek*, May 17, 2010; "Restoring Honor" rally footage, August 28, 2010, http://www.c-spanvideo.org/program/HonorRall; "Manhattan Declaration: A Call of Christian Conscience," released November 20, 2009, http:// www.manhattandeclaration.org/man_dec_resources/Manhattan_Declaration_ full_text.pdf; Sarah Posner, "The Original Culture Warrior," April 26, 2012, *Salon*, http://www.salon.com/2012/04/26/the_original_culture_warrior/singleton/.

EPILOGUE

1. Samuel G. Freedman, "In Surprising Shift, Many Evangelical Voters Are Turning to Santorum, a Catholic," *New York Times*, March 24, 2012; Steve Ford, "Santorum's Theology of Dominion," *Raleigh* (NC) *News and Observer*, February 26, 2012, http://www.newsobserver.com/2012/02/26/1881521/santorums-theology-of-dominion.html; Ashley Parker, "Romney Assures Evangelicals That Their Values Are His, Too," *New York Times*, May 13, 2012; Kasie Hunt, "Mitt Romney Meets with Billy Graham," Associated Press, October 11, 2012; Eric Marrapodi, "Billy Graham Site Removes Mormon 'Cult' Reference after Romney Meeting," CNN Belief Blog, October 16, 2012, http://religion.blogs.cnn. com/2012/10/16/billy-grahams-group-removes-mormon-cult-reference-from-website-after-romney-meeting/; Eric Marrapodi, "Billy Graham Buys Election Ads after Romney Meeting," CNN Belief Blog, October 18, 2012, http://religion.blogs.cnn.com/2012/10/18/billy-graham-buys-election-ads-after-romney-meeting/; Billy Graham Evangelistic Association advertisement, *St. Louis Post-Dispatch*, November 4, 2012, A9; Tim Townsend, "Catholics Intensity Furor over Mandate," *St. Louis Post-Dispatch*, June 20, 2012; Erika I. Ritchie, "Rick Warren Cancels Obama-Romney Forum at Saddleback Church," *Orange County Register*, August 22, 2012, http://www.ocregister.com/news/forum-369266-warren-civil.html; Jo Becker, "An Evangelical Back from Exile, Lifting Romney," *New York Times*, September 23, 2012; Matthew Bowman, "Is This the Mormon Moment?" *Time*, September 27, 2012, http://ideas.time.com/2012/09/27/is-this-the-mormon-moment/; Michael Gerson, "Ideology without Promise," *Washington Post*, September 21, 2012.

2. Stephen Mansfield, "Religion and the 2012 Presidential Race, Part I: Is Barack Obama a 'Born Again' Christian?" *Huffington Post*, May 22, 2012, http://www.

huffingtonpost.com/stephen-mansfield/religion-and-the-2012-presidential-race-obama-born-again_b_1530508.html.

3. Laurie Goodstein, "Study Finds That the Number of Protestant Americans Is in Steep Decline," *New York Times*, October 10, 2012; Tim Townsend, "More Americans Choosing None as Religious Affiliation," *St. Louis Post-Dispatch*, October 14, 2012; "Young Evangelicals in the 2012 Elections: A Study Sponsored by Sojourners," October 16, 2012, http://sojo.net/sites/default/files/YEStudy Final.pdf; Sandi Villarreal, "Young Evangelicals, Election 2012, and Common Ground," October 16, 2012, http://sojo.net/blogs/2012/10/16/young-evangeli-cals-election-2012-and-common-ground; Jaweed Kaleem, "Jim Wallis Talks Faith's Role in Politics, Gay Marriage and Immigration," *Huffington Post*, April 5, 2013, http://www.huffingtonpost.com/2013/04/05/jim-wallis-faith-politics-immigration_n_3024458.html.

4. Cathleen Falsani, "What Is an Evangelical, Anyway?" September 18, 2011, http://sojo.net/blogs/2011/09/18/what-evangelical-anyway; Michael J. Altman, "The Invention of American Evangelicalism," Religion in America blog, June 22, 2012, http://usreligion.blogspot.com/2012/06/invention-of-american-evangelicalism-or.html; Marcia Pally, *The New Evangelicals: Expanding the Vision of the Common Good* (Grand Rapids, MI: Eerdmans, 2011), 19, 119; Thomas Albert Howard and Karl W. Giberson, "An Evangelical Renaissance in Academe?" *Insider Higher Ed*, February 24, 2012, http://www.insidehighered.com/views/2012/02/24/essay-need-evangelical-scholars-reclaim-christian-thought-fundamentalism; "An Evangelical Manifesto," May 7, 2008, http://www.anevangelicalmanifesto.com/docs/Evangelical_Manifesto.pdf; Brian McLaren, "A New Christian Convergence," July 26, 2010, http://www.patheos.com/Resources/Additional-Resources/New-Christian-Convergence.html; Jane Mayer, "Bully Pulpit: An Evangelical Talk-Show Host's Campaign to Control the Republican Party," *The New Yorker*, June 18, 2012, 56–65; Mike Lofgren, "GOP Insider: Religion Destroyed My Party," *Salon*, August 5, 2012, http://www.salon.com/ 2012/08/05/republicans_slouching_toward_theocracy/; Timothy Noah, "Language Cop: 'Christian,'" *The New Republic*, March 27, 2012, http://www.tnr.com/blog/timothy-noah/102074/language-cop-christian; Timothy Dalrymple, "The Legacy of an Activist Career: An Interview with Jim Wallis," August 9, 2010, http://www.patheos.com/Resources/Additional-Resources/The-Legacy-of-an-Activist-Career-An-Interview-with-Jim-Wallis.html; "Ted Haggard, Gary Busey on 'Celebrity Wife Swap,'" *Huffington Post*, November 22, 2011, http://www.huffingtonpost.com/ 2011/09/22/ted-haggard-gary-busey-on-celebrity-wife-swap_n_975433.html; David Kuo and Patton Dodd, "God's Quarterbacks: What Tebow and Roethlisberger Reveal about Evangelical Politics," *Washington Post*, January 6, 2012, http://www.washington-post.com/opinions/who-is-gods-quarterback-tebow-roethlisberger-and-american-evangelicalism/2012/01/05/gIQAS6VcfP_story.html; Carla Hinton, "As an Ailing Billy Graham Ages, Who Advises Leaders Next?" McClatchy-Tribune Business News, January 17, 2009.

INDEX